The Accountant's Tale

The Accountant's Tale
A Reading of the History
of Biblical Religion

Andrew P. Porter

WIPF & STOCK · Eugene, Oregon

THE ACCOUNTANT'S TALE
A Reading of the History of Biblical Religion

Copyright © 2021 Andrew P. Porter. All rights reserved. Except for brief quotations in critical publications or reviews, no part of this book may be reproduced in any manner without prior written permission from the publisher. Write: Permissions, Wipf and Stock Publishers, 199 W. 8th Ave., Suite 3, Eugene, OR 97401.

Wipf & Stock
An Imprint of Wipf and Stock Publishers
199 W. 8th Ave., Suite 3
Eugene, OR 97401

www.wipfandstock.com

PAPERBACK ISBN: 978-1-6667-1778-5
HARDCOVER ISBN: 978-1-6667-1779-2
EBOOK ISBN: 978-1-6667-1780-8

Manufactured in the U.S.A.

Biblical quotations are from the Jerusalem Bible, c New York: Doubleday, 1966.

Contents

Acknowledgments   viii

1   Getting Started   1
    1.1   Ways to Think in Theology   1
    1.2   First Questions   2
    1.3   The Shape of the Story   4
    1.4   Some History of Religions   7
    1.5   Chalcedon   10
    1.6   The Basic Question of Religion   14
    1.7   Some Presupposed Choices   14
    1.8   Understanding a Strange Culture   16
    1.9   Social Construction and Sacred Canopies   18
    1.10   Covenant Renewal   19
    1.11   Problems to Come   22

2   The Common Documents   25
    2.1   The Priestly Creation Story   25
    2.2   The Origin of Sin Was Not a Fall   26
    2.3   The Name   28
    2.4   The Ten Commandments   29
    2.5   The Shape of the Exodus   31
    2.6   The Atrocities   34
    2.7   David's Shenanigans   36
    2.8   Job and His Friends   36
    2.9   Deutero-Isaiah   38
    2.10   Qoheleth and the Wisdom Literature   39

3   The New Testament   40
    3.1   The Exodus in the Gospels   40

	3.2	Problems with Miracles	42
	3.3	Exposure, Limitation, and Need	44
	3.4	Christians and Jews in the New Testament	46
	3.5	A Responsible Liberty of Interpretation	49
4	**The Common Era**		**54**
	4.1	The Disasters of the First Century	54
	4.2	Christianity as Atheism	57
	4.3	The Mishnah and the Talmuds	58
	4.4	The Oven of Achnai	60
	4.5	The Marcionite Crisis	62
	4.6	The Trinity	63
5	**The Medievals**		**66**
	5.1	A Focus on Aristotle	66
	5.2	Proofs of God	75
	5.3	More Miracles	78
	5.4	More Atrocities	81
6	**Modernity**		**82**
	6.1	The Domestication of Transcendence	83
	6.2	The Way to Modern Science	88
	6.3	Darwin and Evolution	94
	6.4	Reform Judaism	97
	6.5	Liberal Theology	99
	6.6	The Birth of Biblical Criticism	103
	6.7	The Discovery of History	106
7	**Postmodernity**		**111**
	7.1	Kierkegaard and Heidegger	113
	7.2	The Neo-orthodox	115
	7.3	The Many Faces of Interpretation	121
	7.4	Analytic Philosophy and its Kin	124
	7.5	Biblical Literalism	126
	7.6	Pathologies of Proofs	129
	7.7	Revisiting Sociology of Knowledge	135
	7.8	Postmodernism So Far	138

8	Some Applications	140
	8.1 Returning to Miracles	140
	8.2 Literalism and the Resurrection	157
	8.3 The Gospel of Peter	162
	8.4 Not as Literalist as They Think They Are	164
	8.5 Violations of Laws of Nature	172
	8.6 Acts of God	176
	8.7 Confessing the Resurrection	180
	8.8 Exposure, Limitation, and Need	184
9	Problems in the Culture	188
	9.1 Naturalism, Nominalism, Materialism	188
	9.2 Individualisms	193
	9.3 Confusions About Religion	196
	9.4 Seeking Meaning in the Sciences	199
	9.5 Loss of the Humanities	200
	9.6 A Technology of Disrespect	202
10	Problems Not Faced in the Church	208
	10.1 Basic Life Orientation	209
	10.2 The Heart of Historical Religion	211
	10.3 Evading History	214
	10.4 Christians and Jews	217
	10.5 Unbelievable, Offensive, and in Bad Faith	222
	10.6 Religious Autoimmune Disease	224
	10.7 The History We Live In	227
	10.8 Some Christian Answers	233
11	Conclusions	235
	11.1 Collecting Themes	235
	11.2 Our Problems, in Retrospect	237
	11.3 Our Present Plight	238
	11.4 Questions	243
Bibliography		251
Index		268

Acknowledgments

It was Edward Hobbs's insight into how biblical religion handles the pains of life that made it possible to ask the sort of questions in this book.

Though there are many parts to the puzzles that follow, sociology of knowledge is probably the biggest. One person more than anyone else guided me through the work of Peter Berger, and that was Shawn Sullivan. He doesn't know what came of it, so he is hardly responsible for the claims made here. But my gratitude is no less, and wrestling with Berger's critique of biblical religion (one largely ignored by theologians) was life-changing for me. Peter Berger himself was gracious enough to answer questions, which was more than I was entitled to. Ted Peters reminded me of some of this.

Denis Roby was kind enough to read and mark up manuscript printout, with many incisive comments. Over the years he has shown me the way into much literature that I would not have found on my own. I was supremely fortunate to have Mark Fischer read the text also, with an eye and ear shaped by decades of teaching philosophical theology. My friends rarely agree with me completely, so what follows is my responsibility, not theirs.

John M. Ellis was most helpful in explaining and expanding his published work on the nature of language. Barbara Green, OP pointed out the magnitude of the problem in comments on literalism in the Catholic Church. Gregory Rocca and Michael J. Dodds, OP helped with Aquinas and the transmission of Aristotle to the Christian West. Margaret Brenman-Gibson put me onto her husband's work and, more generally, was one of God's finest gifts to the people around her. Anthony Kenny made useful comments on his own work. Jonathan Weitsman is my principal source for help with all things Jewish.

Some parts of this book are cut and pasted from other pieces of my own writing without further acknowledgment than this.

It is not clear that much of it is new or original. It is a call to recover resources from the past and apply them in new ways in the present. While the order of topics is historical, this is not a history but merely some observations of a few themes that have appeared during the course of biblical and Christian history.

This book was typeset with LaTeX on Slackware and Debian GNU Linux boxes.

Chapter 1

Getting Started

1.1 Ways to Think in Theology

Theology can be approached in many ways. I have in the past quoted a joke about a man who wanted to hire someone good with numbers.[1] He interviewed a physicist, a mathematician, and an accountant, and asked each one in turn, "What is 2 times 2?" The physicist's answer was intuitive, the mathematician's was long and complicated, and the accountant replied, "What do you *want* it to be?"

Each of these three approaches has parallels in theology, and they are all necessary. The physicist is not dumb or uneducated. The mathematician is necessary and not useless. And the accountant is not dishonest. The physicist knows best what it feels like to believe. The mathematician is the only one who really appreciates the philosophical subtlety and risks of belief. And the accountant may be the only one who really knows what it means to be honest about biblical covenant in the history of religions.

The normal or traditional way to proceed would be to start with the physicist for an intuitive explanation of the faith, and then, for a rigorous philosophical explanation, to follow with the mathematician. The accountant would be left out, and with him most biblical criticism. That is not the way of this book. To put it in clear but technical language, it is a question

---

[1] A more extended version can be found in my *Elementary Monotheism*, volume II, *Action and Language in Historical Religion*, 226. Online at http://www.jedp.com/alhr.pdf. I don't think the joke is fundamental or exhaustive of the possible ways to do Catholic theology. It was merely convenient, because there are obvious analogs of the physicist, mathematician, and accountant in Catholic theology. And the analogy with the mathematician (though not our problem in this book) is a stretch.

of whether to do history within the larger context of philosophy (the traditional way) or do philosophy within the larger context of history (slightly postmodern). I choose the second, philosophy within the larger context of history[2] read as a history of human actions — which means human *choices*. A little bit about basic philosophical commitments may come in later writing, but even in that problem, we will be trying to understand our not understanding of God. Comprehending God is not possible. So the immediate task is to understand some of the history, how the choices in the Bible and since it have shaped our present problems.

One idea may be hinted in anticipation: We never know all there is to know about ourselves, about what we are doing, about the world around us. But we can know enough, enough to get through life one day at a time. This underlies all that follows. Language gives us not just knowledge (and with it, ignorance) but also ambiguity, and where there is ambiguity, there is choice. Hence the accountant's question.

1.2 First Questions

Once, after I enjoyed the privilege of listening to a class of highschool philosophy students describe their reading (Marlowe's *Faust*), their instructor asked me, with anticipatory canary-feathers all over his mustache, "is there a God? Does God exist?" or something like that.[3] I replied that that is the wrong place to begin. First, you have to answer two much more basic questions. (1) Is human life a part of nature alone, without history, or is human life fully understandable only in terms of history (of which nature is only a part)? (2) What do you want to do about the pains of life? How do you want to handle them? Are you interested in putting some sort of positive construction on them, or are they just barren, to be avoided if possible? Do the pains of life spoil life? Or is life good in spite of the pains? Is life good even in full view of its pains? Can the pains be integrated into a good life?

To begin with "God" is to jump to conclusions before the meaning of the words is even clear. As with the mathematician who began with presuppositions that come long before 2×2, we have a lot of work to do first. The choice between nature and history can be made as you like, but

---

[2] This book, among others; *In the Beginning, Exodus; The Bible Then and Now* also told the history.

[3] I am indebted to Gary Parlapiano for the invitation to visit his daughter's class.

1.2 First Questions

it is a choice between quite different worlds and quite different ways of being human. Nevertheless, the pains of life have to be dealt with, one way or another. There are many ways to do that.

The story, in two sentences, is first a narrative and then a challenge:

> A long time ago, some people stumbled into a world-affirming historical basic life orientation, in full view of the pains of life.
>
> Do you want to be a part of it or not?

What's your pleasure? What will you do with your life? As the accountant said to the prospective employer, "What do you want it to be?" If this blithe summary is to make any sense, it will eventually need a lot of explaining. Much of that will have to wait for an inquiry focused on transcendence. Some of it has already appeared in other books. This book is about only one part of the problem: the human choices made in biblical religion.

A word of caution is in order, both to see the scope of the problem and to see the limitations of the present inquiry. We shall be focusing on some of the many varieties of a very simple question. It could be asked of anybody, and anybody could answer, though mostly people don't worry about such theory.

> What is the meaning of life?
> And where does it show itself in the world?

We expect theoretical or philosophical or theological answers, and this book will for the most part follow that tradition. But real life is not so simple or so clear. Clearings where ultimate reality shows itself can be much more interesting than the toy appearances that philosophers and "traditional" theologians so love.

Let a story illustrate. Once upon a time, I was minding my own business, watering potted plants on my back porch. Through thick foliage and across the back fence, I could hear (but not see) a conversion between two people; call them A and B. They were hammering a new roof on the house over the fence. A was recounting to B another conversation, between C and D, who were not present. C had been going on and on for a long time, mostly about football. Finally, D asked, in rapt awe, "Don't you have a life other than football?" C answered, "Football *is* my life!"

The lesson is that answers to the question above, where does your proposed ultimate reality show itself in the world, are not necessarily philosophical or theological. C's answer cannot be mistaken for a proof, or even an argument, or any other form of philosophical theology. It cannot be domesticated by academic bullies. It is impossible to duct-tape it to a chair and beat it with rubber hoses to make it confess the meaning of life.[4] Nevertheless, in this inquiry, we shall for the most part follow the tradition — our asking will be in philosophical and historical terms, in the spirit of "go first to the lost sheep of the House of Israel" (or the lost sheep of the house of theology?). Yet many who are not quite as "secular" as they appear yearn for some street-signs in life, something to tell them where they are on the path of meeting the pains of life, and doing so with resources from biblical history. That will come, and it will show theology and theologians as often dispensable (or just useless).

Be not misled. C knows far more about football than I do, I was always a lousy athlete, and I don't even know how to *watch* a football game.[5] Billy Collins hoped his poetry students would learn to water-ski past the poem, waving to it on the shore at high speed, enjoying themselves. That is something C could do, and I do only clumsily. That, too, will come. For now, let me speculate. What C saw in football was skill and grace ($\chi \acute{\alpha} \rho \iota \varsigma$, a word from the heart of the New Testament) — and the "right stuff."

1.3 The Shape of the Story

This book has a relationship to its predecessors and successor(s) that needs to be spelled out. It is not just that this book is the Accountant's Tale, where *Basic Concepts* (or *Waters* and *Unwelcome Good News*) were the physicist's intuitive approach, and *Unanswerable Questions* will stand in for the mathematician. There is another sequence into which the story fits, with a different logic. It is historical. The challenges to theology in the modern world can be sorted into four stages. (There were other challenges before the modern world, but these four, the most recent, will give us quite enough work to do.) This book is about the third stage, and *Unanswerable Questions* will say a little about the fourth.

In the first, in the seventeenth century, the challenge came from the new physics. The problem was how to make sense of acts of God, divine

---

[4] Billy Collins, "Introduction to Poetry," source and date unknown.
[5] Listen to Andy Griffith, "What it was was football." It's on the Net.

1.3 The Shape of the Story

providence, in terms of the new physics. Divine presence hovered above divine providence. That story is told in various places and reviewed below in some brief remarks about science. The key to unraveling the puzzle of science can be found in extending the distinction between Chalcedonian and monophysite theology beyond Christology. That much is widely known, however poorly it is understood. That was the first modern stage of challenges to modern theology. One could go back before the modern world, I suppose, and say that Aristotelian naturalism was the challenge in the thirteenth century, but there were many other challenges before the seventeenth century — and before the thirteenth as well.

In the second modern stage, every beginning seminarian learns in basic Bible starting with the Documentary Hypothesis that the real challenges come from historical scholarship, starting in the nineteenth century. Those lucky in their teachers learn that the challenges to theology come not from physics but from critical history, historical and cultural relativity, and religious pluralism. Seminarians with literalist instincts complain, in lampooning their Bible teachers, "First, we destroy your faith." If their teachers understand, they can show the students how biblical religion still makes sense. For all its historical relativities, for all the revisions entailed by critical history, and for all the challenges of religious pluralism, biblical religion is still the affirmation of life in this world, as history, not just nature, and in full view of its pains, pretty much as it always was, though not *explained* as it always was. In that characterization, it is still a viable basic life orientation, perhaps more so than it has seemed to literalists. Critical history vindicates the historicality of historical religion; literalist accounts are neither coherent nor credible.

The third stage of challenges to theology unfolds from the second when the relativities of the second stage lead to the challenges that come from the sociology of knowledge. Reality is, for the sociology of knowledge, a human social construction.[6] Many think that means nihilistic relativism, the position that there is no truth and no basis for criticizing either theory or practice. I think that is a mistake. It silently presupposes a platonist conception of truth as absolute, not relative to history or culture. There are other, and better, conceptions of truth. A better response to "everything is a social construction" would be to face the question that follows immediately

---

[6] Not just for sociology: Martin Heidegger's philosophy moved in the same direction, as Thomas Sheehan has pointed out in a summary appraisal. But Peter Berger, the sociologist of choice, didn't deal with philosophy.

from that: why are some social constructions better than others?

With that question comes another: *How* does reality enter into our human social constructions? I have deliberately alluded to Berger and Luckmann's title, *The Social Construction of Reality* (see sections 1.9 and 7.7 below). Its sequel is Peter Berger's *The Sacred Canopy*, about the phenomenon of covering up the human freedom in the social constructions of reality, in order to evade responsibility and evade the anxieties that come with responsibility. The present book is in a sense a meditation on sacred canopies: the history of social constructions and of forgetting (and occasionally remembering) that they *are* human choices. The second question, the fourth stage of modern challenges to theology, asks how ultimate reality enters into our social constructions. That is deferred for later. Even then, I don't think I have very good answers, since we are always left dependent on grace, much though we would rather not be. The fourth challenge invites theology to re-understand transcendence.

It would be tempting to introduce God at the beginning also, and so jump to the fourth stage of challenges to theology. I think that would be to get ahead of our logic. It would be to rely on intuitive concepts that surreptitiously introduce assumptions that ought to be examined more carefully.[7] True, we have already rushed in (as philosophers are prone to do), and used the word "God" — but what does that mean? What is to be said to the naive secular who says, "God? God?! I don't know that word; how do you spell it?" We owe the logic (and inquirers) a candid and careful answer, and that, too, must wait for the mathematician, or his stand-in, as best I can conjecture, in *Unanswerable Questions*. A foretaste appeared briefly in *Basic Concepts*, chapter 6, "A Little About God." Hence we start with a historical account, in which God appears in the third person and then only in a kind of indirect discourse: So-and-so believed in a reality whom they called "God." For the moment, it is not obvious what they were doing. That will come out slowly.

In the parable, the mathematician starts with modern set theory. We shall proceed as if the mathematician started in the ancient world, with a *history* of the concept of number, coming to its groundings in set theory only late in the story. That is, we shall follow the career of world-affirming

---

[7] The physicist is necessary, as C. S. Lewis argued in effect in *The Abolition of Man*, especially the essay, "Men Without Chests." Beginning answers are intuitive, grounded in well-trained instincts, and to a certain extent, emotional. More can be found in my *Basic Concepts of Biblical Religion*.

historical religion (WAHR) from its beginnings through many haps and mishaps, to the present, to the small extent that the history of historical religion is even understood. This means that in many places in our story, in order to keep the present account to a manageable size, we will have to refer to other accounts of the history. In the end, we will have traded one set of problems (science) for the consequences of critical history, now seen as exposing the Church's responsibility in its own history. Out of that will grow yet another problematic (about transcendence), one that I don't understand very well. Perhaps that is as it should be: one of the marks of transcendence is that it cannot be fully understood.

The original contrast to world-affirming historical religion was world-affirming nature religion (WANR). There are other kinds of basic life orientations (BLOs), though they are beyond this book's interests.[8] A basic life orientation is an appraisal of whatever is the ultimate reality (u-r) in life and the world, what matters and what doesn't, what it means to be successfully human, what failure might mean. There are many possible BLOs, but in this book we focus on those that take life as both historical and good: biblical religion. We mostly bracket questions about God — tolerating intuitive answers and postponing deeper inquiry for later.

The rest of this chapter provides some context. It is not a larger context in philosophy but rather in history. We tell some of the end of the story at the beginning, in order to see where the story is going.

1.4 Some History of Religions

"Religion" is a term of interest to religious studies departments, a matter of custom, convention, and academic comity agreements. The trouble is that not all religions are "religions." A decent if rough and loose definition of religion would be basic life orientation (BLO), possibly including a mode of recognition and intention (MORI), but many BLOs don't have a MORI. One could gloss MORI as "organized," but many people get along quite well without *organized* religion, and if you were to suggest that their lives have no coherence, they would rightly take exception.

There is another definition of BLO that helps, though it is also a definition of theology: Theology is the use of language to make a home for man

---

[8] What Merold Westphal called "exilic" religions are the prominent alternative, but for the moment, we have enough problems just with biblical religion.

in the universe.[9] This definition has problems. The first is that it is leaky: not every use of language to describe things in the world qualifies as theology. The second is that many instances are ambiguous: do the differential equations of physics[10] make a home for man in the universe or are they just science? That depends on how you read them and for what purposes. The third is that theology conventionally, in the Christian West, is taken to be theoretical, but many BLOs have no trouble creating a world without resorting to theory at all.[11] So we might say that theology (the articulation of a BLO) is the use of language at the "top level" to turn the universe into a world, a home for man. What is the top level? Sometimes that's hard to say.

The beginnings of the history of religions in the nineteenth century may be left to specialists. There are several typologies of religions that are helpful for us. Merold Westphal, in *God, Guilt, and Death*, lays out the differences between religions of nature, of history, and of escape from the evils of this world.[12] He called them mimetic, historical-covenantal, and exilic religions. But there are more choices than just these three. Luther Martin, in *Hellenistic Religions*, surveys some BLO options that Westphal does not cover. In particular, he deals with what we would call secularism and new-age mysticism.

Begin with religions of nature. Originally, in the neolithic, the only way questioning the world could arise was in regard to nature. How are we supposed to fit into nature? The world was just nature; history (and other complex concepts) were invisible.

As a contingent fact of history, the earliest forms of nature religion were all in some sense world-affirming. They provided ways of grieving for the pains of life, but on the whole, the natural world was a good place to live. All was not love and peace, however. Tribalism has a natural and logical place in nature religion. In a Darwinian social context, it makes perfect sense to eliminate the competition in order to propagate in-group genes in place of out-group populations. Finding reasons to get along with other groups took a long time, and it came after the transition to historical

---

[9] I am indebted to Edward Hobbs for this definition.

[10] General relativity, the "Standard Model," or String theory, and so on; whatever one takes as basic in physics.

[11] Art is one way of making sense of the cosmos without the hazards of philosophy or theory. Those hazards are not trivial. Philosophy can easily wrap itself around its axle.

[12] Merold Westphal, *God, Guilt and Death*, chapters 9–11.

1.4 Some History of Religions

religion. Be all that as it may, a world-affirming BLO in nature (world-affirming nature religion, WANR) can be summarized thus:

> Your job is to fit into nature naturally,
> disturbing natural harmonies as little as possible,
> and mending disturbances of nature as needed.

For a nature religion, that is what human fulfillment *is*. Where writing and literacy are rare and geographical horizons are limited by lack of technology for extensive travel (effectively before iron), history was invisible. In nature, things happen "naturally," that is, they are somewhat predictable, even if the regularities of nature are also sometimes random. Things that defy prediction — later intelligible as history — were beyond knowledge, surds, evil, impossible to make sense of.

That's all fine, but as we know, both writing and iron became available, and so with broader horizons and writing came both an expanded world and history. Sooner or later, somewhere, consciousness of history was inevitable. At first history was just the deeds of conquering emperors. It was also, for many, especially their subjects, a world of hurt and misery. The world of the neolithic was replaced with civilization. The costs of civilization were not nice at all: empire, slavery, atrocities, and worse. Yet the possibility of a happy world was not forgotten.

In a world around an empire (here, Mesopotamia or Egypt), subject peoples entered and left the imperial power often. And when history became visible, it was inevitable that somewhere, sometime, someone would find blessing in accidents of history, even though the accidents of history cannot be comprehended in terms of natural regularities. To affirm life in this world, those accidents would have to become the beginning of a world-affirming *historical* religion.

What we have just described approximates the Exodus. It is what holds the Common Documents together, the documents that are shared in common by the Church and the Synagogue. A few dozen families (at a minimum; maybe more) got out of Egypt, the imperial power, under disagreeable circumstances. That much is so commonplace as to be unexceptionable. If more warrant were needed, there is plenty of evidence of Egyptian cultural influence in the Common Documents. So something like the Exodus cannot responsibly be doubted as a historical "fact," even though we don't know the details with any confidence. (The hydrodynamic special effects are commonly mistaken for the theology in the texts, but they are not.) What was unusual is that these people's literary executors tell us that they were *grateful* to escape from Egypt. We come to more of this below, but for now, as we shall explore in more detail, it is enough to forecast that the Exodus is what holds the story together. We shall revisit this history in sections 2.5, 3.1, 10.7, and 11.3.

1.5 Chalcedon

Merold Westphal spoke of historical-covenantal religion as traveling through history in company with a transcendent Other.[13] The question of transcendence will accordingly be with us, often unnamed and in the background, for the rest of our inquiry. To make sense of it, we take out of order an obscure council, here instead of in the chapter on the Common Era. It met in the fifth century, and it dealt with an issue that runs through the entire history, from beginning to end. It has come back as a persistent theological neuralgia in the modern world. Hence Chalcedon can serve as a guide to our theological method. In its superficial form, the problem shows itself in so-called "miracles," which appear to the modern mind to be violations of natural laws, but the problem goes much deeper than just "miracles." The problem arose in another form in the Council that met at Chalcedon, an Asian suburb of Constantinople, in 451 CE: how to make sense of Jesus Christ as both divine and human without falling into absurdity or other errors. Our problem is a generalization of the christological problem: how to make sense of divine presence and divine action in general, beyond the doctrine of the Person of Christ.

Ultimate reality shows itself in the world, pretty much by definition. Though people do not agree on what u-r is, it is always possible to ask someone,[14]

> "What is it about life and the world

---

[13] See Westphal, *God, Guilt, and Death*, 231, "... meet the God of creation in ever new historical encounters." He cites Deuteronomy 5.2–3, "[HaShem] our God made a covenant with us at Horeb. It was not with our fathers that [HaShem] made this covenant, but with us, with us who are here, all living today." Jerusalem Bible, altered in the divine Name. Westphal, 234: "he will not abandon them, but will continue to guide and accompany them through the uncharted existential wastelands of historical existence." Passim, in the Bible, "I will be your God and you will be my people." Westphal, 251, on reconciliation after sin, about God and Israel: "The two agree to put the past aside, so as to resume their journey through historical existence together."

[14] Cf. p. 14.

1.5 Chalcedon

that leads you to say such-and-such about ultimate reality?"

The question is asked about the world as it is, not some world of wishful thinking. For the present inquiry, u-r shows itself in the world without tampering with nature, simply because (in the world of modern science) there are no exceptions to natural laws. From another perspective, u-r, by its appearances in history transforms the very being of people, the world, and other events in history.

As said, the problem arose in working out a philosophical account of the Incarnation, in the Definition of Chalcedon. The council fathers there said, in effect, that two realities are both fully present in the one Lord, neither reality truncated or compromised to make room for the other, because the two realities are of qualitatively distinct orders of reality. It would be a category error to think that transcendence has to interfere with the intramundane world.

We shall follow a Chalcedonian method in our inquiry. There are then two ways to talk about any phenomenon in the world: in terms of its worldly aspects and the same phenomenon in the perspective of transcendence.[15] The worldly account may work from the history of religions, or the natural or social sciences, or literary criticism, or history, or any other intramundane perspective. To say that the phenomenon is "just" its intramundane aspects, as modern naturalistic atheists argue against biblical religion, is not an argument; it is a demand. In effect, the demand forbids the asking of unanswerable questions, but unanswerable questions arise within human life whether they are permitted or not. The demand to ignore them may politely be refused. One and the same phenomenon may be questioned in many ways, including some that lead to unanswerable questions. Language (especially in colloquial theology), raises problems at this point, because it *appears* to answer unanswerable questions. Its semantics is odd, in part because it is always ironic, and its irony has been forgotten. I agree with the atheists against pretending that unanswerable questions are answerable, but disagree with simply dismissing them. It should be possible to understand a little about our not-understanding of ultimate reality.

In summary, then, in a Chalcedonian method there are two sorts of

---

[15] That does not take transcendence as a dual world in which one may park natural causes, with effects in this world, thus shielding causes from inspection or criticism. I want no part of supernatural dualism, which will become clearer as this inquiry progresses. By contrast, one feature of transcendence (but only one) is just irony.

questions about any worldly phenomenon: asking about its intramundane aspects and asking about its transcendent aspects. Neither rules out the other, and a complete treatment includes both, though often we don't have a complete treatment.

While outside Christology the problem shows itself superficially in questions about miracles, at more depth, it is about acts of God, about how to interpret language of acts of God, and so about transcendence. How are we to make sense of transcendence? A better treatment of that must wait, but some of it will appear in this book.

The principle is that there are two realities in one phenomenon, if we may borrow new terms for an old idea. In the Definition, it is two φύσεις in one πρόσωπον, one ὑπόστασις, usually translated as two natures in one person. We need terms (*reality*, *phenomenon*, or just *thing*) that are usable in a context wider than the Person of Christ. Neither reality interferes with the other, both are fully present, intact, and unaltered. The two realities are the this-worldly aspects of things and their transcendent grounding. What the principle rules out is confusing acts of God (and especially *causation* by God) with the way worldly causes and changes work. The world works in its normal ways. Transcendence is not interference with the world, it is something else.

So, to make it clear that we are speaking of theology outside of Christology, one might speak of monophysite theology of action and chalcedonian theology of action, rather than christologically monophysite or christologically chalcedonian theology, thus generalizing beyond the origins of the distinction in Christology.

Look at some developments that came later from the principle in the Definition.

To extend the principle from Christology to acts of God more generally has obvious implications for miracles: whatever else the miracle texts may do or mean, they are not credible reports of violations of laws of nature. Extending Chalcedon opened the door to treating nature as having its own integrity, one that God intended and respects. The principle, so stated, is approximately what Thomas Aquinas stipulated in the *Summa Theologica*. "Gratia non tollat naturam, sed perficiat": grace does not interfere with nature, but perfects it.[16] The text in question 62 continues, "... grace

---

[16] The translation of "tollat" is loose. The English Dominicans translate it as "destroy nature." Thomists tell me that this principle is stated in many places, but two that are easy to find are 1.1.8 ad 2 and 1.62.5, corpus.

1.5 Chalcedon

perfects nature according to the manner of the nature; as every perfection is received in the subject capable of perfection, according to its mode." What should be noted here is that Thomas's conception of nature and the natural was different from ours. For him, the paradigm typical of nature was life as in Aristotelian biology. Generalizations have infrequent exceptions, and that enabled him to read "miracle" texts literally in ways that have become impossible after seventeenth-century science.

The principle that gratia non tollat naturam bore fruit later when the integrity of nature took the form of exceptionless mathematical consistency in modern physics. The understanding of nature has changed greatly over the course of history, and Chalcedon has made it possible to separate changes in the natural sciences from changes in theology. When the philosophy of nature changes, the theology of transcendence will of course change also, but the effect is not disastrous. Transcendence shows itself in the world as it is, and when that world changes, transcendence can adjust without interfering with the natural sciences. (Influence in the other direction is possible also.)

The principle of Chalcedon was carried forward with mixed consistency later. Sometimes the temptations and seductions of monophysite theology of divine action were too much. In the seventeenth century, it supplied the presupposition for Deism.[17] Acts of God are then violations of laws of nature. For those who believe in the modern supernatural, they do happen; for Deists, acts of God do not happen. Chalcedonian action theology does not understand acts of God this way, and so the dilemma does not make sense.

Chalcedon spoke of two *fuseis* in one *hypostasis*. That, too, can be generalized: the ontology of a thing can be complex. A thing can be different things for different purposes. This will bear fruit in the postmodern world with hermeneutics, where questions about the what-is-it of a thing can have many answers. It will enable the disentanglement of the discourses of the natural sciences and human action, a disentanglement that is not yet complete. This line of questioning will eventually come to a changed understanding of acts of God.[18]

---

[17] This was only one ingredient in the changes of that century; we shall see others in the changes on the way from the thirteenth to the seventeenth century.

[18] Cf. section 5.6 in *Unanswerable Questions*.

1.6 The Basic Question of Religion

Let me emphasize what was already said above on p. 11, for it amounts to a basic principle in philosophy of religion. The most basic commitments of biblical religion are to the goodness of this world (that's what makes it *created*) and to its essentially *historical* character. The most basic commitment of philosophy of religion is methodological. It begins with the shape or form of questioning about ultimate reality:

> Tell us where (or how) in the world your proposed ultimate reality shows itself. What is it about life and the world that induces you to characterize ultimate reality as you do?

This question is the Basic Question of Philosophy of Religion, if that is not too pompous a name for it. The name is useful as a label. We saw it on p. 3 and 11, and we shall see it again (p. 153) and cite it occasionally. The question is directed to us as much as to any others. People don't agree about ultimate reality, and they don't agree about what kinds of things do and don't happen in this world. What is more, they don't agree about what form transcendence might take (if there is any transcendence), but that is rather advanced compared to this initial step into the basic questions of philosophy of religion. Answers to the Basic Question are always circular, for they are already assumed before one can begin to answer. Whether the circularity is a problem depends on whether the answer is taken as a proof or as an explanation. If the answer is read as a proof, the logical circularity is vicious; if the answer is read as a mere explanation, the logical circularity is hermeneutical.[19]

1.7 Some Presupposed Choices

The inquiry that follows in this book is about biblical religion of the Christian variety, though significant parts are shared with rabbinic Judaism. Some of the central commitments may not be as familiar as one could wish. Best to stipulate at least some of them at the outset. Biblical religion affirms human life in this world as good, in full view of its pains,[20] and as unfolding in history,[21] not just part of nature. We do not affirm the

---

[19] The hermeneutical circle first appeared in Gadamer's *Truth and Method*, and we see it again in more detail on p. 143 below.
[20] See Porter, *Unwelcome Good News*.
[21] See Porter, *In the Beginning, Exodus*.

1.7 Some Presupposed Choices

pains of life because we like them (we don't) or because they feel good (they don't), but because they bear blessings — clearly in some cases, and we trust in other cases. That entails some kind of transcendence. Transcendence is a word fraught with many meanings, but here, if one pursues the inquiry, one usually finds unanswerable questions, of which more in *Unanswerable Questions*, the sequel to the present study.

To embrace life, pains included, is to deal with the characteristic or cardinal pains of life: Exposure, Limitation, and Need. These have an origin in an Indo-European cultural context in which all of reality is divided into three parts, as the Trinity paper makes clear.[22] In a real sense, Edward Hobbs's work has made possible inquiries such as this book, and it is important to see why and how. If we are to accept the theology of the Priestly editor and the Yahwist in Genesis 1–3, that the created world is good, pains included (though not everything done in it is right), then the next question has to be faced: what to do about the pains of life, specifically Exposure, Limitation, and Need. We shall come upon that tripartite division of the pains of life frequently as this study unfolds. If we trust that they bear blessings (some obvious, some not), we can proceed in a way that is not possible if they are written off as evil.

Asking how radical monotheism would look in a non-Indo-European culture is work for someone fluent in at least some non-Indo-European cultures; it is not something that I can do. In some cultures, the Indo-European distinctions have simply been imported without attending to cultural differences, and that may have been adequate.

That should make clear at least three or four easy ways to get out of biblical religion, for those not interested in it. One can say, I'm not interested in all that pain, or history is bunk, or the Bible is about the wrong history, or transcendence is nonsense. Since these choices are starting points, it is a logical error to try to refute them in favor of biblical religion; starting points cannot be reasoned *to*, only *from*. Thus we safeguard the confessional liberty of interpretation open to everyone.[23]

We accept one central presupposition of the natural sciences (one that the sciences get from theology, by the way), namely that there are no exceptions to natural laws.[24] This lies under one theme of the present work, the implications of so-called "miracles." Acts of God are not to be un-

---

[22] Porter and Hobbs, "The Trinity and the Indo-European Tripartite Worldview," *Budhi* (Manila) Vol. 3, nos. 2&3 (1999) 1–28.

[23] *Basic Concepts of Biblical Religion*, section 5.6, "Hermeneutical Circularity."

[24] See my *By The Waters of Naturalism*, and *Where Now, O Biologists, is Your Theory?*

derstood as interference with natural processes, hence the Chalcedonian method announced above.

We also accept that Christianity begins in the same place as rabbinic Judaism, namely, the Exodus, Monarchy, Exile, and Second Temple Judaism. This is not Marcionite theology.

1.8   Understanding a Strange Culture

Understanding biblical cultures and texts is a problem for us because biblical cultures were so different from our own. So a question arises, how can we learn from a culture so different from our own? The problem, unrecognized, arose with miracles and modern objections to miracles. Before the modern period, miracles were simply accepted. With the new sciences, they became a problem, and in so doing exposed widespread problems in theology.

The issue has attracted much discussion. For the present study, an essay by Edward Hobbs will help: "Recognition of Conceptuality as a Hermeneutical Tool."[25] A culture has a repertoire of concepts with which to understand the world, and those taken together are its *conceptuality*. Hobbs speaks first of language, not conceptuality, and indeed, language and the difficulties of translation supplied his central analogy for understanding conceptuality.

> In any attempt to interpret a document from another time or another culture, a major barrier to the attempt, in addition to the usual problems of interpretation, is the *difference* between the author's language and ours, between his culture and ours, between his assumptions and ours, between his way of looking at things and ours.[26]

One might add that in closely related languages such as English and French, cognate words often mean very different things, and translation by cognates can be highly misleading. Similar problems dog NT translators. Another kind of problem arises when the other conceptuality simply has no counterpart in our own. Hobbs's example (466–467) is ghosts, in Hamlet: Shakespeare and all his contemporaries believed in ghosts, but they are not really a part of the play's message. To think that we would have to

---

[25] Hobbs, "Recognition of Conceptuality as a Hermeneutical Tool."
[26] Cross, *Texte und Untersuchungen*, 466.

1.8 Understanding a Strange Culture

believe in ghosts to understand Hamlet would be a serious mistake. It is simple (but still pertinent) to point out that it is possible to understand the role of ghosts in that world without actually believing there are ghosts in our own world.

All of this is preparation for the issue with which Hobbs began, namely, trying to understand the question an alien document itself asks, in the terms of its own time, terms that may possibly be translatable into our own terms. Not how does the alien culture *conceive* its world, but how does it *understand* its world? Hobbs readily admitted that *understand* has many meanings other than the one he was interested in, but his definition is clear enough:

> By an *understanding*, I mean a relationship one takes up toward one's existence; or a construction of the meaning-significance of one's universe as it is engaged with the self and the self with it, in terms of which every decision is made; or a relationship between the self and its universe in terms of which all decisions are made. In other words, I am using the word in its primordial sense — that which *stands under* — stands under choice and action. This is given as sense I.9 in *The Oxford English Dictionary*. It is not so much an attitude, as what underlies all attitudes. It is not primarily an intellectual matter, since it concerns the heart more than the head. An understanding is not an opinion, but rather the basis for action. It is at stake whenever one comes to a decision about anything affecting the self and its relationships, for to make a decision based on another understanding is to assume or take up that other understanding. And it is not a question of what theories one holds, but of the core of one's choices. It is the question of one mode of selfhood rather than another.[27]

Hobbs next remarked that such an understanding correlates with one's *gods* — in cultures that think in terms of gods. Not all do.

We may summarize in order to give some elasticity to our own terms, at a corresponding cost in precision. The question then occurs as what do we want to keep from biblical cultures, and what is just different in ways that no longer make much claim on us? Things may be more complex when the

---
[27] Cross, *Texte und Untersuchungen*, 472–3.

features to be left behind were themselves left behind in the course of biblical history. One prime example may be found in the hallmarks of nature religion that were slowly left behind by our forbears in the development of Israelite religion from the time of the Judges to Second Temple Judaism.[28]

1.9 Social Construction and Sacred Canopies

There are many ways of asking about intramundane phenomena, one of which is the history and formation of religions. Sociology of knowledge is one example of that. Why include a twentieth-century development (sociology) at the opening of a story that begins more than three thousand years ago? It tells us a little of where we are going. Sociology of knowledge tells us something about the choices people make in turning the universe into a world. Those choices (as in answers to the accountant's question) shape the story. We include here only the consequential results of the sociology of knowledge; the details of its development can wait for section 7.7.

The central results are two: (1) Human worlds are human social constructions, the result of collective human choices. (2) People would like to conceal that aspect of their world(s) and pretend that their choices are in fact objective and necessary. Why? Because seeing their own hand in making their world (a) makes them anxious, and (b) enables them to make trouble. To acknowledge that our world is our work, not that of an objective reality over against us, is the door into a kind of loneliness, and that leads to anxiety, sometimes intolerable anxiety. A functioning society requires the cooperation of its members, and they can be induced to cooperate much more efficiently if they don't know they have any choice in the matter. Once they discover that they could choose differently, they are free (logically, at least) to become uncooperative, which they readily do, not least because rights and responsibilities are distributed somewhat unevenly. People don't always get what they want and don't agree about what they (or others) deserve.

Sociology deals with human phenomena under the aspect of sociality. Knowledge is one such phenomenon, and the sociology of knowledge attempts to explain the social sources, production, distribution, consumption, and uses of knowledge. What that knowledge *does* is make a home

---

[28] For a list of some of them, see p. 230 below.

for man in the cosmos. That structuring defines roles, apportions power and resources, and defines failure and success in human living.

One of the fundamental results of the sociology of knowledge is that knowledge is knowledge of a *world*, and to the extent that it is comprehensive, coherent, and integrated, knowledge of a world is *religious*. It shapes a BLO, and that is (by definition) the work of religion.

If we say that a human world is a human choice, that raises obvious problems, some of which must be postponed until we have more resources for addressing them. My purpose here is to mark the problems so that the reader can follow them as they thread through the events that follow, from the beginning in the Common Documents to our present post-modern culture.

The thread that runs through the present book is human choice, choice not seen, often choice covered up in bad faith. The central result of the sociology of knowledge, the human social construction of worlds, appears in the Bible. It is called covenant.

1.10 Covenant Renewal

There is a feature of the Exodus story that deserves to be singled out for emphasis. It makes an important contrast to modern reasons for being part of biblical religion. It could be treated as unremarkable, until one notices that practice since the medievals has been quite different. The difference is simple enough: moderns have arguments for believing in God, but there are no such arguments in the time of the Exodus.

The pattern is simple enough. There are many leaders of the people in the course of the story, and when the leader is about to die, there is an assembly of the Israelites, a settling of accounts and some last words. When the assembly takes the form of a covenant renewal ceremony, among the last words there will be a question put to the people: Which gods will you serve? Then so-and-so "was gathered to his fathers" and the next leader takes over.

What is striking in contrast to medieval and modern usage is that participation in the covenant is a *choice*, not a deduction, nor any other kind of inference. Covenant is not justified. Aquinas gets it right, at least in principle: in the *Summa*, he knows that Christian theology presupposes commitment, which is a choice (1.1.8), not something that could be justified. Yet faced with medieval challenges from non-Christians, Scholastic theology inevitably responded in ways that could be interpreted as justifying itself, even if, strictly and technically read, it did not do that. Modern usage is even more overt. For moderns, it is possible to "prove" that God "exists," and "prove" that Christianity is the one and only divinely mandated religion. When modernity was reduced to incoherence, postmodernity found itself bewildered, unable to make sense of biblical religion.

Merold Westphal remarks the contrasts, both with nature religions and with modern rationalism, in the chapter on historical-covenantal religion in *God, Guilt, and Death*.[29] The challenge of the covenant (and the Law that enables its keeping) are not addressed to everybody. The surrounding Canaanites could perhaps be faulted for offenses against what was later known as "natural law," but certainly not for disobeying the covenant or its laws, because they were not party to the covenant. Westphal speaks of the covenant as a way to get through "the uncharted existential wastelands of historical existence." The surrounding nature religions simply dismissed history as absurd. The unpredictability of history was evidence of its evil.

The covenant is a personal relationship between a transcendent Other and a people. It is like a marriage, among other metaphors for it. It is not addressed universally to everybody, though in later history, anybody could join. There *are* other gods but they are forbidden to the covenant people. This is simple logic: you can take the meaning of life anyway you like, but if you want to be a part of the covenant people, the meaning is a transcendent Other, a companion traveling through history.

> We do not read, it would be self-contradictory and therefore irrational to have any other gods before me. We read instead, "I am the Lord your God, who brought you out of the land of Egypt, out of the house of bondage. You shall have no other gods before me."[30]

The logic of covenant is the logic of a promise: it is personal and it is irrevocable.

The first and greatest of the Deuteronomic sermons is of course the book of Deuteronomy, Moses' farewell discourses. Moses rehearses the history in which the law and covenant were given. He repeats the Law itself (hence *Deutero*nomy), 12–26, culminating in the Short Historical Creed, 26.5–10. There are dire consequences for breaking the promises

---
[29] Merold Westphal, *God, Guilt, and Death*, 234.
[30] Westphal, *God, Guilt, and Death*, 234, quoting Exodus 20.2–3, and Deuteronomy 26.

1.10 Covenant Renewal

undertaken in covenant, a theology that is not shared among all voices in the Common Documents (see section 2.8). It is a choice (Dt. 30.15 ff.), just as Westphal observes.

Joshua takes over and, in his own farewell at an assembly of all the Israelites at Shechem (Joshua 23–24), he reviews their history. Then he puts them to the question:

> But if you will not serve [HaShem], choose today whom you wish to serve, whether the gods that your ancestors served beyond the River, or the gods of the Amorites in whose land you are now living. As for me and my House, we will serve [HaShem] (Joshua 24.15, JB, altered in the divine Name).

Judges is a cycle of stories of faith and unfaith, told briefly. Samuel is more complicated. Much of the work of 1 Samuel is to legitimate the move from the judges to the monarchy. The text and its editors are ambivalent about the change. In 1 Samuel 12, Samuel convenes an assembly, the monarchy is ratified, and Samuel both reproaches and pardons the people for choosing a king. (Here, as in other places also, several divergent theologies are presented.) It is not Samuel's dying words; he doesn't die until 1 Samuel 25.1. But this assembly is pretty much his last work, and the people's response is in its way a covenant renewal. We have progressed noticeably in the history of religions: Westphal says the covenant at the Exodus is not negotiated; this one (the monarchy) is very much the result of a struggle with God.

The kings usually do not have farewell sermons or covenant renewal ceremonies. The Deutenonomistic Historian does not approve of most of the kings; their behavior brings disaster on the monarchy. But when Josiah's priests discover the book of the Law in the Temple, there is once again an assembly and the covenant is renewed (2 Kings 22–23). After the monarchy has ended and the people are trying to recover in the Persian period, under Ezra and Nehemiah, there is another covenant renewal in Nehemiah 8–10, legal details in chapter 9, and the people's voluntary choice in 10.1.

Consciousness of covenantal choice has varied over the years. Usually, the only perceived author of a new covenant was God (see Aphrahat, p. 214 below); the human hand was invisible and unnoticed. Joshua 24 is quite exceptional, and it was never generalized in the Bible beyond the Deuteronomic theology's needs. Sociology of knowledge is a twentieth-century discovery, and theology has been slow to respond, though a few have seen the problem.[31]

1.11 Problems to Come

Some issues will recur throughout the rest of the story, some are inchoate here and waiting to appear later. The problem is a mishandling of anxiety, which will frequently become the root cause of problems in theology.

We have already seen, in prospect, that covenant is a confessional commitment, not something derived from logic. It is a choice. It manifests in a responsible liberty of interpretation: the covenant community has a discretionary authority in the conduct of its covenant. This leads to anxiety, and theology has all too often tried to cover up its choices and responsibilities in order to evade that anxiety. Two examples are the handling of "miracles" and the attempt to prove the so-called "existence" of God and correctness of Christianity.

Miracles come from ages long gone, and what they meant then is seldom clear now. Theology (and popular piety) all too often tried to objectivate the "miracles" in order to use them as proofs of faith and thereby evade the anxiety of faith. The ancient world had little concept of natural law as we know it, and it would be unfair to bring their texts to arguments about natural law or exceptions thereto.[32]

The other perennial way to escape the anxieties of a confessional commitment is to try to "prove" the correctness of Christianity. We shall see enough of that in chapters to come.

When biblical religion moved from its Hebrew origins into the Greco-Roman world, a dilemma became apparent, and both sides of the dilemma were well populated. Westphal characterizes biblical religion as a covenant community traveling through history in company with a transcendent Other. There are more ways than one to do that. At least two matter here. To do what someone else wants is to relate to that other person, in a way that makes the other present. As a consequence, accompanying a transcendent Other takes the apparent form of keeping the Other's Law. In the perspective of the history of religions, it was a humanly constructed Law, which puts the covenant participants in the position of asking ulti-

---

[31] One is Kaufman, *Essay on Theological Method*.

[32] The problem is not limited to the ancient world. Many today still think like the ancients about alleged miracles.

1.11 Problems to Come

mate reality to enter into their socially constructed reality. The other way to accompany the transcendent Other is to take particular chosen events in history as the presence of the Other, manifest in a human person (Jesus, as it happened) to whom the believer relates directly. Again, covenanters are in the position of asking ultimate reality to enter into their socially constructed reality. In both strategies, the humans are at the mercy of the other party to the covenant — ultimate reality. *Both* strategies are open to abuse in efforts to try to get control over the immanent presence of transcendence. In a sense, the history we are embarking on is a history of precisely that kind of abuse. Attempts to get control over transcendence are attempts to evade anxiety.

Two ways to do that stand out. In the first, Christian theologians think it is possible to begin de novo with Jesus. This is semi-Marcionite theology.[33] In semi-Marcionite theology, the inheritance from Second Temple Judaism is marginalized or ignored. When the Common Documents are still read, it is as if they are a commentary on the New Testament, not the foundation on which the New Testament is built. Even scholars in the modern world who should know better still do this.

The second way involves other conceptual errors as well, so it is somewhat complicated. We have seen it in the section above on a Chalcedonian method in the construction of transcendence. Once again, monophysite theology (whether in the doctrine of the Person of Christ or about divine action more generally) works to get the believer out of anxiety. It renders the transcendent as enough like the intramundane to make it predictable and controllable, at least conceptually. The traditional way to express the problem is in a concept of *analogy*, and there are ways to protect analogy from abuse, but that topic lies beyond this book.

The anxiety that lies at the origin of these problems can be seen in God's word to Moses at the Burning Bush, though not in the usual translations. Moses asks God's name. The answer is usually taken as a license for Greek ontology ("I am who I am") but this is not very helpful. John Courtney Murray glossed the Hebrew as "I shall be with you as who I am shall I be with you" — not entirely grammatical in English, but he claimed the Hebrew was already somewhat odd.[34] This calls out our anxiety as much as it names God. Anxiety did not become a thematic problem in phi-

---

[33] Fully Marcionite theology is rare. Other than Harnack, few names come to mind.

[34] Murray, *The Problem of God*, 10–11. See further comments at p. 10 above and at p. 28 below.

losophy until the modern period, with Søren Kierkegaard, returning much amplified in Heidegger. More of this below.

Some of the problems may be listed here; we shall see them as the history unfolds:

> residual traces of Marcionite theology;
> monophysite theology (and metaphysics) of divine action;
> trying to get out of the pains of life *ultimately*;
> not seeing how a historical life orientation works;
> a sacred canopy;
> confusing analogy, or taking analogy as univocal;
> proofs of God instead of confessional theology;
> naturalism, nominalism, materialisms, individualisms;
> turning away from existential phenomenology,
>   back to analytic philosophy of religion;
> metaphysical squalor: transcendence has lost its intelligibility.

We are embarking on a history of historical religion, following the accountant's question ("What do you want it to be?"), tracing some of its answers and evasions in the history of Christianity.

To give some indication of what's not here, there is a vast discussion of religiosity in a secular age (Charles Taylor's work is exemplary) that provides a depth and detail that this study cannot. For the most part, the present study traces problematic engagements in the life of the church at a level that is not nearly so subtle.

Chapter 2

The Common Documents

2.1 The Priestly Creation Story

The last editor writes the first preface, and so it was with the first Bible, the Pentateuch or Torah, but that recognition did not come until the nineteenth century. That editor will later come to be recognized as the "priestly editor." He (or more likely they) wrote around the time of the Babylonian Exile and assumed the worldview of the Babylonians of the sixth century BCE.

Our theme is openness and ambiguity in biblical religion, and it is present in the texts from the beginning. For one cannot really understand these texts unless one knows what is left out. In the first place, everything is declared to be *good*. In the surrounding nature religions, by contrast, some things are good, but not all. (More of that in Genesis 3.) It is a contest of good versus evil, and good wins in the end — sometimes just barely. It is in that sense that nature religion is world-affirming. The purpose of a nature religion is to further the triumph of good over evil, by enabling you to live in harmony with nature. In the nature-oriented beginning, evil could be grieved and remedied, but it was still evil. One marker of the disagreement with nature religions in Genesis 1 is the lack of names for the sun and moon gods; they are just called the greater light and the lesser light. To one from that culture, the omission would have been conspicuous. The priestly editor rejects the naturalistic worldview of good versus evil. It's all good. Clearly, this will not be easy, because the pains of life still hurt, some of them are beyond meaning or explanation, and remedies for them will still be necessary. We have a lot of work to do.

2.2 The Origin of Sin Was Not a Fall

Genesis 2.4 begins a different story of creation, by a different editor, known as the Yahwist, writing long before the Priestly Editor. This is well known in some academic circles but unevenly broadcast to the general population.[1] The two creation stories are mutually inconsistent, the demonstration of which is left as an exercise for the reader. The inconsistency tells us something about both the text and its later editors. That it did not bother them does not mean they were stupid or illogical, it means they were happy to include side by side multiple versions of the story, simply because the different versions all came from the same family — the one covenant people, in all its diversity. Inconsistency in the text means, for us, that it is not to be read as one single simple coherent argument from beginning to end. These texts are the legacy of a people and a tradition and a way of living. If you want to be a part of that way of living, you can be, but it is a choice (section 1.10), not the result of any kind of inference. There are no proofs that this is the one true religion. The texts won't excuse you from the responsibility for your own basic life orientation. Transcendence is present in these texts and stories, but for the moment, all we have is *their* language of transcendence. *Our* language of transcendence is yet to come.

Genesis 3, the story of Adam and Eve in the Garden of Eden, is the work of the Yahwist. This story is generally taken in Christian circles, as in Romans 5.15–20 (but probably not always in Jewish thinking), to be a "Fall." The "Fall" was the origin of sin, which has been passed on from one generation to the next in an inevitable way. In some languages, it is even called "hereditary" sin. Here again, the texts do not say what many readers think they say. In the first place, "fall" is not a word that appears in Genesis 3; that text does not tell us of "The Fall." Whatever Paul's meaning in Romans, "Fall" is also a Gnostic term, later meaning a fall of humanity from a happy spirit world into the world of physical bodies: a world of misery. Unlike nature religions and world-affirming historical religion, Gnosticism was *not* world-affirming. To borrow a Gnostic term, "fall," and project it onto Genesis 3 inevitably reads at least some Gnostic ideas into the text. To be fair, most Christian theology has insisted on the affirmation of the world as good as we saw it in Genesis 1, the Priestly creation story. And so the result was never fully Gnostic. Nevertheless, elements of Gnostic thinking persisted: the idea that human existence was

---

[1] One of the more accessible introductions is Friedman, *Who Wrote The Bible?*

2.2 The Origin of Sin Was Not a Fall

somehow spoiled.

I think there is a better explanation, and one that does not in the least undercut the seriousness of human sin. Genesis 3 is about the origins of sin, but it is also a continuation (or anticipation; the Yahwists wrote before the Priestly editors) of the emphasis on the goodness of human life and the world in Genesis 1. We need something more than taking the myth in Genesis 3 literally. It *is* a myth, not history, though it will turn out to be a myth *about* very real history. The origins of sin are to be found in the same place as the origins of human action, the transition from animal behavior (purely naturalistic) to a kind of action that is not finally explicable in naturalistic terms. That transition was the acquisition of language, which *was* historical, even if we don't know when or how it happened.[2] It is only with language that it becomes possible to ask and answer questions such as "Just what did you think you were doing?" There are many answers (ambiguity is always with us). We have ways of criticizing narratives, which must wait for now. To ask or answer that question is to participate in an activity, one we may as well call *responsibility*. (It is an activity before it is a property that people may or may not have.)

So why is language the origin of *sin*? Because it is the means of distinguishing between good and evil. To acquire language is to eat the fruit of the tree of knowledge of good and evil. Better put, good and evil are the fruit of language. To call the acquisition of language a *fall* is absurd, and to think we could be (or were) creatures *without* sin but *with* language is incoherent.

How is language the means of distinguishing between good and evil? That power lies in its openness and ambiguity. For it is in language that we create worlds, imagine futures, criticize the past, decide what we want, and take offense at what we don't like. It is language that enables us to think about more than what is present in the here and now: the past, the future, and things far away. But that can be done in many ways. Even when a description of a painful situation does not explicitly take offense, it can be *interpreted* as taking offense.[3] While what is actually said is privileged, the privilege is not absolute. Many things go without saying, and they are just as effective even if not spelled out. To say that I don't like something can be legitimately interpreted to mean taking offense at

---

[2] Anthropologists are working on the problem. Be patient.

[3] What is painful is offensible and *whether* offense is taken often depends on *context*, but context is left out, to be supplied by the hearer or reader, and so it is ambiguous.

it. Rarely is the attempt to dislike something without taking offense at it wholly successful. To take offense is to call it evil; to call some good thing evil is one of the original forms of sin. And in a created world, everything is good: that was the point of Genesis 1. Obviously, people disagree about that. Not everything is painless, and not everything is *right*: some things (events, actions) are horrendously wrong. This basic life orientation will not be easy.

2.3 The Name

In Exodus 3.14, at the Burning Bush, Moses asks God his name, and the answer is traditionally translated into Greek, Latin, and other Indo-European languages as, "I am who I am."[4] This is not as helpful as it could be, but it is worth a digression, for a lot of history hangs on it. It has been taken as a license to find a place in theology for a Greek philosophical fascination with questions about Being, being in and of itself. Let me bypass the philosophy of being and just observe that the being of beings always involves contingencies of some sort, and humans have a stake in those contingencies because they are the world we live in. Wherever a *contingency* affects someone's *interests*, it can be *narrated*, and those three features are the constitution of an *act*.[5] The theological tradition takes God to be the author of being, and with that I would agree. So the traditional translation, despite its problems, has some real truth in it. It does, however, bring a lot *to* the text, when readers usually think they are safely finding what is already *in* the text. Hence all readings of this text are responsible acts of interpretation. It could be read differently.

Returning from our digression about being, come back to God's answer to Moses at the Burning Bush. John Courtney Murray gives a better rendering in *The Problem of God*,[6] even if it seems more a paraphrase than a literal translation. It also does a better job of respecting the nuances in Hebrew, a non-Indo-European language and one not particularly interested in Greek philosophy. Murray translates the Hebrew, *eyeh asher eyeh*, as "I shall be with you as who I am shall I be with you."[7]

---

[4] Vulgate: Ego sum qui sum. LXX: Ἐγώ εἰμι ὁ ὤν.

[5] This was argued at length in my *Living in Spin*, 5, 147, and section 5.1.1.

[6] Murray, *The Problem of God*, 10.

[7] Murray doesn't cite the technical literature, but he easily could have. Westphal, *God,*

This is striking enough so that we should back up and look at the context in Moses' encounter with God at the Burning Bush. God has told him to return to Egypt and bring all his friends out here into the desert, abandoning the civilized big-city world (Egypt) for a precarious life of uncertainty in the barren wilderness. Moses is understandably nervous. Two verses earlier, we find out what the real issue is. Moses is trying to get his instructions straight. He says, "Who am I to go to Pharaoh and bring the sons of Israel out of Egypt?" The answer is not what we would expect: "'I shall be with you,' was the answer, 'and this is the sign by which you shall know that it is I who have sent you ...'" (Jerusalem Bible, Exodus 3.11–12)." God's answer touches the nerve of Moses' anxiety: will he (and we) be alone, or is God *with* us? Hence Murray's translation, "I shall be with you as who I am shall I be with you."[8] It is an answer within a non-answer. It names our anxieties, our relation to an Other who is not like human others. It is also a brilliant insight: what possessed the Elohist (the author of most of this text) to speak of God like this? To say that the text was divinely inspired burkes the issue and hides our responsibilities. In the history of religions, this is a new idea, and it has a human origin, for which we *are* responsible.

2.4 The Ten Commandments

Here they are, in order:

> (1) You shall bow down to no other god,
>   for [HaShem's] name is the Jealous One;
>   he is a jealous God.
>   Make no pact with the inhabitants of the land,
>   or, when they prostitute themselves
>   to their own gods and sacrifice to them,
>   they may invite you ...
> (2) You shall make yourself no gods of molten metal.
> (3) You shall celebrate the feast of Unleavened Bread ...

Guilt, and Death, 238, note 82, and citations therein. Westphal has for *eyeh asher eyeh*, "I will be there (for you) as I choose to be there." Von Rad, *Old Testament Theology*, 1.180–1, has much the same idea, with considerable discussion.

[8] Even Murray's translation is forced by Indo-European languages to make time and tense distinctions that may not be in the original Hebrew, but I don't know how to deal with that issue.

> (4) All that first issues from the womb is mine:
>   every male, every first-born of flock or herd.
> (5) For six days you shall labour,
>   but on the seventh day you shall rest ...
> (6) You shall celebrate the feast of Weeks ...
> (7) Three times a year all your menfolk
>   must present themselves before the Lord [HaShem],
>   the God of Israel.
> (8) You must not offer the blood
>   of the victim sacrificed to me
>   at the same time as you offer unleavened bread ...
> (9) You must bring the best of the first-fruits of your soil
>   to the house of [HaShem] your God.
> (10) You must not boil a kid in its mother's milk.
>   (JB, Exodus 34.14–26, altered in the divine name)

Hey, wait a minute!

Those are not the Ten Commandments that I remember!

That's not what I had to memorize as a kid!

Nevertheless, they *are* in the text, and inasmuch as they are the second edition, don't they supersede the first edition, the ones on the tablets Moses broke when he saw the Golden Calf?

By now the pattern should begin to be clear: We are dealing with multiple witnesses, different versions of the faith.

A trick question for you: how many commandments are there in the Ten Commandments? Answer: at least eleven. Protestants and Catholics number them differently (at least the ones in Exodus 20, the ones we are most familiar with). It doesn't particularly matter how you number them, though I grew up with the Protestant numbering, in which no other gods and no visible images are the first and second commandments instead of the first and its included corollary. Some of my fellow Catholics would, I think, like to hide the fact that the prohibition of visible images applies even to images of the One God, not just images of other gods. Perhaps that is because there are so many offenses against this commandment in Catholic history. Michelangelo's Sistine ceiling is only the most famous, justly revered, some of the finest Christian art. Once when I was saying my prayers before Mass in St. Louis cathedral in New Orleans, I looked up and who should be looking down on me but God himself! This artistic tradition is older than Michelangelo and continues still. Visible representation of God is not a good idea despite the genius of the art, even in priceless works that should nevertheless be treasured. Visible representation of God blunts precisely the anxiety of the presence of God that we saw in the text of Exodus 3.14 above. Perhaps the best response to breaking the second commandment is like that of Jesus to the woman caught in adultery in John 8: you are amply forgiven, but don't do it again.[9]

Return to the differences between the first and second editions of the Ten Commandments: The editors knew more than they tell us. Preserving multiple witnesses to faith, not all of which are mutually consistent, is exactly the biblical tradition.

2.5 The Shape of the Exodus

The Exodus story begins in Genesis and continues through 2 Kings, that is, all of the Pentateuch and the Former Prophets. The actual "exodus," Exodus 1–15, is merely the center of the story. Genesis is the preparation, and the story of the Monarchy is the outcome. The Exodus requires the prior context in the lives of the patriarchs, and its purpose is to fulfill the covenants with the patriarchs: the erection of the Monarchy, whose history is an essential part of the Exodus story.

In brief skeletal outline,[10]

> Israel begins in the Promised Land
> > with the patriarchs
> Israel goes down to Egypt
> > and there becomes a mighty nation;
> the management in Egypt changes,
> > the new management is unfriendly.
> The Israelites complain,
> the Boss brings Israel out of Egypt,
> > feeding them in the desert,
> > with many trials.
> Eventually they come into the Promised Land,

---

[9] There is another solution, for art that is portable (rather than attached to a building): simply moving the art to a museum avoids a host of problems. For example, while imagery is not a problem with Barnett Newman's Stations of the Cross, putting them in the Smithsonian keeps them out of many pointless controversies. The Church's debt of gratitude to New York Judaism for the Newman Stations is beyond calculation.

[10] The shape of the Exodus is mirrored in the Gospels; see section 3.1.

>   crossing the Jordan at Jericho,
>   settling in the land of Canaan;
>   Israel asks for a king.
>   The monarchy begins with Saul and David,
>   and through many cycles of faith and unfaith
>   eventually brings disaster upon itself.

This, especially the parts before the Monarchy, encapsulates the Short Historical Creed in Deuteronomy 26. That short text supplies the narrative structure of the major parts of the Common Documents, and everything else is fitted logically into that narrative structure.[11]

This has the shape of a Shakespearean tragedy: there is a prolog (Genesis 1–11), sort of like seeing Hamlet's ghost but before any development. The first act poses the problem: having enough children to make life worthwhile (Genesis 12–50). The second act develops the story (Exodus through Judges). The third act pivots in a way that determines how the story plays out: (1–2 Samuel). The fourth act is the beginning of the descent into disaster (1 Kings 1 to 2 Kings 17). The fifth act is the final disaster itself (2 Kings 18–25).[12] It may not be an accident that many narratives follow such a pattern. Indeed, much of the story *was* plotted — by an author or group of authors, the so-called Deuteronomist, or just "D," one of J, E, D, and P. He (or they) wrote more than just the book of Deuteronomy, for his friends continued the story in what is known as the Deuteronomistic History, i. e., the Former Prophets, from Joshua to 2 Kings. So the structure of the story is intentional, which makes it less surprising that it is like Shakespeare's structures.

The third act pivot (1 and 2 Samuel) resolves some of the ambiguities in the story thus far, but it also prepares for what follows. It makes the narrative categories concrete, it shows us *how* those narrative categories and tensions must be handled in the fourth and fifth acts. Even here, multiple voices are respectfully recorded, as in the dispute about whether to have a king at all in 1 Samuel 8–12. Those voices have been integrated into the larger story in a way that serves *its* development; we do not have them in older or more original texts.

One might complain that the greater Exodus story was not written like

---

[11] Von Rad, the title essay in *The Problem of the Hexateuch*.

[12] Given the structure of Shakespeare's tragedies, it is fairly easy to spot the same structures in the greater Exodus. See William Gibson, *Shakespeare's Game*.

2.5 The Shape of the Exodus

a Shakespearean tragedy and, of course, there is a sense in which that is true. It is too long. Way too long. It has too much extraneous material in it: genealogies, shopping lists, liturgical instructions, cosmologies, real estate deeds, not to mention the laws, which Christians overlook and the rabbis treasure, for differences of reason to which we come below.

Yet differences of genre aside, the Exodus for reasons intrinsic to narrative has some of the same features of a drama. In Shakespeare, the plays presuppose a prior equipoise, some system of contingencies and interests that are in balance with one another and, if left to themselves, likely to continue in the future much as in the past. William Gibson observes that the plays begin with a "happening," an event that disturbs the prior equipoise, and from that disturbance follows the story as it unfolds. On the stage, it takes two or three hours, that's all the audience has paid to see. In the Common Documents, it takes many hundreds of pages, with many digressions.

Yet the prior equipoise is easy to identify, if one knows what to look for. It is a world with a naturalistic worldview, a world whose life-orientation is focused on nature. In nature, things happen naturally, and that is not just a vapid tautology. In nature, things *have* natures, and their natures determine how they move. Even the indeterminate is random in ways that are typical or characteristic of the beings we see. (In physics, that randomness is still mathematically intelligible, as in statistical mechanics.) In this conception of nature, real action, action that is neither random nor determined, is not natural, it is a disturbance of nature. We will see details below, in section 6.7. For now, the disturbance (Abraham needs children) does not begin to tell us what it will develop into: a world-affirming *historical* orientation, a world in which history makes sense, in which history is more than a meaningless surd within nature.

As Dryden says to General Murray about 14 minutes into *Lawrence of Arabia*, "Big things have small beginnings." Why do some small things (and not others) become the beginnings of big things? That is a matter of narrative, and narrative is the origin of action as much as action is the origin of narrative.[13]

---

[13] This was the central thesis of *Living in Spin*. The relation between narrative and action is ontologically and hermeneutically circular.

2.6 The Atrocities

Biblical religion evolved over a period of more than a thousand years, from before Samuel and David to the Disasters of the First Century, and there was more in that development than meets the eye. The Common Documents are a record, from many voices, of the transformation of a nature religion into a world-affirming historical religion. As part, but only one part, of that evolution, many remnants of nature religion survived well into the Persian period and after. The most embarrassing were the atrocities. We never hear them on Sunday mornings, and for good reason.

Biblical actors have a better excuse than the later atrocities committed by the Churches against rabbinic Judaism and other Christians. In the first millennium BCE and even more in the second, they could plead that they were new to world-affirming historical religion and didn't quite yet know what it entailed. The Churches in the second millennium CE have no such excuse.

The list below tells only a few of the atrocities, along with some other episodes where the deity commands things we would regard as unethical:

>   Genesis 19, the destruction of Sodom
>   Genesis 22, the binding of Isaac
>   Genesis 34.25, slaughter of the males of Shechem
>   Exodus 17.8, slaughter of Amalek
>   Exodus 32.25, Levites slaughter the faithless
>   Numbers 21.21, Sihon and Og
>   Numbers 15.16, God: harry the Midianites
>   Numbers 25, the Baal of Peor
>   Numbers 31, vengeance on Midian
>   Numbers 31.16, slaughter of the women
>   Numbers 33.2–6, drive out aboriginals
>   Deuteronomy 2.26, Sihon again
>   Deuteronomy 3.1, Og again
>   Deuteronomy 7.1–6, "lay them under the ban"
>   Deuteronomy 7.22, "God will destroy..."
>   Deuteronomy 20.10–15, slaughter/enslave enemies
>   Joshua 6.17, Jericho under the ban
>   Joshua 8.26, Ai under the ban
>   Joshua 12.7, more kings conquered
>   Judges: many wars, some victories

1 Samuel 15, Samuel hewed Agag in pieces

This is hardly a complete list and, as said, we mostly shield ourselves from reading it. By contrast, if one lives in a lectionary, or reads all of the Pentateuch once a year instead of just snippets from it, the atrocities eventually become oppressive and appalling. That we today do not regard these texts as "operative" (to use an American political expression of prevarication) does not face their full import. As said at the beginning of this section, the texts from Genesis through II Kings and on through the Persian period provide a history of the evolution of historical religion out of preexisting nature religion. That is true enough, but it is easy to dodge an implication that should be spelled out. We can read these texts as authoritative scripture but *not* as "dictated" by God. They are a transcript of what people then heard (or thought they heard) from God. They are a history of growth in faith but not of instruction for us. I think this is as true for rabbinic Judaism as it is for Christianity. For both of us, what needs emphasis is the history of companionship between the community of the faithful and the transcendent Other, and that is a history of love, even if the Other has a larger and more generous perspective than the humans involved. The presence of the Other does not deify the human covenanters.

These atrocities, both those recounted and those commanded, are a sample of the laws or deeds that we would consider unjustifiable. In the law, there are many capital offenses that we would consider not worthy of death; some we would not count as offenses at all.

Many individuals did indefensible things that were nevertheless typical for that age; Jephthah's vow and sacrifice of his daughter is only one of the more picturesque. Did the editors approve? Since the Deuteronomistic Historian shaped his tale as cycles of faith, unfaith, disaster, and repentance, it is doubtful that he (or they) really approved of Jephthah's behavior.

The worst, the atrocities, were a normal feature of nature religions; tribalism and elimination of the competition were common. The development in the last millennium BCE, from David and Solomon to the end of Second-Temple Judaism, was a transformation, from nature religion to world-affirming historical religion.

The texts give us a worldview very different from our own, and so it is fair to ask, what do we have in common with them? The answer is that there is a difference between a people's worldview (or even just world) and how they relate to it, as we saw in section 1.8. What we see is the development of world-affirming historical religion, historical-covenantal religion, slowly and by stages.

2.7 David's Shenanigans

Consider David's career, especially the parts that are never read on Sunday morning. The parts that *are* read in Church are fairly pious. A better picture of David gives us an exceedingly crafty politician, always lucky to have others kill his enemies for him. But let me not tell the story, when a better version is available in Stefan Heym's *The King David Report*. David's successor, Solomon, had a triple legitimacy problem: he had to legitimate the monarchy — at all — against those who preferred to continue with judges. He had to legitimate the House of David against the House of Saul, and he had to legitimate himself against his older brothers. What resulted was,

> The One and Only True and Authoritative, Historically Correct and Officially Approved Report on the Amazing Rise, God-fearing Life, Heroic Deeds, and Wonderful Achievements of David the Son of Jesse, King of Judah for Seven Years and of Both Judah and Israel for Thirty-three, Chosen of God, and Father of King Solomon[14] ...

Heym meant the book as a satire on Josef Stalin, a modern-day Solomon (see 1 Kings 1–2, 12).

2.8 Job and His Friends

At this point, a number of conversations in theology proceeded in several different directions. One leads through Qoheleth to Job and Deutero-Isaiah, and thence to the New Testament.[15] The other, also from Qoheleth, leads to the Wisdom literature. I pass over the Megilloth and the Chronicler's History, beloved as they are, because they would take us too far afield.

---

[14] Heym, *The King David Report*, 9.
[15] This observation comes from Samuel Terrien.

2.8 Job and His Friends

First look at the book of Job, a disagreement within the tradition: the Deuteronomic theology and its critics. The dispute between Job and his friends offers many lessons. One that overly pious readers don't notice is that the Bible contains many theologies and they do not all agree. Job's friends are not alone; their theology is characteristic of the Deuteronomic tradition and it occurs in other places as well (e.g., Psalm 37).

In Deuteronomic theology, the wicked get what they deserve and likewise the righteous. For the Deuteronomists, there is no injustice in fate or happenstance. Job knows better, and his protests make a claim on us today. Deuteronomic theology survives in all theodical attempts to justify the pains and evils in life, a feature of Analytic philosophy of religion.

Some replies parallel Job's, of which one of the clearest is D. Z. Phillips' *The Problem of Evil and the Problem of God*, but he is hardly alone. (Terrence Tilley could be mentioned also.[16]) Theodicy is characteristic of the modern world, and Phillips' arguments against it impeach the mainstream modern conceptions of God. They all speak of God as if He could be known as we know phenomena in this world, without the precariousness of mystery.

The God of Analytic philosophy of religion is hard to distinguish from someone with a fiction writer's power over history and events. But that way leads to moral incoherence, and even Analytic philosophers have begun to suspect that they may not be able to understand God after all.

The other point to be made about the many voices in the Bible is that none are to be thrown out or decanonized. They all have a place, and they get their meaning from their place in the conversation with those who disagreed with them. Even the Deuteronomists are not always wrong. As beloved as Deuteronomic theology is in rabbinic Judaism, it is not the only theology in the Common Documents.

Whereas Jacob at the Jabbok struggled with God and won, Job struggles with God and gets no answers. This is a considerable development. In Qoheleth, all is vanity, and the humble soul might as well live with that, gracefully if possible. The author of Job asks, but what about all the pains? Numerous times, I have characterized biblical religion as affirming human life in this historical world, in full view of its pains. You have a responsible liberty of interpretation in the conduct of a covenant, but that still leaves the problem of pain. Something has to be said about it. Job comes up empty and therein lies his lesson for us.

---

[16] Phillips, *The Problem of Evil*. Tilley, *The Evils of Theodicy*.

We all deal with the pains, both practically in our lives and communally in our explanations. I would say theoretically, but my point (and Job's) is that our theories have no ground to stand on. We end up holding the bag, so to speak. Ultimate reality tells us little, and that does not make it evil or malicious, but it does make it holy — and in that holiness, somewhat frightening. Hence the Common Documents' reverence for "fear of the Lord," a part of their theology that is usually overlooked.

The sequence from Qoheleth to Job to Deutero-Isaiah was used as an argument for sequential dating of those texts by Samuel Terrien.[17]

2.9 Deutero-Isaiah

Isaiah is usually divided into two or three parts, the second beginning at chapter 40, and the third at chapter 56. The second and third are post-exilic, though there is some post-exilic matter in 1–39 also. The problems in Deutero-Isaiah are new. Isaiah of Jerusalem, as 1–39 is known, is preoccupied with the problems of the monarchy under Hezekiah and the kings before and after him. In Deutero-Isaiah we see (or hear) a concern to eliminate other gods, and with that concern the problem of suffering. The first is a variation on earlier themes, the second we inherit from Job. Rejection of other gods appears in more than one form in the Pentateuch and Former Prophets. The Yahwist lampoons them (in Genesis 31.34–35, the idols have to hide in a porta-potty); the Deuteronomists take them very seriously, as dangerous popular abominations. Deutero-Isaiah, like the Yahwist, lampoons them: Isaiah 44.9–20. We have come, at this stage in the development of world-affirming historical religion, to a sense that one must make a choice. The character of the one God is different from and incompatible with that of the other gods, the gods of nature and nature religion. It is not yet clear how that will play out, and it would be unfair to project onto Isaiah a twentieth century theology of "radical monotheism" (H. Richard Niebuhr); we are not there yet.

What preoccupies the Isaianic tradition at this point is pain, suffering. The four Servant Songs are only the most visible texts. The problem of pain is there in the beginning, when Isaiah comforts the exiles in Babylon, promising return to the land of Israel. But in the end, he knows (and we know) that mere reprieve from today's suffering is not enough. Hence the Servant Songs, which are open to multiple interpretations, even on

---

[17] See Samuel Terrien's Introduction to Job, in *The Interpreter's Bible*.

the plain sense of the texts. The Servant suffers, and his suffering will benefit others (us). Whether the Servant is an individual or the people of Israel itself is not entirely clear. This explicitly departs from the idea that one person's suffering for another (whether just or unjust) is barren of good. How it might bring good Isaiah does not tell us — wisely, since it virtually always is a moral surd, something that doesn't make sense, raising unanswerable questions.

We use the Servant Songs to make sense of Jesus and the Passion, but they were not intended that way. That will take the conversation that began with Qoheleth and Job and was radicalized in Deutero-Isaiah on to its next steps.

2.10 Qoheleth and the Wisdom Literature

The route from Qoheleth to the Wisdom literature offers us a much needed cautionary perspective. Qoheleth sees pointlessness in life and blames it on vanity. This is not wrong, but the phenomenon is richer than he saw. The remedy is a certain reticence, compunction, and humility before the mishaps of history and life. In that reticence is a respect for the unanswerableness of the questions we raise — questions we *have* to raise. What follows in Sirach is a collection of maxims for how to stay out of trouble. They are very sensible, but they retreat from the real challenge of moral absurdity. For that, we need to return to the trajectory from Deutero-Isaiah to the Gospels, if possible without forgetting the lessons of Qoheleth. Usually, they were forgotten.

Chapter 3

The New Testament

3.1 The Exodus in the Gospels

In section 2.5 we saw the structure of the Exodus and how it binds together the Common Documents as a coherent literary collection. There is a structural parallel between the plots of the Synoptic Gospels and the Exodus.[1] The key is to identify Jesus as the new Israel, or the new Joshua (the names are even the same in Greek).

> Both Israels start out in the Promised Land
> both go down to Egypt
>   there is a slaughter of innocents in both cases
> both are tested and fed in the desert
>   one for 40 years, one for 40 days
> both reenter the Promised Land
>   crossing the Jordan at Jericho,
> and after a period of activity,
> both go up to Jerusalem
> and a triumph of sorts.

There is an inescapable irony in the endings of the Gospels. The Exodus story has been retold with the ineffable pain of Deutero-Isaiah rather than the triumphalism of the King David Report. Disaster has been reunderstood as triumph. That vision is precarious, and forgetting its precariousness is the way to serious trouble. We come to more on that when we

---

[1] It is incomplete in Mark, but Matthew and Luke saw what Mark was doing and supplied the missing parts at the beginning.

3.1 The Exodus in the Gospels

look at the problem of the miracles in the Gospels in section 3.2, and some attempts to make sense of it, in section 8.1.

The structural parallel between the Gospels and the Exodus was seen by Meredith G. Kline in 1975,[2] but Edward Hobbs described it twenty years earlier in his University of Chicago dissertation on Exodus typology in the Gospel of Mark.[3] Hobbs' position has changed in details but not, I think, in regard to the importance of Exodus typology in the Gospels.[4] Indeed, the problem of accounting for the structure of the Synoptics has attracted much attention without a consensus theory emerging. Nevertheless, the centrality of the Exodus has survived in that conversation.

Whether or not to read the Gospels as Exodus typology has a simple consequence. On one reading, the traditional reading, the "Old" Testament is about predictions of Jesus, and it is merely prolog for the Gospels. On the other reading, Exodus typology in the Gospels, the Common Documents are not just prolog, they are the *model* and foundation for the Gospels. The Common Documents were not written with Jesus in mind, as if by some magical or preternatural "inspiration" by God. They were written about their own concerns and for their own times. The writers knew nothing of Jesus (whatever may be said in another voice about divine intentions), and it is not fair to begin interpretation of the Common Documents with prior knowledge of Jesus.

Note a feature of the difference: The kind of challenge the Common Documents make is radically changed. In the traditional reading, they can be used as "proofs" of the divinity of Christ, etc. In the typological reading, they are not proofs, they are an invitation to faith, a faith that began with the Exodus and continues with Jesus (and with the Mishnah). But they do not get the believer out of responsibility for his faith, should he accept the invitation the documents and history make. To make an obvious parallel, the claim that one cannot really understand the Gospels without prior knowledge of the Exodus is like the observation that Monty Python's *Life of Brian* makes little sense without prior knowledge of the Gospels. The Synoptics are parody — *holy* parody — but parody nonetheless. Exodus typology in the Gospels is hardly new in biblical scholarship. Patristic exegesis knew it well, but it was mostly forgotten after the middle ages. It has been recently rediscovered and radicalized, though it is still not much

---

[2] Kline, "The Old Testament Origins of the Gospel Genre."
[3] Hobbs, "The Gospel of Mark and the Exodus."
[4] Private communication.

known in the popular understanding of the New Testament.

3.2 Problems with Miracles

If there is one problem for theology in the modern world that stands out, it is the question of what to do with the miracle texts in the New Testament. It is the reason theology has lost its credibility for so many. These texts were presumably believed literally before the modern period, though that assumption is open to question. In the modern period, they have been read literally and that reading accepted "as gospel" or else simply rejected as false. The change has accompanied a changed concept of nature and of what is naturally possible.

We do not yet have the resources we will need to make sense of the miracle texts. The underlying principle was sketched in section 1.5. The problem runs through the Church's history, as we shall see in section 5.3. Resources to address it will come with modern scholarship, in section 8.1. In the meantime, we find ourselves in the middle of the Gospels, and some things must be said, for the miracle texts are clearly very important. I would not accept the move of Liberal Theology, writing off the miracles as unscientific confusions of a former age, with no theological significance. They do come from an unscientific age, but they are nevertheless theologically significant. They are not nearly as unaware of the meanings of what they wrote as Liberal theology takes them to be. It is Liberal theologians, not the Gospel writers, who are naive.

The issues raised by miracles in the New Testament are not what they appear to be (the historicity of apparent events) but rather a question of the larger context in which to read the texts. They are not proofs but invitations to faith and challenges to choose. How do you *want* to read them? That question will be with us for some time.

The invitation to faith focuses on the person of Jesus. They are not histories or biographies in the modern sense. Many questions that we would instinctively ask, they do not answer. In the miracle texts, a client with a problem gets the problem solved by the product being advertised, usually with something preposterous happening along the way. The thrust of the texts, in summary, is that Jesus cleanses, raises, and feeds Israel. This is Exodus typology: Where God, through Moses and Joshua, rescued Israel from Egypt in the past, he is doing the same thing again. That message is clear enough, though making sense of it in its details is much harder.

3.2 Problems with Miracles

Are the miracle texts to be taken literally (assuming we even know what it would mean to take them literally)? This is a problem for us because the evangelists appear to believe the "miraculous" healings literally, even if we don't.

The texts are similar to TV advertisements.[5] For the present, suppose one *were* to read them as like TV advertisements (after all, an invitation to faith is sort of like an advertisement). What then is the *product* being advertised in these texts? It is not named, not in the theoretical terms that would make us happy in our own time. A hint appears in the beginning of Mark, in the call to *metanoia* (1.5); literally, *change of mind. Metanoia* is usually translated as repentance (for sins), and while that is not wrong, it is not quite the sense in question here. Repentance for sins (followed by forgiveness of sins) is often the preparation for the healing that follows. The word *metanoia* and its derivatives appear only a few times in Mark (at the beginning), a little more in Matthew, and more in Luke and elsewhere. It is not a marker of emphasis, and it usually is translated as repentance *for sins.*

Yet there is another sense of the word at stake in these texts, as change of mind. The clients who buy the product are "saved," but are they saved *from* their pains, or *in* their pains? That depends on how you read the preposterous in the middle of the miracle texts. If you want to be saved *from* your pains, you pretty much have to read the texts literally. If you are willing to be saved *in* your pains, the literal reading doesn't help. Here we extend the exploration begun in Job and Deutero-Isaiah. This is what it means to affirm human life in this painful world as good, without resorting to Deuteronomistic theology that tries to justify the pains of life. You have a liberty of interpretation in dealing with your pains, and Deuteronomistic theology (somewhat like karma) is not the only option available.

If read as advertisements, the miracle texts challenge us, precisely because they put us to the question: Are we saved *from* the pains of life, or *in* the pains of life? The texts do not compel an answer; you have to choose. In that challenge, the Bible doesn't give us simple answers to our questions, it prods us in our questioning. This is an instance of the general ambiguity present in a world-affirming historical basic life orientation.

The move from being saved *from* the pains of life to being saved *in* the pains of life is precisely what Mark 1.5, 1.15, and 6.12 are advertising:

---

[5] We return to this in section 8.1, p. 145. The similarity was first noticed by Edward Hobbs.

metanoia, a change of mind — change of mind about ultimate reality.

3.3   Exposure, Limitation, and Need

In section 1.7, p. 15, I promised more about Exposure, Limitation, and Need. They are themes in the New Testament, usually unlabeled. Even though we have not yet reviewed the resources of modern scholarship, it is possible to note the emergence of Exposure, Limitation, and Need here. Their principal locus is in the miracles, but the teaching will support our reading of the miracle texts, in a preliminary way in this section, and in more detail in chapter 8. The challenge of the miracle texts begins with clients who face pains of one sort or another. In the process of *metanoia* they come to find salvation. On my reading, contrary to literalists, they find salvation in those very pains, rather than from them. That is not easy, nor should it be made to seem easy. The pains remain painful, and wrongs remain wrong. Bearing them doesn't make them go away.

Look again at the miracle texts. What sort of pains are dealt with in them? In the healings, some are raised, some are cleansed. The others that deal with human need are feedings.[6]

What about the teaching? In some we are enjoined to face up to the truth about ourselves. In some, we are enjoined to accept limitation with gratitude and joy (Matthew 20.1–16). In some we are enjoined to help our neighbor in need. Call these three sorts of pains Exposure, Limitation, and Need. They were spotted as a series by Edward Hobbs, who characterized them as "(1) exposure of the self; (2) contingency or limitation; and (3) need of others for our aid."[7]

The teaching repeats or reinforces the issues in the miracles, where Jesus cleanses, raises, and feeds Israel. Cleansing, raising, and feeding are remedies for Exposure, Limitation, and Need. Does the teaching mean we are supposed to get *out* of Exposure, Limitation, and Need or to find

---

[6] There are other "miracles," notably having to do with water: walking on water, stilling a storm. This is an Exodus theme. I don't know what to do with the withering of the fig tree.

[7] Hobbs originally published this claim in "An Alternate Model from a Theological Perspective," in Herbert A. Otto, ed., *The Family in Search of a Future* (New York, Appleton-Century-Crofts, 1970). They are repeated in Porter and Hobbs, "The Trinity and the Indo-European Tripartite Worldview," *Budhi* (Manila) Vol. 3, nos. 2&3 (1999) 1–28; on the net at http://www.jedp.com/trinity.html. The Indo-European cultural background for this Trinitarian theology was traced in that paper. The same material is covered, with credit to Hobbs, in my own *Elementary Monotheism*, vol. I.21–26, section 3.1.

3.3 Exposure, Limitation, and Need

God's good blessing *in* them? Answering that question is not a matter of finding the proposition that answers it correctly. It is a lifetime of struggle, sometimes technically known as *conversio morum*, conversion of life or conversion of habits. You can struggle with God but I would hazard that it is wrong to set *conditions* on God. The model is Jacob at the Jabbok (Genesis 32.23–33), not Jacob's conditional promise of loyalty (Genesis 28.20–21) at Bethel. At Bethel, Jacob says, "If God goes with me and keeps me safe on this journey I am making, if he gives me bread to eat and clothes to wear, and if I return home safely to my father, then [HaShem] shall be my God." (JB) This is a poor theology. Getting from the understanding of God at Bethel to that at the Jabbok demonstrates considerable maturation.

All three of Exposure, Limitation, and Need (and their underlying conceptualities of order, action, and sustenance) are ambiguous. To be exposed is to be shown as one is, rather than as one pretends to be, but there is ambiguity in both pretense and reality. We have ways of criticizing narratives and often need to work to get the story straight. But even then, there can be multiple narratives, multiple accounts of human actions that are all simultaneously true, though not all "matter" equally. The Limitations of life are seldom unequivocally clear, and we usually have a liberty of interpretation in dealing with them. We have choices, in other words, as when one goal can be had at the expense of another, though not both together. And even in others' Need we find the same ambiguity. What are someone's real interests? How do we balance one person's interests with another's? We have conventional ways of resolving some of these ambiguities but not all of them.

Last and deepest is the ambiguity in looking for blessing in the pains of life, in seeking good in them rather than from them. That is inherent in radical monotheism as H. Richard Niebuhr described it. There are many ways to seek good in the pains of life.

That commitment is not uniquely Christian. Though it is not theoretical in the Common Documents, examples of each of Exposure, Limitation, and Need can be found there. It does appear in the abstract (not as a series) in the Talmud, at Berakoth 60b.[8] The rabbis ask whether we are to offer up a blessing (a berakah) for the evil in life as we do for the good. St. Paul in Romans 8 is subtle and nuanced by comparison. The rabbis leave no wiggle room and simply answer in the affirmative. *How* we are to do that

---

[8] Soncino Talmud, Seder Zera'im, Tractate Berakoth 60b, 379.

is another question, one with many answers. These themes that appeared only implicitly in the narratives of the New Testament will develop and become explicit in the history that has followed since.

3.4 Christians and Jews in the New Testament

All that ambiguity shows itself at the root of one major question in the New Testament and its aftermath. How do we handle the disagreements between Christianity and rabbinic Judaism? The New Testament is a collection of documents telling the emergence of Christianity from Second Temple Judaism. It was a bitter quarrel, and we have only one side of it. "The Jews" don't get much favorable treatment, an issue to which we shall return more than once. The possibility raised in the texts but usually denied or evaded is that the covenant community could split into two *legitimate* daughter religions. Second Temple Judaism was destroyed by the Romans, and both the New Testament (after Paul) and the Mishnah grew out of that destruction: What do we do now?

Romans 9–11 is one example where the NT deals with relations to "the Jews." It is also one of the few that does so thematically and does so with even minimal charity toward non-Christian Judaism. There are many more places in the New Testament that qualify as anti-Jewish polemic, but they usually don't speak explicitly about the covenant with Judaism. Paul in Romans 9–11 is not sweet on synagogue Judaism, but he is more nuanced in his disagreements than most other NT texts, and he does grant that the covenant with Judaism is not annulled. The verses 9.1–5 are actually rather complimentary to the Judaism of Paul's time, as he is proud of his Jewish roots there.[9] So in a sense, Romans 9–11 may be the least anti-Jewish of the texts that bear directly on relations between emerging rabbinic Judaism and Christianity.

These chapters can be interpreted many ways, often requiring that some texts be subordinated to others; it is not clear that there is a single consistent and coherent answer to all the questions we would bring to these three chapters. Clearly, Paul is not in a good humor about "the Jews." The issues as always were about the Law and liberation from the Law, and the place of Jesus. One could put it as a choice, "Christ or kashrut (and circumcision)."

---

[9] Beck, *Mature Christianity*, 81.

3.4 Christians and Jews in the New Testament

Most readers have taken these chapters to mean that in the end, all Jews will convert and become Christian, though the text does not actually say that. My first source is Krister Stendahl's discussion in *Paul Among Jews and Gentiles*. Nevertheless, Paul does say that the covenant with "the Jews" is not annulled, not in the least. Yet Christian readers commonly take 11.23–24 and especially 11.26, "... and so all Israel will be saved" to mean that at the end time, all Jews will become Christians. What follows illustrates both the problem and a solution. Norman Beck points out a problem in the recent translations. Romans 11.28 in the RSV reads:

> As regards the gospel they are enemies *of God*, for your sake; but as regards election they are beloved for the sake of their forefathers. [29] For the gifts and the call of God are irrevocable.

I have italicized two words that are not in the Greek, which has ἐχθροὶ δι' ὑμᾶς not ἐχθροὶ θεοῦ δι' ὑμᾶς. To find a correct translation, one must go back to the Authorized Version or the Douay-Rheims because almost all the translations after 1920, the RSV included, have corrupted the text; they all have inserted "of God," so that the text reads "enemies of God." The Authorized Version (King James) got it right. The Douay-Rheims got it right; the Vulgate got it right. Even Luther, no lover of Jews, got it right.[10] The mistranslation has come upon us insidiously and unconsciously but not innocently. It is anti-Semitic, and it coincides with the modern resurgence of anti-Semitism. We all thought anti-Semitism crested with the Shoah, but we were wrong; it continues into the twenty-first century with renewed and appalling virulence.

Norman Beck gives an extended discussion of Romans 9–11 and these verses in particular. The Greek is ambiguous, but Beck goes around the ambiguity of *echthroi*:

> Therefore a literal translation would be something such as
>
> "with respect to the gospel they are *not loved* (estranged, alienated) because of you, but with respect to the election they are *beloved* because of their ancestors." (111)

As he says, "the adjectives *echthroi* and *agapētoi* are rather sharply contrasted."[11] He renders *echthroi* as "not loved" in order to bring out that

---

[10] Beck, *Mature Christianity*, 110–12.
[11] Beck, *Mature Christianity*, 111.

contrast. I actually prefer the meaning in common translations, "they are enemies for your sake," which suggests that God has made them your enemies in order to do something good for you. What that good is, we shall see soon enough.

In any case, things begin to make sense. If we assume a responsible liberty of interpretation on the part of the covenant people, it is easy. We still have to find that responsible liberty of interpretation, but that is not difficult.

There has been a little progress recently. Late twentieth century translations of Romans 11.28 all get it right. And at Vatican II, there were moves toward dismantling the tradition of anti-Jewish theology. Nostra Aetate (4) speaks of "the spiritual patrimony common to Christians and Jews" and it denies that Judaism is responsible for the death of Christ. If there really is such a common patrimony, that poses for us the problem of how to make sense of the division of that patrimony. Addressing that will take us to the roots of historical-covenantal religion, in ways that we have largely forgotten.

The issues that Paul raises in Romans 9–11 touch broader questions. Anti-Jewish theology is only one. Central is religious choice (which we have already seen in Joshua 24), the anxiety that comes with it. Christians have all too often tried to cover up religious choice with a "sacred canopy." The issues that Paul has raised will take us to Exposure before we are done. The social construction of religions will be one of our enduring themes. And in Paul's comments on the incipient parting of the ways between Christianity and rabbinic Judaism we see a characteristic bitterness, self-certainty, and lack of self-criticism common when a new religious movement is born.[12]

What we have in the separation of Christianity from rabbinic Judaism raises the possibility of multiple covenants — a possibility denied by both parties. It is an example of the phenomenon we started with, in the accountant's response to his prospective employer's question about 2×2: "What do you want it to be?" In effect, we have bumped into a *responsible liberty of interpretation*.

---

[12] Cf. Norman Beck's comments.

3.5 A Responsible Liberty of Interpretation

It is time to explore the possibility that we just called a "responsible liberty of interpretation." It is in the texts, explicitly in places, though the New Testament does not provide a *theory* of responsible liberty. It is even limited and opposed in some places in the New Testament and certainly limited and opposed by later readers. It is shared with other sources in first-century Judaism, and it grew and developed in rabbinic Judaism as well as in Christianity. Reflection in depth does not come for several centuries, and while there may be Christian sources, the most magnificent text is in the Babylonian Talmud. We come to that in section 4.4.

My principle disagreement with the tradition is a simple one, and it follows the pattern in this book: in many places, the tradition did more or less the right thing but did not carry it far enough. In other places, the tradition was simply wrong (e.g., the atrocities, or sacred canopies), but there are resources within the tradition to correct the problems. Paul claims a responsible liberty for Christians, but if it is granted to Christians, why isn't it granted to the rest of first-century Judaism also? I think it is, and Paul all but admits as much in places. First, let us see the places where a responsible liberty is explicitly granted in the New Testament. Prominent themes are the forgiveness of sins, the "Power of the Keys," freedom from the Law, freedom vis-a-vis God, discretionary authority in the conduct of the Church's affairs, forbearance towards others, and a liberty in covenant that includes the Jews. These are the place to begin. They are interrelated.

Jesus' opponents in the Gospels seem to think that forgiveness of sins is available only from God, or available through the keeping of the Law. This may well be a caricature of first-century Judaism, but it is the evangelists' position that we are interested in, not the historicity of those they argue against. In the Gospels, the forgiveness of sins is freely available, and it is subject to human discretion. It is free for the asking, and what the Church decides is binding. This is known as the "Power of the Keys," and it appears in Matthew 16.13-20, esp. 16.19, repeated in Matthew 18.18 and in John 20.22: "Whatever you bind on earth shall be considered bound in heaven; whatever you loose on earth shall be considered loosed in heaven." It appears in other words in Mark (2.7) and Luke (5.24) also. There could not be anything clearer or more explicit in a grant of discretionary authority to the human community of faith.

There is more than meets the eye in this simple claim of authority to forgive sins. To forgive sins is to revise narratives and the commitments and obligations of the offender and offended. In a philosophically simple world, that could be missed. It is the opening to a much richer world, as we saw in *Living in Spin* and shall see in *Unanswerable Questions.*

The forgiveness of sins is a concrete instance of something much broader, freedom from the Law, from kashrut, circumcision, and the sabbath restrictions. This appears in the Gospels in the healings on the sabbath and in the Benedictus, but it becomes thematic and emphatic in Paul. In the Gospels, the Law was made for man, not man for the Law (Mark 2.23–28, Matt. 12.1–8, Luke 6.1–5). It is in Romans and it is the theme of Galatians. The Greek word is *eleutheria,* freedom. Galatians 1.5 in the AV speaks of "the liberty wherewith Christ hath made you free." The Greek is something like "the *eleutheria* for which Christ has *eleutherized* us."

What Christian readers don't want to hear is that Christ has eleutherized rabbinic Judaism just as much as he has the Church. The liberty is given also to the other covenant inheritors, who became rabbinic Judaism. How could it not be? Paul himself says that the original Exodus covenant still continues. The Gospels say that if you do not forgive others, you will not be forgiven. By analogy, that applies here also: if you claim a freedom and liberty for yourselves, you have to allow it for other (i.e. non-Christian) Jews also.

Paul is hardly a moral nihilist, he does not say nothing matters and anything goes — in his words, "sin the more, that grace may abound." He is still opposed to the vices, and he gives several long lists. What Paul opposes is an *abuse* of the Law. In the history of Christian theology, this quarrel and these texts have taken on a life of their own and grown in the telling. The question is whether obedience to the Law gives the believer a moral claim on God, and the answer is, obviously, No. Put the Law (halakah, kashrut) in another perspective: It is not something ethical, it is designed to shape lives, it is liturgical, and in my limited observation, it works. It is no more universally binding than Catholic liturgics. Many Protestants would find the Catholic sacramental system bewildering but, like kashrut, it does work. Hence a careful reading shows that Paul's opposition is to Judaizers but not to "The Jews."

Another theme, briefly, appears in the words, "ask and it will be given unto you" (Matt. 7.7, 19.19, 21.21–22; Mark 11.24; Luke 7.1–10, 11.9). This is a stance toward God that is quite different from the obedience of slaves or servants. It presupposes that humans have, and God trusts them

3.5 A Responsible Liberty of Interpretation

with, enough sense to make reasonable choices for themselves.

The Church explicitly claimed a discretionary authority in the conduct of its own affairs in texts other than the power of the Keys. In Acts 1.15, that authority is exercised in the selection of Matthias to replace Judas. It is exercised again in the Council of Jerusalem, Acts 15.28, when gentile converts are dispensed from most of kashrut. Only the prohibition of eating blood and food dedicated to idols is retained. Free choice is not restricted to the Church as a whole; Paul in 1 Corinthians (7.25) extends it to individuals in at least some matters. Forbearance toward others, a theme we shall see again,[13] is enjoined in Romans 14.1 ff. and 15.1–3.

Relations with "the Jews" appear everywhere, but they are thematic in Romans 9–11. Christian anti-Jewish theology assumes that the covenant with "the Jews" was superseded when the gentile stock was grafted onto the Jewish root-stock (Rom. 11.16 ff.), but Paul says, quite to the contrary, "Is it possible that God has rejected his people? Of course not" (11.1). Readers often think that Romans 11.25–32 means that eventually all "the Jews" will convert to Christianity, but the text does not say that and it makes better sense on the reading that the Exodus covenant inherited from Second Temple Judaism extends to rabbinic Judaism as well. (See the discussion of Krister Stendahl and Norman Beck, above.)

Outside of Paul, Hebrews 8.8–12 cites Jeremiah 31.31, promising a "new covenant." The community of faith travels through history in company with a transcendent Other, and the openness of history and openness to change does not come to an end. The promise is not of a final solution good for all time and independent of history or culture, as a prevention of further change. It is a promise that ultimate reality will be with its people through whatever changes may come.[14] Christian theology is divided about this. The possibility of such presence of God in changing covenants rises to view in Aphrahat, a fourth-century bishop, only to be denied in the next breath (p. 214 below).

There is more than meets the eye (or ear) in a passage we have already seen. The prelude to the power of the Keys in Matthew 16.15 comes from Mark (8.28–29) and is repeated also in Luke (9.20), in the question, "Who do you say that I am?" Since the phrasing is different from Joshua 24.15,

---

[13] When we come to the Oven of Achnai.

[14] What does not change in God is his faithfulness and his presence. Personal presence may involve a great deal of change, as many texts witness. In another sense, God does not change because he is outside of time. And some would see God as unchangeable in a Platonist sense, though I would not.

"choose today whom you wish to serve" (JB), the parallel is easy to miss. The principle is simple enough: covenantal religion is a free choice, not the result of any kind of logical inference. Merold Westphal remarked the distinction, as we saw on p. 20 above, in regard to the covenant renewal assembly in Joshua 24.

A responsible liberty of interpretation is implicit in the texts in yet another way. Theologians are divided about whether to read the Gospels as a proof of the divinity of Christ or to read them as an invitation to faith. Exodus typology in the Gospels, an integral feature of reading them as an invitation to faith, is an invitation to an *exercise* of a responsible liberty of interpretation.

We moderns, as readers, clearly exercise our own liberty when we disregard new "law" in the New Testament as in Paul's injunction to silence women (1 Cor. 14.34–35). One could find other examples. So *we* clearly claim a liberty for ourselves, in addition to such claims in the texts. The Church has always claimed authority over the Scriptures in disputes with those who hold that the Scriptures interpret themselves and are authoritative over the Church.[15] This is generalized in ways that could make some uncomfortable: the Breviary for December 31 says, "We ask you to extend the liberty of our sonship in you to all people."[16]

There is also opposition to a liberty of interpretation in the New Testament. All the passages that say salvation is available *only* through faith in Jesus Christ have been used by readers to disinherit rabbinic Judaism from the covenant. Those made anxious by the responsible liberty have done their best to restrict it. They limit infallibility to the Pope, though Augustine somewhat ambiguously says that liberty is given to the whole Church.

> And because of that role which he alone had, he merited to hear the words: "To you I shall give the keys of the kingdom of heaven." For it was not one man who received the keys, but the entire Church considered as one. Now insofar as he represented the unity and universality of the Church, Peter's preeminence is clear from the words: "To you I give," for what was given was given to all. For the fact that it was the Church that received the keys of the kingdom of God is clear

---

[15] Interpretive authority over the Scriptures does not abolish responsibility to the Scriptures, be it noted.

[16] Breviary, Advent and Christmas, 474, in the intercessions for Morning Prayer.

> from what the Lord says elsewhere to all the apostles: "Receive the Holy Spirit," adding immediately, "whose sins you forgive, they are forgiven, and whose sins you retain, they are retained."[17]

In other words, do not rest interpretation on one or two texts alone, but consider the import and implications of the whole of the New Testament.

We have said a great deal about a "responsible liberty of interpretation" without saying much about the "responsible" part. We are responsible to our fellows in covenant and to God. How that responsibility is to be exercised seems to me to be not a matter of formulas, calculation, or logic but of personal relations. In another vein, one ought to remember that there is more to covenants than the human communal discretionary authority given in a responsible liberty. Ultimate reality will interpret your proposed covenants by its lights, not yours. You can set the value of π to 4 if you like, but that doesn't mean u-r understands "$\pi = 4$" the way you do. So the general caution (the responsibility part) in a liberty of interpretation is "be very, very careful when you declare a covenant."

---

[17] The Breviary patristic lesson for SS Peter and Paul. Augustine, Sermo 295: 1–2, 4, 7–8, PL 38, 1348–1352. Breviary, Ordinary Time I, 1506.

Chapter 4

The Common Era

4.1 The Disasters of the First Century

Disaster forces change and usually choice: What to do about the disaster? There was disaster enough from 67 CE to 135 CE: Two Jewish revolts, the destruction of the Temple in 70 CE, the failed second revolt, and a Roman regime that drove Jewish observance out of Jerusalem. The loss of the Temple was effectively the end of Second-Temple Judaism. There were many constituencies in first-century Judaism, especially if one counts the diaspora as well as the land of Israel. Christians were only one. In the long term, only one other survived: the Pharisees, who became rabbinic Judaism.

It was thus in the loss of the first Temple, when the Babylonians conquered the kingdom of Judah. Eventually, under the Persians, choices were made about what to save — and the canonization of the Pentateuch was the result, along with saving as much of the prophets as could be salvaged.

Other choices also were forced in the First Century. Within the Christian movement, the gospel of Mark was a response to two things — the loss of the Temple and the theology of the heirs of the disciples. Mark doesn't like the disciples; they are not too smart and they want power.[1] Luke treats them better. For our philosophical purposes, more modest than those of the New Testament scholars, it is enough to say that the Church had to decide what to keep for the long haul — both texts and institutions. The memories of the first generation were fading (or just as often, growing in the telling),

---
[1] Weeden, "The Heresy that Necessitated Mark's Gospel" and *Mark: Traditions in Conflict*.

4.1 The Disasters of the First Century

but they had to be saved or else they would be lost. Peter Berger describes the phenomenon as "objectivation."[2] Objectivation is a process by which acts in the past that were perhaps intended but not thought out in detail survive beyond their original actors. They become social institutions, external to individuals, and available for internalization by later members of the community. One of Berger's central contentions in his early writing was that social institutions are social *constructions*, though people often try to hide their social-constructedness.

This was true of texts as much as of social structure, roles, and practices. It was always a question of what do we want to keep, what is beyond saving? What matters? What doesn't? There have been many conjectures about the origins of the structure of the Synoptic Gospels. I will name only one, Meredith Kline's account of the origins of Old Testament typology in the Gospels. We have seen it already.[3] Before the Gospels, there were only memories, oral tradition, and a few letters, mostly from St. Paul.

The transition from memories to texts has to accomplish four things. What goes for texts goes for acts as well. Conversation gets saved in text; acts get saved in a similar way, often by means of texts. Paul Ricoeur shows five ways in which conversation and act have to be abstracted out of their original happening to a wider audience.[4] They are meaning, origin, speaker, world, and addressee. He groups them under four headings. (1) He takes meaning and origin in space and time together. The events originally had a place only in their own time; they have to be moved from that origin to a meaning in all history. They have to be "saved" for later believers. What we have in the Gospels is the *meaning* of the events in Jesus' life, not the actual happenings themselves, not their physical particulars, not their context in a background of limited relevance. (2) Reference to persons is obvious in speech but not in text; "what do *you* mean?" and "what does *that* mean?" coincide for speech but not for text. In saving the speech or act, the relative importances are reversed: what the words mean surpasses what the author meant. In conversation, the speaker can rescue the meaning; in text, only the meaning can rescue the meaning: text requires an act of interpretation of an importance that speech does not. A little differently, events and personal encounters that in their original happening were significant only for those present have to acquire a wider

---

[2] Berger and Luckmann, *The Social Construction of Reality*.

[3] P. 41 above.

[4] Paul Ricoeur, "The Model of Text." See Rabinow and Sullivan, *Interpretive Social Science*, 75–80.

significance for everybody, for those who come after. Their meaning has to make itself clear to all; it cannot be saved or re-explained by the original participants. (3) The original background of the events and their relationship to it is lost, and it has to be replaced by a wider relationship to history and the world. This is a transition from context taken for granted to the world, after the original context is forgotten or lost. (4) The acts that were originally transacted between a few people have to acquire a universal address, challenging and engaging all who can understand them.

Institutions, such as the Eucharist, get consolidated, simplified, and structured.[5] Ricoeur did not use Gregory Dix's account of the origins of the Eucharist as an example of the transformation he described, but he could well have.

What went for the Church went for the Synagogue as well. When the Romans expelled the Jews from Jerusalem, the rabbis were forced to make similar choices. Late in the first century and early in the second, the rabbis had to decide what texts to keep as central and what texts could be left to fend for themselves. According to a popular legend, they met in Javneh on the shore of the Mediterranean but the supposition of that council apparently has weak support. In any case, the rabbis did not keep the whole of the Greek translation of the Common Documents, the Septuagint, and some texts were long lost to history and recovered only recently; e.g., the original Hebrew of Sirach. The resulting canons of the Common Documents were different in the Church and the Synagogue. Inasmuch as of the three divisions of the Scriptures (the Torah, the Neviim, and the Ketuvim) the last, the Writings, were of recent distribution, the rabbis saved them from a scattered and haphazard fate.

I speak of the Disasters of the First Century, but the last of them came only in 135 CE, well into the second. Still, it was about a century from the death of Jesus to the death of rabbi Akiba. The first Jewish revolt (67–73 CE) had ended in disaster, but its failure did not extinguish hope. The failure of the second Jewish revolt (132–135 CE) did that. The Romans did a fairly thorough job of destroying anything in the land of Israel that could serve as a focus for any more Jewish revolts. They turned Jerusalem into a Hellenistic city, with a temple of Jupiter where the Jewish Temple had stood. The second Jewish revolt was against that project, started in

---

[5] Gregory Dix, *The Shape of the Liturgy* tells the story well. The early texts outside of Paul and Mark come from the canon of Hippolytus (approximately the source behind Prayer 2 in the Novus Ordo), and a few other second-century texts.

132 by Simeon Bar Cochba, who claimed to be the Messiah.[6] There was no more Second-Temple Judaism after 135 CE.

4.2 Christianity as Atheism

It is worth note in passing that the first Christians were sometimes accused of being atheists. That is not just a confusion about worshiping the "wrong" gods; it perceived something important about biblical religion. The texts are noted in Bauer's Lexicon, at "$\check{\alpha}\theta\epsilon\text{os}$." The accusation sometimes included Jews. Christians were uncooperative with the established polytheistic reciprocal recognition of all the gods, and so the full weight of the charge of atheism fell on them. The word was used outside Christian literature, so it had recognized meanings already. Josephus knows the issue; it is also in the *Martyrdom of Polycarp* and Justin's first Apology. *Martyrdom of Polycarp* IX.2: Polycarp is offered acquittal by the magistrate if he will only say, "Away with the Atheists!" Christians sometimes returned the insult, so the meaning of the word was open to divergent understandings.

The Common Documents in places take an attitude toward other gods that indicates a difference in character between the biblical God and the other gods, but this was rarely worked out philosophically. Theologically, it has attracted attention from time to time, especially in our own time.

These few texts cannot by themselves bear the weight that later arguments might put on them, as if they were a license for H. Richard Niebuhr's remarks in "Faith in gods and in God." They don't go that far, but they are worth note as the start of ideas that grew later. Aquinas speaks of God as not "existing," and twentieth-century theologians have recovered his insight.[7] The point is that there is no being, entity, or person in this or any other world that is divine, because the biblical God is not one being among other beings. Theological opinion is, of course, divided, and I take sides in the disagreement.

One might ask, beyond the texts cited, why the issue arises. I think what's at stake is the anxiety at the core of human existence and good and

---

[6] Oxford Dictionary of the Christian Church, "Bar-Cochba."

[7] Aquinas, *Super Sententiarum* 1.8.1.1 ad 4. That paragraph is discussed in the beginning of my *Basic Concepts of Biblical Religion*; extensively by Gregory Rocca, *Speaking the Unknowable God*; and John Courtney Murray, *The Problem of God*. H. Richard Niebuhr, in *Radical Monotheism*, 122, offers similar thoughts.

bad ways to meet anxiety. Anxiety leads to transcendence. But all that is yet to come, in the postmodern period, our own time.

4.3 The Mishnah and the Talmuds

The first half-dozen centuries of the Common Era saw much writing by Christian theologians, a body collectively known as the Patristic literature. The Jewish counterpart to the New Testament was the Mishnah, a collection edited and canonized by the end of the second century by a rabbi known as Judah the Prince (among other titles).[8] Like the New Testament, it answered the question, "What do we do now, after the destruction of Second-Temple Judaism?" Two traditions of commentary on the Mishnah eventually developed, one in Jerusalem (fifth century),[9] another, later, in the Babylonian diaspora.[10] They are known respectively as the Palestinian (or Jerusalem) Talmud and the Babylonian Talmud; the Yerushalmi and the Bavli. The later one, the Bavli, usually gets more attention than the earlier. There was more rabbinic literature than just the Mishnah and the Talmuds; in *Unanswerable Questions* we shall see part of it, the great rabbinic commentary on Genesis, on things created before the creation of the world.

The Mishnah was probably collected and edited for reasons similar to the New Testament: to save traditions that otherwise would have been lost. I do not know better reasons. The Talmuds were undoubtedly in some measure not just solutions to internal Jewish problems but also responses to the external context, which was largely Christian.

The Talmudic literature is of interest for several reasons. It is simply part of the story of latter-day biblical religion, which includes rabbinic Judaism as much as Christianity. It parallels and corroborates the Christian developments in some places (see p. 45 above). It exemplifies the responsible liberty of interpretation that we have already seen in the New

---

[8] Yehuda ha-Nasi in Strack and Stemberger, *Introduction to the Talmud*, 89.

[9] Strack and Stemberger, *Introducton*, 304, date Genesis Rabbah between 400 and 450 CE and put it as nearly contemporary with the Palestinian Talmud, but their comments on dating the Palestinian Talmud (199) are less optimistic. The fifth century will have to do until better research is available.

[10] Strack and Stemberger, *Introduction*, 225–226, say that the composition of the Babylonian Talmud was not an organized process with an ending. The beginnings were in the second half of the first millennium; more than that I, an outsider, am not competent to say. The text may not have become stable until printing, and then only slowly.

Testament. Scholarship of the Talmuds has undergone significant changes, in directions that bear on our central theses. I don't think Christians read the Talmud much before the nineteenth century. That century, with critical history, saw Christians turning to the Talmuds to answer questions about Judaism in the time of Jesus.[11]

Changes in perspective today exemplify a changed relationship between Christianity and rabbinic Judaism. Günter Stemberger (1980) revised H. L. Strack's *Introduction to the Talmud and Midrash*. One result is that the rabbinic literature is now a little more accessible to Christian readers. Another result is that Talmudic scholarship, like biblical scholarship of both testaments, is today a joint Jewish-Christian affair. Participation is uneven, but scholars of both religions are present in every area. Jacob Neusner's Foreword to Strack-Stemberger gives a history of those changes. *All* of these texts are now things that humans wrote, not texts that God delivered to us from on high. And ordinary standards of historical evidence and inference apply, to all these texts, biblical, rabbinic, and patristic.

The differences between the New Testament and the Mishnah and Talmuds represent a choice that can be summarized briefly as "Christ or halakah?" Contrary to St. Paul, kashrut is not works righteousness, it is a liturgical activity. On p. 33 above, we said that Christians overlook the Law and the rabbis treasured it. Why? What is the difference, in the choice between Christ and halakah?

What can be said here is only a foretaste of what is to come; we will need resources from twentieth-century philosophy and even then we shall be extrapolating. In Heidegger, human existence is defined as the sort of being that has an interest in its own being. Quite true, but other humans have an interest in my being, as I do in theirs, and this interinvolvement is essential to the nature of personhood. It applies in particular to human relations to God: In the biblical tradition, the human covenant community travels in pilgrimage through history in company with a transcendent Other.[12] Being-with Jesus the Lord is everywhere in the New Testament. What is harder to hear is that keeping kashrut, halakah, is also a form of being-with, not a kind of legalistic claim against God. When human activity is "doing what another wills or wants," it becomes a form of being-with

---

[11] One text that stands out is the *Commentary on the New Testament from Talmud and Midrash* by Herman Strack and Paul Billerbeck (1922), but it is only typical, not unique.

[12] Merold Westphal, *God, Guilt, and Death*, 222, and chapter 11.

God. That is how halakah sanctifies life. One might observe here that there are more ways to do that than just one.

4.4 The Oven of Achnai

There is a passage in the Bavli that carries on from the responsible liberty of interpretation that we saw in the New Testament. It is not exactly theoretical, because it proceeds by way of stories that illustrate a few maxims in the Mishnah. Theory, if any, is yet to come from phenomenology in our own time.

The text begins in tractate Baba Metzia, 58b.[13] The Mishnah is about negotiating in good faith in commercial transactions, but it grows to forbearance toward others in general, especially in what is said. This is worth some emphasis, for one of the lessons to come is about how to conduct a disagreement with courtesy and respect. By folio 59b (p. 352), the example is a dispute about how to clean an oven. Are we to take it apart and clean each tile separately or can we just spray Easy-Off on the intact oven? Rabbi Eliezer ben Hyrcanus is in a minority of one. He demands a naturalistic witness and a carob tree is transplanted a hundred cubits. The others reply that halakah (and covenant more generally) are not a matter of anything naturalistic. Again, Eliezer commands a stream to flow backward and it does. The answer is the same. So also with asking the walls to fall. Eliezer asks for a sign from heaven, which testifies that he is right. The majority reply that such questions are not to be decided by voices from heaven (presumably God's, in this case). We have arrived at the responsible liberty of interpretation. Footnote 2 cites Exodus 23.2, and the modern editor continues, "Though the story is told in a legendary form, this is a remarkable assertion of the independence of human reasoning." The Talmud here quotes Exodus as "After the majority must one incline," and the modern editors do not raise questions about the text. The paragraph that follows is quite striking:

> R. Nathan met Elijah and asked him: What did the Holy One, Blessed be He, do in that hour? — He laughed [with joy], he replied, saying, "My sons have defeated me, My sons have defeated me." It was said: On that day all objects which

---

[13] The Soncino Talmud, Seder Nezikin, vol. I, Baba Metzia, 347–356.

4.4 The Oven of Achnai

R. Eliezer had declared clean were brought and burnt in fire. Then they took a vote and excommunicated him.

The editors' footnote says, "Lit., 'blessed him,' a euphemism for excommunication." The text continues:

> Said they, "Who shall go and inform him?" "I will go," answered R. Akiba, "lest an unsuitable person go and inform him, and thus destroy the whole world."

The modern editors in a footnote add, "I.e., commit a great wrong by informing him tactlessly and brutally." The text continues:

> He donned black garments and wrapped himself in black, and sat at a distance of four cubits from him. "Akiba," said R. Eliezer to him, "what has particularly happened to-day?" "Master," he replied, "it appears to me that thy companions hold aloof from thee." Thereupon he too rent his garments, put off his shoes, removed [his seat] and sat on the earth, whilst tears streamed from his eyes. The world was then smitten: a third of the olive crop, a third of the wheat, and a third of the barley crop. Some say, the dough in women's hands swelled up.[14]

Rather than disagreeing with courtesy and respect, the Church has all too often enforced its will through violence. It is enough to part ways when a disagreement makes it impossible to continue together. In a sense, then, schism is not the great evil it is thought to be. Peaceful schism is much better than violent forcible orthodoxy.

The main theme — a responsible liberty of interpretation — is much in the air these days. We easily forget the responsible part. In many places, I have invoked the covenant community's responsible liberty of interpretation, and always cautioned, you can declare any covenant you want, but remember that ultimate reality will interpret your covenant by its hermeneutic, not yours. This surely applies to the lessons in Galatians and the Power of the Keys.

---

[14] Soncino edition, 59b, 353–354.

4.5 The Marcionite Crisis

The Marcionite crisis is another example of choices made by the Church. Marcion started a movement in Rome in the middle of the second century.[15] What matters for us is that he wanted to abandon the received Scriptures (the Common Documents) altogether and proposed deleting anything that felt Jewish from what was yet to become the New Testament.[16] He put the Church to the question: What texts and traditions do you want to keep, and how do you see your relationship to the inheritance from Second Temple Judaism?

Marcion's answers were negative, but the Church kept the received Scriptures in a canon approximating the Septuagint, more even than the rabbis kept. Nevertheless, the Church drifted into a theology in which the Common Documents were marginalized as the "Old" Testament. It was read with a hermeneutic that limited it to predictions of Jesus, rather than being the typological basis for the New Testament. In effect, the settlement of the Marcionite crisis kept the received scripture — but marginalized it and made it secondary to the New Testament. This is the presupposition of several regrettable developments in theology. One of them goes by the name of "supersessionism," the thesis that the covenants in the Common Documents (and along with them, rabbinic Judaism) have been superseded by Christianity. This is one root of Christian anti-Jewish theology, anti-Semitism, and a long history of atrocities.

The second regrettable move in theology grows out of the first: the idea that one can start de novo with Jesus and come to the Common Documents later, if at all. Unnoticed is a trail of theological developments with pathological consequences, some of which were not exposed until the twentieth century.

There is a third consequence of the Marcionite crisis, and this one was all to the good, though it could be developed more: Latin-speaking Christianity in the West has always been willing to learn from the Greek-speaking East, and from Judaism, even though the West seldom learned Hebrew or Aramaic.[17] This openness to other cultures and even other reli-

---

[15] The article in the *Oxford Dictionary of the Christian Church* has details, some rather uncomplimentary.

[16] For Marcion, the Jewish inheritance was about a God of wrath and punishment, not of saving grace at all. This is not my reading, but it still widely available today. J. N. D. Kelly tells the story of the New Testament canon briefly in *Early Christian Doctrine*, 56–60.

[17] This is the thesis of Rémi Brague in *Eccentric Culture*.

4.6 The Trinity

gions has generalized and borne fruit in the interest of Western scholars in other religions and in many ecumenical and interreligious conversations.

When the Church no longer prays the Psalms entire over a week or a month, it is easy to forget the importance of the Exodus. The Psalter is soaked in the Exodus. We get snippets in the Mass, but snippets don't help much. We never get enough to hear what the Psalms are really about. Only the Breviary has the full Psalter (or most of it), but how could the Breviary make any sense on semi-Marcionite assumptions? Full Marcionites are rare; Adolf Harnack was one, and there aren't many others. But half-Marcionite theology is quite sufficient to inflict the damage of supersessionism.

4.6 The Trinity

The origins of the doctrine of the Trinity provide an example in support of the theme of this book, a history of Christian social constructions of reality. The conjecture has been presented elsewhere, sometimes on the Net, and so the summary here will be brief.[18]

Later than the Marcionite crisis came two or three centuries in which, among other matters, the Fathers refined the doctrine of the Trinity, in order to make the faith clear and to rule out such misunderstandings as were known to them. The roots and results of that process are worth some brief attention because neither (as we would see them) were obvious in the third to fifth centuries. Indeed, even today, they may not be obvious, but we have resources for an inquiry beyond the patristic structure of the problem. It will vindicate the Fathers, I believe.

The obvious roots are in the New Testament: "the grace of our Lord Jesus Christ, the love of God, and the fellowship of the Holy Spirit" in the ending of Second Corinthians, and "in the name of the Father, the Son, and the Holy Spirit," the ending of Matthew, and other places. Not quite so obvious is the trinitarian structure of the work of Jesus in the Gospels, cleansing, raising, and feeding Israel. In section 3.3 above, we took that to mean embracing Exposure, Limitation, and Need.

Not obvious at all are the cultural roots of this tripartite instinct. Those

---

[18] Hobbs, "An Alternate Model," in Otto, *The Family in Search of a Future*. Porter and Hobbs, "The Trinity and the Indo-European Tripartite Worldview." The argument appears also in *Elementary Monotheism*, chapter 3; in *Unwelcome Good News*, chapter 3; in *By The Waters of Naturalism*; and in other places.

have come out in twentieth-century anthropology.

There are for present purposes two parts of the concept of the Trinity: its roots in biblical monotheism and its roots in the Indo-European tripartite ideology. Biblical religion contributes the idea that God provides (and provides good) in the pains of life as much as in the pleasures; hence the concern to embrace Exposure, Limitation, and Need. The tripartite ideology sees everything in the world in terms of three functions: order, action, and sustenance. In the Indo-European pagan world, in the pantheons of its various cultures, two gods presided over order (cosmic and juridical); one god (with assistants) presided over war; and many gods provided fertility, sustenance, health, and beauty, etc. In that pagan world, the gods provided only in the pleasures of life, not in the disappointments. The disappointments were barren. In biblical religion, they are fertile.

In the early Christian versions that we have, Jesus, the incarnate Logos, does the work of the first function, having to do with order: He judges and redeems, he deals with the problem of sin, in Exposure. God the Father acts in Limitation, and God the Holy Spirit in human Need. The practical details are somewhat more complicated than that, as sketched in Porter and Hobbs, cited above. The three Persons of the Trinity sometimes trade work, but tripartite thinking runs through it all.

The transformation of Hebrew- (or Aramaic-) speaking Jewish Christianity into Greek-speaking and somewhat philosophical gentile Christianity was a long process and somewhat disorderly. The tripartite ideology was not originally a theory, certainly not a thesis. It was a genre, appearing in the structures of narratives. Narratives can be told (and retold) in many ways, but there had to be some faithfulness to the original events and accounts of those events. The move to philosophical precision in the fourth and fifth centuries was by way of reshaping narratives. It was not originally theoretical; certainly not in the New Testament.

Take stock of where we are in our own exploration of human choices in biblical religion in the Common Era: The Trinity appears, in the light of a conjecture from anthropology, to be shaped in part by the culture into which Christianity expanded in the Greco-Roman world. I am not in a position to test that conjecture, so it remains only that — a conjecture. It is nevertheless plausible. What questions arise if it is confirmed?

One that seems to arise for hasty readers is whether this is not just modalism. But modalism is a disorder of the doctrine of God as he is in himself, and neither Edward Hobbs nor I have ever written about God

4.6 The Trinity

as he is in himself.[19] This questioning in our Trinity paper was about what God *does*, not about what God *is*. And inasmuch as tritheism would be influenced by the Indo-European tripartite ideology just as much as orthodox Trinities or modalism, the objection seems odd. Too many other questions need to be addressed before we could say much about God as he is in himself.

How can the doctrine of the Trinity be *true* if it is a cultural construction of Indo-European Christians? That is like asking how the position of a body in Cartesian coordinates can truly be some (x, y, z), when other coordinate systems could be used also. And there are many other coordinate systems, as any student can attest.

What would the monotheistic world-affirming stance toward the pains of life look like in a non-Indo-European world? We (monolingual I-E speakers) cannot answer that question. That inquiry must be left to scholars fluent in at least some non-Indo-European cultures.

What about the variant forms of the Trinity in the actual history of the Christian church? Many were considered, and I trust that the Church's choices were reasonable. This is an instance of the response to social constructivism, "Why are some social constructions better than others?" We usually have answers.

---

[19] If I could change only one thing in the Trinity paper, it would be to leave πρόσωπον untranslated. The traditional translation is *person*, but that is the last meaning in all the dictionaries. None of my teachers were happy translating πρόσωπον as person. Some of the other meanings are theologically pertinent.

Chapter 5

The Medievals

5.1 A Focus on Aristotle

My principal sources for the Scholastics are in the secondary literature, and so the remarks here are limited by that restriction. I do not have a Thomistic education and so have to rely on others for guidance, of whom the Dominicans are the most conspicuous. They provide maintenance for the broadest philosophical tradition in the history of Catholic theology. I hope my gratitude is commensurate with that service; the results are my responsibility, not theirs. That said, what follows is, I hope, respectful, though in places I disagree with the Thomistic tradition. It is more a question of how to extend that tradition into the present, how to apply it in the twentieth and twenty-first centuries, than whether to continue in the tradition of (for example) moderate realism. Between moderate realism and nominalism or platonism, I happily side with moderate realism, of which Thomas was one exemplar. Where I come down between realism and idealism I do not know and do not understand. One man's idealism is not always another's. If I am an idealist, it is the idealism of existential phenomenology rather than any of the earlier or more traditional forms.

In the twelfth century, texts of Aristotle became available and were translated into Latin, and the results were synthesized with already available theology. By the thirteenth century Aristotle was widely disseminated and the focus of much controversy. Thomas Aquinas was at the center of this conversation. He was most conspicuously successful in integrating Aristotle and Christian theology, modifying Aristotle where necessary, building on The Philosopher wherever possible.

5.1 A Focus on Aristotle

In the present story, this episode is one example of handling challenges well rather than turning away from challenges or just retreating from earlier achievements — my principal complaints against our own time.[1] Indeed, if Thomas's example had been followed, if his instincts had been pursued further, much trouble later might have been avoided. That is not to say that his solutions for his problems work today as solutions for our problems.

In the terms of his own time (and what other terms should he be judged by?), his achievements were impressive. In effect, Aquinas can stand as a challenging model for us — we would do very well if we could do for our own time what he did for his. That is not quite the same thing as retreating into the thirteenth century and trying to use Thomas's philosophy to solve our problems. It is also not to deny that on some easily available interpretations of both Thomas and many popular twentieth-century philosophers, Thomas handles some of our problems better than our contemporaries do. Nevertheless, Thomas's problem was Aristotelian naturalism; our problems are history and hermeneutics.

What follows is not a retelling of the story of the recovery of Aristotle and assimilation of his work. Others have done that well, and Richard Rubenstein and Fernand van Steenberghen will have to suffice here.[2] Steenberghen is both shorter and sometimes more technical, though not always as detailed as Rubenstein. What follows is a non-Thomist's perspective on Thomas through the lens of a few modern problems. It is an outsider's appreciation and only gives a few places where Thomas's example could help us today.

Let me pick four issues of convenience. Later, it will be possible to inquire how Aquinas was subverted by those who came after him. (1) Thomas saw the confessionality of Christian commitment: commitment is chosen, not something derived. (2) In Thomas's view, grace does not interfere with nature. (3) An understanding of causation is critical to making sense of divine action in our world. Thomas's understanding of causation is one stage in the history of philosophy, and it offers some very salutary lessons for us. (4) In recognizing that we do not know *what* God is,

---

[1] Twelfth and thirteenth-century scholarship open to the challenge of Aristotle is one example of the character of biblical religion when it is willing to criticize itself. That shows up earlier in the prophets, and later in nineteenth-century liberal biblical criticism.

[2] Rubenstein, *Aristotle's Children* and Steenberghen, *Aristotle in the West*. This narrative and its larger context have attracted a fair amount of criticism recently, but that controversy lies beyond the present book.

Thomas protects the transcendence of God from reduction to an intramundane phenomenon. It would be easy to find other places where Thomas's position compares favorably with some modern philosophers, but that is enough for the moment.³ Present interests are limited to a few themes in the history of theology, patterns of success and of resources neglected.

(1) Confessionality: In the opening question of the Summa, Thomas asks whether sacred doctrine is a matter of argument (ST 1.1.8). The answer is qualified. Given premises *within* doctrine, one can argue. But the premises *of* doctrine are taken on faith. Here Aquinas sees that biblical faith is a confessional commitment, not something derived from any kind of reasoning. Yet somehow the word got out that it is possible to prove (or at least argue) that God "exists," Christianity is the best religion, etc. Instead, Aquinas is consistent with Joshua 24, though he doesn't cite that text.

What, then, about arguments? Steenberghen observes that the *Summa Contra Gentiles* (SCG) was not directed at Muslims but to Christians faced with Muslims.

> It is only too clear that St. Thomas's work was not intended to be put into the hands of Moslems, but it was intended for the use of Christian missionaries engaged in the evangelisation of the Moorish peoples.... We need only read the introductory chapters (Book I, chapters 1–9) to find that the *Summa Contra Gentiles* is addressed, not to pagans or to Christians who have followed them in their errors, but to the "friends of wisdom," to Christians who respect the Scriptures and are dedicated to the defence of the truth of Catholicism (chapter I).⁴

The SCG may not have been intended for polemical use, but it was put to polemical use anyway. The line between explanation and argument is easily blurred, and then crossed surreptitiously. It may be useless to argue with nonbelievers, but one still has to explain to the faithful why we disagree with those other people, whoever they are. The problem is that philosophical explanation can then be taken to other people and used as

---

³ See e.g. Kenny, "Aquinas and Wittgenstein." Kenny has not been entirely happy with this article in hindsight (private communication), but it is nevertheless a decent illustration of the sort of questions that can be raised. I am grateful for it.

⁴ Steenberghen, *Aristotle in the West*, 194–195.

5.1 A Focus on Aristotle

an argument, even though it is wrong to argue about confessional commitments.

Even to explain to the faithful what is wrong with idols courts exactly this risk. There is a difference between theoretical arguments against idols (or equivalently, other gods) and ridicule.[5] But that is not an argument and cannot easily be twisted into an argument. When theological or cultural adversaries demand that partisans of world-affirming historical religion justify themselves, two things are presupposed. Usually neither presupposition is recognized. The first is that doctrine (and its basis in faith) are indeed a matter of dispute, contrary to Aquinas in ST 1.1.8. The second is a demand to accept the challenger's starting point as the basis of a life orientation. In effect, it is a demand to accept the other's basic life orientation, concealed in the presuppositions of a challenge: "Justify yourself on the basis of *my* presuppositions ... " But those presuppositions usually depart from a biblical life orientation. They suspend its affirmation of this world as good in full view of its pains, or look outside history (and its transcendence) for the meaning of life, or look within nature for meaning instead of to history for transcendence.

In such a situation, an argument can be heard (and used) in more than one way, in more than one context, with more than one sense, with more than one audience. This ambiguity is part of the distributed ontology of human action (see *Living in Spin*), but that understanding of action was hardly known or spelled out in the thirteenth century. It is the sort of thing people know, but do not *know* that they know. Thomas looks pretty good in his intuitive ability to navigate around the illogic of arguing about what is not a matter of argument. Not all of his contemporaries and successors did as well.

(2) Thomas says in more than one place that grace does not interfere with nature. This is the problem of world and transcendence, or for this book, a Chalcedonian method in making sense of transcendence. We have already seen this and spelled it out as a general canon of method. See p. 12 above, in section 1.5.

Recast the reception of Aristotle into Chalcedonian terms: Aristotle's philosophy was almost entirely about the intramundane. It convinced its readers because for them it provided better explanations than anything else available. That said, in a Chalcedonian method, explanations of the world

---

[5] In Genesis 31.34 they have to hide, helpless, as noted above.

come and go, and the later ones are usually better than the earlier ones.

The Christian understanding of transcendence was not in the thirteenth century consistently Chalcedonian. To be Chalcedonian, the presence of God is something that transcends intramundane phenomena, rather than being a part of them. But as transcending them, transcendence (as we can know it) is relative to intramundane phenomena, simply because they are what it transcends. ("Relative to" does *not* mean "a function of," a mistake that would return to naturalism and abolish any real transcendence.) For Aristotle, it was all part of one coherent and unified reality. This does not entirely fit a Chalcedonian method, in which the intramundane and the transcendent have somewhat different logics. For Aristotle, the world, in the sense of all-there-is, was a coherent unity. Such transcendence as there could be was at most an extension of the intramundane.

Chalcedon itself extended to the doctrine of the Person of Christ and no further. As things have often worked out, even today, even that much is frequently compromised. Aquinas saw the way to the solution, I think, when he said that grace does not interfere with nature. That much is on the way to a generalized Chalcedonian method, but his nature was not our nature. For Aristotelians, nature is susceptible to generalizations but not to exceptionless mathematical laws as we know them from seventeenth century physics. In consequence, it is much easier to accommodate miracles in an Aristotelian world than in the modern world. The problem was not so acute for him as it is for us.

Indeed, to be fair to the thirteenth century, there are places where it is difficult to see how they could have done differently, given the assumptions available to them. Theology was sometimes used to correct natural "science," which had proposed "aseity of matter, eternity of the world, creation by intermediaries or progressive emanation, [and] denial of providence."[6] None of these ideas today could be supported empirically[7] and so the problem does not arise for us as it did in the thirteenth century. All of these ideas were available then, and were credible "science" — by their standards. To get some perspective on changes in science from one age and theory to another, one might consult A. G. Pacholczyk, *The Catastrophic Universe*. It is a long history of discontinuous changes between successive cosmologies.[8] Many, in hindsight, had very precarious support.

---

[6] Steenberghen, *Aristotle in the West*, 153.

[7] Save possibly eternity of the world in Fred Hoyle's astrophysics, which could be supported empirically but isn't.

[8] Pacholczyk, *The Catastrophic Universe*.

5.1 A Focus on Aristotle

Today, to constrain the particulars of astrophysical cosmology by theology would seem to be perverse; and even Hoyle could be assimilated if necessary. Then, constraining cosmology within the limits of theology was built into "the way things are" in presuppositions so deep as to be inexhumable. Today, to set theology and astrophysical cosmology in opposition should be seen as a category error, one easily refuted by the existence of two mutually inconsistent cosmologies in the first two chapters of Genesis. In the thirteenth century, it would have been difficult to disentangle scientific cosmology from the theology of creation. Today, it can be done, though not all succeed.

(3) Thomas on causation raises questions that came before him and endure to this day. My source is Michael Dodds.[9] Aristotle and Thomas made distinctions among causes that have been lost in the modern world, and sometimes they lump together different causes that the modern world distinguishes scrupulously. Some of the "four causes" have been lost or ignored in the modern world, which focuses on efficient cause, losing interest in the others. Formal and final causes have been ignored, banished, or just abolished.[10] Efficient cause has been narrowed to its meaning in the modern physical sciences, from which all other instances are required to be derived. Problems in those derivations will have to wait for a later chapter. For the moment, Aristotle and Aquinas simply lump all efficient causes together. Dodds' account is in *Unlocking*, pp. 33–41, "The modes of causality: necessity, contingency, freedom, and chance." The issue is what to do about apparent exceptions to otherwise applicable causal explanations. Behind this discussion lies unstated the modern issue of exceptions to natural laws, but to foist that onto Thomas would be an anachronism. We have said that Thomas's nature is more like generalizations that have occasional exceptions, and the exceptions do not undermine or invalidate the generalizations themselves.[11] I think there is something more in Dodds' account. We live in an age that is in awe of the regularity of the physical world. It puts us up against unanswerable questions. We both depend on consistent exceptionless physical causality and we have no answers to *why* physical laws have no exceptions. This situation is partly of our own making but not

---

[9] Dodds, *Unlocking Divine Action*.

[10] The Aristotelian tradition is right to insist on the importance of the problem of formal causes, but I would argue that formal causes are not always Aristotelian in a number of respects. See *Living in Spin*, sections 3.2.1, 3.3.1, 3.3.2.

[11] This is closer to developmental biology than it is to Newtonian physics.

entirely so. Modern physics is a human social construction but it survives the test of the question, "Why are some social constructions better than others?" Why does *this* one work so well is a question that we can neither answer nor get behind. It simply has to be accepted, at least so far as we know now. Someday, the problem will doubtless be re-posed, and our own existential sense of uncanniness in the world will have to move on to other phenomena. It will not go away; it is part of the human condition, and the uncanny in the world is always relative to humans for whom it is part of a world.

Aristotle is different: his exposition of causes is more a taxonomy of grammar and semantics than it is a philosophy of nature or of questions about nature as home for man. It's a good guide to language, but he doesn't deal with the spookiness of modern physical causality. Our issues were not Aristotle's or Thomas's issues. What is not noticed and not obvious is that Aristotle, in Dodds' account, is a good guide to how we *edit* narratives of events, which sometimes involve one or another kind of causation. Much of this has been worked out in *Living in Spin*, in the problem of formal causes and in how we narrate events that we call acts. One of the claims in *Spin* was that events are often open to more than one narrative, and so the resulting contingency can be ascribed to more than one actor.[12] Dodds says as much about primary and secondary causes (29–30). They are, for us, transcendent and intramundane causes.[13] I have called that an instance of a Chalcedonian distinction, though Aristotle and Thomas do not see the issue in Chalcedonian terms. In any case, the whole problem of primary and secondary causes is treated loosely enough so that the distinctions we need cannot be raised. Still, some credit should be given: Thomas had a way, however loose, of distinguishing between divine and intramundane causa-

---

[12] This should be easy to understand on the basis of the ontology of action in *Living in Spin*, but it is not easy at a theoretical level in philosophy of action today, even though we easily handle it with great sophistication at a practical and colloquial level. Aquinas doesn't like ambiguity in human actions, but sometimes tolerates it. See Pilsner, *The Specification of Human Actions in St Thomas Aquinas*, 82. Thomistic philosophy of action makes distinctions of considerable precision, precision that I leave to specialists. It is fair to observe, though, that its examples all illustrate the editing of narratives, but the editing *itself* is never thematic, and that is why ambiguity is so hard to handle in Thomistic accounts of action.

[13] It is important not to forget that merely among intramundane causes, there can be many. One could as an example cite Collingwood, *Essay on Metaphysics*, chapter 31, but that chapter draws only on practical reason. *Spin* found more ambiguous intramundane causes than that.

tion. Though it was lost in the beginning of the modern period, Thomists have protested long and loudly against modern scientism that would abolish the distinction and render divine presence and action inaccessible to our post-modern world. Modern philosophers commonly look for a way to understand divine causation as like intramundane causation, and Thomists have rightly demurred. In general, I would say that Thomistic philosophy still does better than many or even most contemporary philosophies on some issues, being surpassed only by existential phenomenology, but phenomenology is still very much an unfinished work in progress. This strikes me not as an argument for going back to Thomas and the thirteenth century but a call to do for our own time what he did for his.

(4) Aquinas says that we can know nothing about *what* God is.[14] Not only do we not know what God is, Aquinas comes within a hair of saying we don't know *that* he is. He does say that God does not "exist" in any sense of *exist* that could apply to things in this world, quoted below. (And what does it *mean* to say God exists in some other sense of "exist"?) The remedy for most of these difficulties lies in the concept of analogy, and how analogy works is a separate issue.

Look at *Super Sententiarum* 1.8.1.1 ad 4; the crucial phrase is "Ipsum esse ... ab ipso removemus." What appears in English as *exist(ence)* is in Latin just *esse*. The Latin verb *to be* is as rich in meaning as its English counterpart. It does not give nuances or make distinctions of meaning between *is* (mere predication) and *exists*. Here is Gregory Rocca's translation of the relevant passage, with a little context:

> When we proceed into God through the way of negation [*via remotionis*, not *via negationis*], first we deny of him all corporeal things [or corporeal realities]; and next, we even deny intellectual things as they are found in creatures, like goodness and wisdom, and then there remains in our understanding only the fact that God exists, and nothing further, so that it suffers a kind of confusion. Lastly, however, we even remove from him his very existence, as it is in creatures, and then our understanding remains in a certain darkness of ignorance according to which, as Dionysius says, we are best united to God

---

[14] Murray, *The Problem of God*, 69–70. Placher, *Domestication*, chapter 2, on Aquinas.

in this present state of life; and this is a sort of thick darkness in which God is said to dwell.[15]

In the *Summa Contra Gentiles* 1.14, a later work, we remove from God anything that could be seen in common with creatures. In effect, it concurs with the *Super Sententiarium* in all but the last step, removing even "existence" from God. It is probably a fair reading to infer from it that nothing about God's "existence" (if he has any) is shared in common with that of creatures.

It might help to draw Aquinas's presuppositions into the light if we could suggest something in contrast. Aquinas is representative of the entire tradition, and the tradition starts by speaking of God as one speaks of another (human) person, and then explores the differences between the semantics of 'God' and that of human persons. My instinct is different and not well worked out. We may see something of it later on. I follow the example of D. Z. Phillips in observing that we ask about God not as one among other persons but after other persons have done all they can.[16] More of that inquiry belongs with postmoderns rather than with Scholastics, but noting it provides a contrast with the presuppositions of the Scholastics.

Aquinas meeting the challenge of Aristotle is one example of the Church doing the right thing in handling its obligations. This needs some emphasis, because in this book we spend more time on engagements that were handled poorly than on those that were handled well. Aquinas is an example of how to handle challenges well. Well, but not perfectly: he is easily subverted.[17] Our challenge is to do for our own time what Aquinas did for his. He had to meet Aristotle; we have to meet phenomenology and hermeneutics, critical history, and the disorderly twentieth century.

---

[15] Rocca, "Aquinas on God-Talk," 648–649. Aquinas's Latin can be found at http://www.corpusthomisticum.org/snp1008.html. Super Sent., lib. 1 d. 8 q. 1 a. 1 ad 4. This passage was cited in the prolog (p. *x*) of *Basic Concepts of Biblical Religion*. It sets the stage for the entire problematic of making sense of God in biblical religion, though it takes a lot of work in the history of religions to get from the beginning in nature religions to Aquinas's insight in this passage. See also Murray, *The Problem of God*, 70–72, for another translation and comments.

[16] See my *Basic Concepts of Biblical Religion*, section 6.2, "Unanswerable Questions." It cites Phillips, *The Problem of Evil*, 133-134.

[17] See sec. 6.1, on the domestication of transcendence by Aquinas's commentators.

5.2 Proofs of God

The middle ages saw the beginning of a phenomenon that does not occur in the Bible and is uncommon in the patristic and rabbinic literature: attempts to "prove" the so-called "existence" of God. There are examples before Anselm, though the question acquired a significance in his writing that was rare before him but frequent after him. Some observations are appropriate here, to be revisited in section 7.6 when we are acquainted with the twentieth-century development of "proofs" for the "existence" of God.

Anselm's ontological "proof" for the "existence" of God has occasioned brisk discussion, both pro and con, ever since his time, with growing interest in the last century. That said, the confessional features of his text have been ignored, while interest has concentrated on his alleged logic for its own sake.[18] What is most conspicuously ignored is that his talk about the "existence" *of* God occurs in the larger context of prayer *to* God.

> Speak now, my whole heart! Speak now to God, saying, I seek thy face; thy face, Lord will I seek (Psalms xxvii.8). And come thou now, O Lord my God, teach my heart where and how it may seek thee, where and how it may find thee.[19]

Anselm is seeking God, and asks for help in understanding God; I would add *insofar as understanding is possible.* He continues:

> Lord, if thou art not here, where shall I seek thee, being absent? But if thou art everywhere, why do I not see thee present? Truly thou dwellest in unapproachable light. But where is unapproachable light, or how shall I come to it? Or who shall lead me to that light and into it, that I may see thee in it? Again, by what marks, under what form, shall I seek thee?[20]

All excellent questions, even today. They go well beyond the seeking that one can find in many places in the Psalter, and anyone who knows the

---

[18] Ermanno Bencivenga is a notable exception: he canvasses the whole of Anselm's writing, of which the ontological argument is only a small part. The whole deeply colors that small part. See his *Logic and Other Nonsense*. Bencivenga knows well (for Anselm says so) that the ontological argument is not really a proof, and is not intended as one; faith is presupposed. Bencivenga's thesis is that it is dubious logic. Indeed, many have defended themselves against *all* proofs in Anselm's words, "fides quaerens intellectum."

[19] Proslogium, chapter 1, in *Saint Anselm: Basic Writings*, 3.

[20] Anselm, *Saint Anselm: Basic Writings*, 3–4.

Breviary can recognize where Anselm is coming from: years of living in the Psalms in the Daily Office. Nevertheless, Anselm's answers are not helpful to me, and I think better answers are possible.

How and why does the problem of God in the form of a question about *existence*[21] arise for Anselm, when it was not a problem in this form for theologians before him? Questions about how we know and name God are biblical. Questions asking where God is when we need him, and if he is here, what is he doing for us, likewise occur in the Bible. These are the four questions that John Courtney Murray collects from the tradition in *The Problem of God*; he shows that they have developed considerably in form since their biblical origins. On his account, the biblical and post-modern problem is different from the medieval and modern problem. "Proofs" of the "existence" of God are part of the Scholastic and modern problematic but not of the biblical and post-modern problematics.

What we can say about thinkers in a past age is always shaped and colored by our own time and our own perspective. The story of Anselm that we can tell necessarily asks and answers some questions that Anselm could not.

Anselm seeks explanations, as in "fides quaerens intellectum," in his words. But the explanation that he finds, "a being than which no greater can be thought," also functions as a proof. It is always possible to confuse an explanation of faith with a proof of faith. This confusion is widespread today but not universal. It was rarely if ever noticed in the modern or medieval worlds. It comes from the radical ambiguity of language. Suppose a telephone salesman for the Tri-Valley Gossip calls and you decline to subscribe. He next asks, *Why* don't you want to subscribe? It is a fatal mistake to give reasons,[22] because he will interpret your reasons not as an explanation of your decision but as moves in a game of bargaining. The ambiguity of explanations, that they can be taken as arguments or proofs, was not *itself* a problem for the Scholastics or moderns. It has become noticeable only in the post-modern period, and even now it is not conspicuous.

For myself, the ontological argument appears to depend on some sort

---

[21] And what justifies translating *esse* and *exsistere* or *existere* as 'exist'? *Esse* has many more meanings than just exist, and the principle meanings for *existere* are "step forth, appear; arise; become; prove to be; be." These would seem to be more about existential phenomenology than analytic ontology.

[22] You can enjoy some real (if brief) entertainment if you simply answer, "Sorry, I don't give reasons."

5.2 Proofs of God

of order relation (greater, lesser) that is never explained and that I do not understand.[23] So strictly speaking, my own response (apart from not believing in proofs at all) is that I don't know what Anselm and his conversation partners are talking about. Even scrupulously construed as an explanation and not as a proof, it still doesn't make sense to me. "Aliquid quo maius cogitari non potest, ut nec cogitari possit non esse,"[24] translated roughly as "something than which greater cannot be conceived, cannot be conceived not to be" is something that for me non cogitari *at all*. I don't know what they are talking about. And I don't have to simply accept the implicit order relation (one with a maximal element) in this discourse — not after Georg Cantor. This is not how I relate to God or understand my own limited non-understanding of God.

Beyond the ambiguity of explanation and proof (or argument) lies another possibility in such discourse, and it is more interesting. Inquiry such as Anselm's seems to presuppose some obligations of responsibility in explaining to ourselves what we are doing: What can we know, and why (or to whom) do we owe an explanation of what we are doing? Further inquiry must await more resources.

The function of proofs is self-comfort, self-reassurance, alleviation of anxiety. A confessional stance is much harder, though more honest and more candid. The function of both argument and explanation *as* self-comfort was probably invisible and unthinkable in the thirteenth century.

Why is Anselm interesting in the present inquiry? Because his argument is ambiguous. (It was also, of course, a watershed.) Its ambiguity was soon ignored — or resolved in favor of taking it as a proof instead of as a soul's self-examination. The ambiguity, though forgotten, was not gone. It is present in all so-called "proofs" of the "existence" of God. That seed, planted in the eleventh century, blossomed riotously in the twentieth.

---

[23] There are other possibilities, inasmuch as I don't think the "ultimate" in ultimate reality is a maximal element in any kind of order relation. It just means that humans make some kind of sense of life, and says nothing about *what* kind of sense. They (we) disagree about what ultimate reality *is*, something that Anselm doesn't reckon with here. If Anselm's comments on God had been framed this way, they would no longer even appear to be a proof, but only a confessional statement, as in fides quaerens intellectum (his words). Oceans of ink might have been saved.

[24] *Proslogium*, 3. Quod non possit cogitari non esse. Found online at www.logicmuseum.com/authors/anselm/proslogion/anselm-proslogion.htm.

5.3 More Miracles

Chalcedon may have disentangled the divine and human *fuseis* in the Person of Christ, but the distinction was not generally extended to acts of God outside that doctrine. The concept of laws of nature did not appear for another thousand years. Philosophical concepts of natural regularity, such as they were, admitted of abundant exceptions. In their Aristotelian form, they were nothing more than generalizations about how nature usually behaves. Scholars read Aristotle, but not the general population.

Popular understanding of anomalous natural behavior in the affairs of men was rich and uncritical. It still is, if one knows where to look.

Miracles in medieval culture were a stage in the development of worldview on the way to problems in the modern world. Benedicta Ward has given us a survey of the medieval mind in its view of the miraculous.[25] Before Aristotle was available, the principle source was Augustine, and Augustine did not think about miracles in the way the scientific mind does. For Augustine, the ordinary in the natural world could be just as miraculous — disclosive of the glory of God — as the extraordinary. Augustine's concept of efficient causation can be quite strange to us. He uses the word 'nature,' but his meaning is not our meaning.

What takes a little while to sink in as one reads Ward's account is how much her questioning is shaped by a scientific worldview. She attempts to understand a world that was not scientific, but the attempt always starts from the scientific concept of order in nature that came only later. A question hovers over her inquiries, "How was their world different from ours?" It has to, because our world is so deeply rooted in our scientific ideas of natural regularity that we are not capable of suspending it. When we visit the pre-scientific world, it will always be as visitors. The pre-scientific worldview in itself, if it could be described innocent of even Aristotelian naturalism, may not be accessible to us at all. If it is, it is so only with great difficulty. The medieval world in its own integrity and wholeness remains elusive.

One can discern lines of thinking in the pre-Aristotelian medieval world that would later be rearranged with a new meaning after Aristotle's naturalism became available, but they did not have such meaning in their native medieval (largely Augustinian) habitat. The ancient world distinguished medicine, magic, and miracles, as Howard Clark Kee has demon-

---

[25] Ward, *Miracles and the Medieval Mind*.

5.3 More Miracles

strated.[26] Their distinctions even sometimes have parallels with our own. What comes as a surprise to us is that they thought exceptions to natural behavior were not necessarily acts of God — they could be caused by sorcery invoking other gods just as much as the biblical God. Such sorcery and divination were forbidden (that goes all the way back to Saul and the witch of Endor), but the forbidden was still entirely possible and credible. For us it is impossible and need not be forbidden. In our own world, attempts to create a magic-capable world in fiction have always resulted in merely a world with a magic that is effectively an unexplained technology. Ironically, our own world, for most of us, has lots of unexplained technology. (Just try to deal with a refractory computer.)

Some things can be made clear about the medieval concept of miracles. They serve the function of clearings, places in life where you can see ultimate reality show itself. They are not violations of natural laws, for the medievals had little or no concept of natural law. We for our part would think many of them to be violations of natural law and, therefore, be skeptical of the reports we have from medieval texts. Whether they took their experiences to be interferences with nature in the sense of dispensations from Limitation is not clear. That is a question of theology, not philosophy of nature. Whether they took their experiences to be proofs of the validity of biblical religion — proofs of faith rather than consequences of prior faith — is also not very clear. These are modern (or post-modern) questions, and the medievals do not ask our questions.

The notion of a clearing, just mentioned, deserves a little more explanation.[27] It is not a medieval concept, for they spoke simply of "miracles," though the etymology of *miracle* could take us to clearings. To propose a definition, a clearing is a place in life, an event, something in the world, or a work of art, in which it is possible to see what ultimate reality really is. A clearing is where u-r shows itself.

There are two kinds of problems here. First, people do not agree on what u-r is, and so one man's clearing may not be another's. A violation of a law of nature (Hume's definition of a "miracle," if you believe in such things), may be a clearing, if it manifests somebody's proposed ultimate reality. People disagree about *which* ultimate reality it manifests, as the Bible well understands and its readers often do not.

The second kind of problem is that people (and cultures) do not agree

---

[26] Kee, *Medicine, Miracle, and Magic*.
[27] Clearings are addressed in *Basic Concepts of Biblical Religion*, section 1.3.

about what kind of things happen in the world, and so the question of whether some happening discloses u-r bumps into the question of how such a happening can happen at all — how it fits into the world. We have seen this issue in section 1.8 above, where Edward Hobbs distinguished between *conceptuality* and *understanding* (sec. 1.8 above). The word 'understanding' has too many meanings to be usable with precision, and so I would suggest *basic life orientation* (BLO) instead. It is someone's appraisal of ultimate reality. The challenge for the modern interpreter then becomes how to discern the BLO of writers from some other time or place, disentangling it, insofar as possible, from their conceptuality. They understood the world in such-and-such terms, but that does not by itself tell us their basic life orientation.

One of the features of a clearing, of reports of an event that functions as a clearing, is a deep-seated ambiguity that attends all matters of interpretation. It is not just that an event, as reported, can be interpreted in many ways. It can be fitted into human lives in many ways. In particular, it is seldom obvious whether the clearing discloses a reality that comes before or after faith. Does it require faith to see the clearing, or does faith require prior experience of the clearing? Or do they happen together? This distinction (which we make) usually did not arise for the Scholastics, though Aquinas saw it correctly at least some of the time. Also lost was the confessional stance of Joshua 24, not to be regained until the twentieth century. If the clearings were in the tradition of that covenant renewal assembly, they would challenge the reader to a choice about BLO.

We will not be able to approach these problems successfully without the recovery (or extension) of a Chalcedonian method in the theology of divine action. That will require modern hermeneutics and phenomenology. The concepts that could have led to the distinction between the two *fuseis* in ordinary acts of God were known to the Scholastics in the distinction between primary and secondary causes. In the years after the thirteenth century, primary causes were conceived (or misconceived) in such a way that they were obsoleted by secondary causes in nature.

The most we can do in this book is look at the miracle texts as challenges and invitations to faith. This book is interested in dismantling sacred canopies and other forms of bad faith, and the evasion of responsibility implicit in taking the miracle texts literally *today* certainly qualifies. How *any* clearings can disclose transcendence must wait for later writing.

5.4 More Atrocities

What, *more* atrocities? Yes, more atrocities. Do your own research.

I do not mean the Crusades; after all, the Muslim Middle East was the result of Muslim conquest by force, which supplies some partial justification for retaking by force lands that were historically Christian and Jewish. The problems were things like mass-murder of Jews on the way to the Crusades, attacks on other Christians, the complicity of some of the clergy.

And above all, heresy hunts: Exterminating heretics should be an eternal shame for the Christians who perpetrated those heresy hunts. Heretics are to be answered, politely and respectfully. Resort to violence is an admission of not having convincing answers.[28] If the body of the faithful choose to commit apostasy, that is their right, as we have said many times in this book: Joshua 24, many places in the New Testament, and the Oven of Achnai in the Bavli. Too bad. Like everybody else, they have to live with the consequences of their choices. It doesn't justify violence.[29]

Controversies over heresy led to the Reformation, and at their worst, to religious wars. Such wars presuppose the denial of a Responsible Liberty of Interpretation that the New Testament claimed and the Bavli in Baba Metzia (section 4.4) used to enjoin forbearance and toleration in religious disputes.

---

[28] The issue in our own time takes a different form. See sec. 10.6, p. 226 on religious autoimmune disease.

[29] What probably *does* justify force is prior violence by other religions.

Chapter 6

Modernity

The transitions from the medievals to modernity and thence to postmodernity are somewhat diffuse. Preparations for both were laid before the changes became apparent. The apportioning of issues to modernity or postmodernity is to some extent arbitrary. In the next two chapters we follow only a few storylines: science and the responses to it, history and the new ways of thinking about it (in this chapter), and twentieth-century phenomenology (in the next). The purpose here is to see how these changes contributed to the theological currents at the focus of this book: semi-Marcionite theology, monophysite theology of divine action, and a feature of theology that has no name but could be characterized as an evasion of confessional responsibility.

In overview, the story of this chapter and the next follows dubious theological moves from the thirteenth century to our own time. The changes were not intended as a way to get out of transcendence; indeed, they were intended to serve transcendence and were usually advanced by faithful Christians and Jews. Nevertheless, they were incoherent, and the upshot was a loss of transcendence. Not even history was left; only nature made any sense, and it came to make sense in new ways that offered a cosmos rich beyond any prior age's imagination — viewed under the aspect of nature, "*sub specie naturae.*" Outside of the natural sciences, the results were generally an impoverishment. Some took this as good reason to move from historical religion to new forms of nature religion, and that kind of naturalism (usually as scientism) is still very much with us and growing today. In the nineteenth and twentieth centuries, the new naturalism came (in the humanities) to be seen as incoherent, and people began to find ways around it and to recover aspects of reality beyond just nature. That process is unfinished, and for the moment it is just a disorderly conversation. It has neither the virtues nor the vices of a comprehensive system. That part of the story has come to be called "post-modern," and it is told in chapter 7.

6.1 The Domestication of Transcendence

Many in the twentieth century have asked themselves how we got into our present predicaments — plural, because problems can be found not just in the sciences or in theology, but even in culture more diffusely defined. Our focus is on theology. William Placher diagnosed the pathology as a "domestication of transcendence," in his book of that name. In a superficial summary, people began to think about God with the same logic they used for persons and things in the world. They tried to use the ordinary logic of intramundane things to understand transcendence, the same logic for both sides of a Chalcedonian account of reality. I don't think that works very well, and it insidiously and surreptitiously moves toward a monophysite understanding of God in the world, undermining Chalcedonian principles utterly. God became just another player in the world. Placher announces his own appraisal of the changes in his forecast to the rest of the book:

> ... before the seventeenth century, most Christian theologians were struck by the mystery, the wholly otherness of God, and the inadequacy of any human categories as applied to God. That earlier view never completely disappeared, but in the seventeenth century philosophers and theologians increasingly thought they could talk clearly about God.

and

> Rather than explaining how all categories break down when applied to God, they set the stage for talking about transcendence as one of the definable properties God possesses — a quality we could understand and that many writers today could then come to find deeply unattractive. In that sense, transcendence got domesticated, and theology suffered as a result.[1]

Placher doesn't solve the problem whose mishandling he chronicles. It's not even clear that it *can* be "solved" — and seeing that is the whole

---
[1] Placher, *Domestication*, 6 and 7.

point. Transcendence is what we cannot understand, and any pretense of understanding it is a sign of serious trouble. It should be possible to understand at least a little about our *not* understanding of ultimate questions, and what we can do about that in this book is limited. To put it a little differently, some questions are unanswerable, but that does not make them uninteresting, and does not mean they should be ignored or dismissed as meaningless. Even that is not for this book but for *Unanswerable Questions*. So for the moment, we parallel Placher's diagnoses and merely say that we relate to some ultimate mysteries on a personal level, without claiming to know much about those ultimate mysteries. That is akin to the position Placher attributes to Thomas Aquinas, though it is here expressed in a different way and with a lot less detail than Thomas left us.

Thomas (and we) may say we do not understand God, but soon after Aquinas, some people thought they could do exactly that.

Disputes in philosophy and theology arose for social and cultural reasons in the thirteenth century, and insidiously spread the presupposition that what both theology and the believer know can be expressed in presuppositions that can be disputed. About *how*, Aquinas gave only unsystematic explanations. Those who came after, Cardinal Cajetan (Tomaso de Vio) conspicuously, systematized what Aquinas did not.

> Aquinas is perhaps best known for his theory of analogy. On closer inspection it turns out that he never had one. Rather he made do with a few remarks and that grammatical astuteness which I have suggested as a replacement for intuition. Others, of course, organized those remarks of his into a theory, and that is what Aquinas has become famous for.[2]

Placher summarizes Cajetan's typology of analogy.[3] What in Thomas was scattered, unsystematic, and a way of insisting that we don't understand God has become in Cajetan's account quite systematic. Moreover, the kinds of analogy Cajetan is most interested in provide the anxious believer with the same sort of knowledge as we get in univocation.

> The possibility that we could meaningfully use a term without really understanding how it applies, which lay at the center

---

[2] Burrell, *Aquinas, God, and Action*, 55. Placher, *Domestication*, 29 and 72, cites Burrell.

[3] Placher, *Domestication*, 72.

6.1 The Domestication of Transcendence 85

> of Aquinas's account of analogical talk about God, seemed to Cajetan unacceptably "confused."[4]
>
> Whereas, push come to shove, Aquinas was prepared to classify analogy as a form of equivocation, Cajetan classified analogy of proper proportionality, the only kind of real interest to him, with univocity....
>
> Far from offering a series of reminders concerning how we cannot understand what we mean when we speak of God, analogy now functioned as a way of explaining just what we do mean.[5]

A figure as influential as Cajetan was Francisco Suarez, a Spanish Jesuit who lived two generations later. In Placher's account, there are places where Suarez, the great commentator on Aquinas, didn't always agree with Aquinas, though that may not have been clear.

> Suarez centered much of his career on commenting on Aquinas, and yet, on the crucial issue of language about God, he appealed to Aquinas's greatest rival among medieval philosophers, John Duns Scotus.[6]

For Thomas, "We cannot imagine what 'being' means as applied to God," and "God's relation to being is just totally different from anything else's relation to being."[7] The issue is univocity in language about God. For Thomas, we don't understand God. Placher's paraphrase above of ST 1.12.13 ad 1, that we don't understand what 'being' means as applied to God, would make a good gloss on the saying in *Super Sententiarum* 1.8.1.1, that God doesn't "exist," and the mind then rests in a certain thick darkness. The *Summa* is a late text, *Super Sententiarum* an early text; the idea has changed its expression some but not really its substance. In any case, for Scotus (and Suarez), not only do we understand at least a little about God, we understand the being or existence of God in the same way we understand the existence of creatures. In particular, in questions about how analogy works, and about how we know God, Scotus seems to be of the opinion that a least a little bit, God "exists" in the same sense of 'exist'

---

[4] Placher, *Domestication*, 73.
[5] Placher, *Domestication*, 74. He cites Cajetan's *Analogy of Names* 6.69.
[6] Placher, *Domestication*, 75.
[7] Placher, *Domestication*, 75, cites ST 1.12.13 ad 1 and ST 1.3.5.

in which creatures exist. Thomas, obviously, if the Commentary on the *Sentences* is to be believed, did not agree.[8]

It is not a theological crime to be a Scotist, and many are; I just don't happen to be one of them. Nor was Placher. The present inquiry is animated by a desire to find for the present century something like what Thomas did for his time.

Placher traces the legacies of not just Aquinas but also Luther and Calvin. With the Reformers, the issues have a different flavor and logic, but they paralleled the Catholics in their attempts to domesticate transcendence. The spirit and temperament of theology in the seventeenth century comes through in a very Reformed idiom, from New England, in the words of Thomas Hooker,

> "I know there is wilde love and joy enough in the world, as there is wilde thyme and other herbes, but we would have garden-love and garden-joy, of God's own planting."[9]

Reflect a little on Placher. The substantive commitments on the way to what we know as Analytic philosophy of religion were first made in the *method* of reasoning, in the style of argument, where they are hard to see and harder to confront in propositions, because they are not expressed in propositions. The Analytic method is the result of a demand, not an argument, and the commitment to a modern method of reasoning is not always spelled out systematically, though Placher found examples in Cajetan, Suarez, and Descartes. Nevertheless, it grew into a culture-wide instinct, something that could not be called out because it was all-pervasive and usually invisible. It was just the way things were in the seventeenth century, but the way things were in the seventeenth century was not how they were in the thirteenth. Even today, people do not always notice the changes.

Aquinas does reflect on the differences between faith, knowledge, opinion, and so on. In his Latin, the focal difference is between *sapientia* and *scientia*. The details are sometimes subtle, but it is fair to observe that even Placher is sometimes misled by the translators. He says,

---

[8] Never mind that even creatures do not all exist in the same way. Martin Heidegger retrieved that insight from Aristotle.

[9] Placher, *Domestication*, 107. He cites Thomas Hooker, *The Soules Implantation into the Natural Olive*, 180.

6.1 The Domestication of Transcendence

In the case of God, faith rests ultimately on such a relationship of trust in God, but in actual practice we end up trusting in propositions — from the Bible or elsewhere — that speak of God.[10]

He gives as backup text the *Summa*, IIa IIae, 1.2, and quotes some of it in a footnote. The title of that question in the English of the Benziger edition of the 1960s reads, "Whether the object of faith is something complex, by way of a proposition?"[11] Of the question of simplicity or complexity Aquinas in the end says, "... in the past both opinions have been held with a certain amount of truth." What matters here is the apparent assumption that to be complex is to be a matter of *propositions*. The Latin is not as obvious, and the translators' choice of words leaves room for comment. It is not out of the question that our conception of propositions (after Boole, Frege and twentieth-century logic) has changed some since the thirteenth century. We cannot pretend ignorance of Frege; Thomas could not know Frege. The word translated as "proposition" is *enuntiabilis*, an adjective that William Whitaker's internet Latin program translates as "utterable," medieval, and very rare.[12] Lewis and Short have for *enuntio*, a related verb, "reveal; say; disclose; report; speak out, express, declare." In other words, just language, in all its forms. This accords with Aquinas (or sources close to him, as where the Eucharistic hymn, Adoro te devote, merely has hearing ("*auditus*"), in the second verse. "Faith that comes by hearing" is much broader than assent to propositions because *language* is much broader than propositions. We have been bewitched by one of our zeitgeists (in the voice of the *Tractatus*) into thinking that anything real can be expressed in propositions. It ain't so.[13] Once Aquinas's Latin is translated to speak of propositions, we are betrayed onto the road to what in centuries later became known as Analytic philosophy of religion, against all of Thomas's substantive commitments.

Much of Placher's reading of Aquinas makes Thomas come down not in any theory but against theories; Aquinas says that discourse about God doesn't work the way theoretical discourse works, but theoretical discourse in the seventeenth century overwhelmed it anyway. Placher gives another

---

[10] Placher, *Domestication*, 33.
[11] Aquinas, *Summa Theologica*, IIa IIae, 1.2, 1170.
[12] http://www.archives.nd.edu/cgi-bin/words.exe?enuntiabilis, accessed 2016-10-06.
[13] See *Basic Concepts of Biblical Religion*, section 5.4, "Living in Language," for the reach of language far beyond mere propositions.

summary of his thesis:

> ... transcendence has often functioned in the Christian tradition, not to make a metaphysical proposal, but as a kind of agnosticism about certain sorts of metaphysical questions.[14]

Later on, he cites Calvin,

> Of these things which it is neither given nor lawful to know, ignorance is learned; the craving to know, a kind of madness.[15]

There is a spirit that runs through all the writers on the way into modernity, and that spirit seeks control. As said above, many of its substantive commitments are hidden in its method, where they cannot be called out and confronted. It is in the nature of disputation that it disambiguates what it argues about and haggles about how to do that. It is hostile to ambiguity, it cannot rest in ambiguity. In ambiguity, one is not in control.

6.2 The Way to Modern Science

Changes in culture that came with the new physics of the seventeenth century raised many issues for theology and faith. From a point of view in hindsight, it began with the new astronomy. In the perspective of the time, it was much more complicated. Nevertheless, to simplify matters, Copernicus demonstrated that a heliocentric account works as well or better than a geocentric account of the solar system. It was just a shift in coordinates, something that students today do routinely without implying anything essential about the systems represented differently in different coordinates. By itself, a change of coordinates would not be of great moment, and that is probably why Copernicus survived. It had to be taken seriously, however, when observations showed that one coordinate system worked better than the other and was simpler and clearer. Change came with Tycho Brahe's planetary observations. They were precise enough so that Johannes Kepler could demonstrate that the orbit of Mars was elliptical. With an eccentricity of 0.093, it deviated noticeably from a circular orbit.[16] In an ellipse

---

[14] Placher, *Domestication*, 9.

[15] Placher, *Domestication*, 58. He cites the *Institutes*, 3.23.8.

[16] The orbit of Mercury has an eccentricity of 0.2, but observations of Mercury were not good enough to be very useful.

6.2 The Way to Modern Science

with one focus at the sun, it eroded the plausibility of geocentric coordinates.

The move from geocentric to heliocentric coordinates brought a mathematical precision that had roots in Ptolemy but was never before extended to sublunar motions. Ptolemaic astronomy, mathematical though it was, was embedded in a larger worldview in which it coexisted with a science of motion based on Aristotelian biology. In the Aristotelian worldview, there are generalizations but no laws in the sense of seventeenth-century physics. Generalizations admit of occasional exceptions and the world is none the worse for it.

Along with the growth of mathematics in the science of motion, the entire Aristotelian schema of explanations was revised. Previously, there were four "becauses" ($αἰτίαι$) or ways to answer why-questions. Of these, both efficient and final causes explained the motion of bodies. In the shift, efficient causes by themselves were sufficient to explain motions. Efficient causes were greatly restricted, and final and formal causes were banished from physics. Francis Bacon was not a mathematician or a physicist, but he is typical of the age in his dismissal of the Aristotelian system of causes.

> In what an ill condition human knowledge is at the present time is apparent even from the commonly received maxims. It is a correct position that "true knowledge is knowledge by causes." And causes again are not improperly distributed into four kinds: the material, the formal, the efficient, and the final. But of these the final cause rather corrupts than advances the sciences, except such as have to do with human action. The discovery of the formal is despaired of. The efficient and the material (as they are investigated and received, that is, as remote causes, without reference to the latent process leading to the form) are but slight and superficial, and contribute little, if anything, to true and active science. Nor have I forgotten that in a former passage I noted and corrected as an error of the human mind the opinion that forms give existence. For though in nature nothing really exists besides individual bodies, performing pure individual acts according to a fixed law, yet in philosophy this very law, and the investigation, discovery, and explanation of it, is the foundation as well of knowledge as of operation. And it is this law with its clauses that I mean when

> I speak of forms, a name which I the rather adopt because it has grown into use and become familiar.[17]

In regard to the motion of bodies, a "fixed law" does the work of both efficient and formal causes, but "the discovery of the formal [cause] is despaired of." Efficient cause was dismissed as "superficial" and of little use in "true and active science." Material cause (what something is made of) was subtle in its Aristotelian form but greatly simplified in and after the seventeenth century. (Modern chemistry, the forerunner of what today we call "materials science," did not come until the nineteenth century.)

Bacon spoke of laws. The concept of law developed from changes in the understanding of the doctrine of creation. That is, the relation of the creator and physical creatures was transformed. It was not just a degeneration from the medieval synthesis, when transcendence and the physical world were easily accessible to one another. Michael Foster told the story.[18] In the change in thinking, the doctrine of creation was cleansed of the Greek elements that took God as a demiurge working with eternally preexisting matter and made God the omnipotent creator of both matter and form. In the older view of "creation," the deity's intentions were manifest imperfectly in recalcitrant matter, much as the drawn figure of a circle manifests approximately a real circle in its abstract and ideal perfection. The human mind has to intuit the intentions of the deity. In the new view, the creator, because omnipotent, produces form-in-matter that obeys his intentions exactly. As a consequence, the scientist can see by observation exactly what was intended. Empirical science was *permitted*, and it gives reliable access to reality. Because the omnipotent deity is free, physical reality could not be derived from any apriori principles. As a second consequence, empirical science became *necessary*. Along the way, ultimate reality (the deity) became consistent and laws of nature lost the openness to occasional exceptions that they had when they were just generalizations on the model of biology. Here is Foster's summary in the third article:

> Hence are derived two assumptions which will easily be recognized to be fundamental presuppositions of modern scientific method: the first the assumption that the scientist has to look nowhere beyond the world of material nature itself in order to find the proper objects of his science, the second (which

---

[17] Bacon, *The New Organon*, Aphorisms, Book Two, no. II.
[18] Michael Foster in *Mind*, in 1934, 1935, and 1936.

6.2 The Way to Modern Science

is really a corollary of the first) that the intelligible laws which he discovers admit of no exception.[19]

Foster's work elicited a few responses but philosophy of science has moved on. There are two reasons that I can think of. James McEvoy commented that this kind of logic (he does not name Foster) tends to simplify matters that were somewhat more messy than he lets on.

> The question as to whether Christian belief has been a favourable, a neutral, or a pernicious factor in the rise of the natural sciences is not one which may be blundered into, nor is it one that can be completely avoided by the historian. Part of its attraction — I abstract from the evident seductive power which it held and holds for controversialists — may perhaps lie in the vertiginous thrill the mind feels in asking it at all: the precipice, the declivities before which the inquirer stands offer a perilous sense of giddy freedom; the wide horizons appearing from the lofty crag give a momentary illusion that the vantage point offers an unsurpassable view of the contours and folds of the historical landscape. It is only in the safe descent to lower levels that the sense of buoyancy is left behind, the vista is replaced with an ever-changing series of perspectives, the eyes attain a sharper delineation of individual features, and the choice of the advantageous path becomes pressing.[20]

From a slightly different perspective and in a larger context, an application may be drawn for our own time, when so-called "scientific atheists" attack Christians for not being scientific. It is important to distinguish what the disagreements are about. Science today does not appear to need support from the doctrine of creation. That doctrine has lately come to mean bad cosmogony perpetrated by an anthropomorphic deity. Nevertheless, restated in the following way, there is some measure of agreement: Ultimate reality is such that the natural sciences are possible, and it is humanly possible to understand the world as nature with the methods of empirical science, resulting in scientific theories that have no exceptions. Science can stand on its own, without support from the doctrine of creation, because the essential part of creation (the goodness of the world as intelligible) has been moved from theology to mere background assumptions about the

---

[19] Foster (1936), 14.
[20] McEvoy, *The Philosophy of Robert Grosseteste*, 211.

world that are necessary if one is to do science at all. An anthropomorphic deity and interference with nature are no longer needed. Atheists and biblical religion disagree at many other points, but not (on the theological assumptions presented here) at this one. Here lie planted seeds that did not germinate until the nineteenth century, for reasons that we shall come to in due time.

Back up to the seventeenth century, the time of which Foster spoke. Problems between theology and science should be obvious, inasmuch as Foster's understanding of a science derived from the doctrine of creation is incompatible with the common understanding of "miracles" as exceptions to laws of nature. That understanding of miracles was implicit though not spelled out before the seventeenth century, but seventeenth-century physics forced scientists and theologians alike to spell out the implications. The physicists tried to demonstrate acts of God in the terms of the new physics but in the end only drove God out of physics, as R. M. Burns explains.[21] They were for the most part believing Christians, so this cannot be construed as an attack on religion by atheists.

Nevertheless, their inquiries expanded into a debate on miracles, as Burns observes in detail. It is not an accident that miracles were the focus of inquiry. This is an example of a more general question that we have asked many times in this book: Where does your proposed ultimate reality show itself in the world? That question asks about *clearings*, not miracles; a clearing is a place where one can see ultimate reality. Clearings were reduced by stages to volokinesis, will-directed motions in violation of laws of nature (Hume's problem). It is worth note that the seventeenth-century physicists also understood something that has largely been lost in the twentieth century: The seventeenth century knew that whether miracles actually happened is a different question from whether miracles came from God or not. The naturalism that takes miracles as such to be evidence of divine presence and action was still in the future when modern physics was new.

Note in passing that Foster's argument has a very anthropomorphic conception of God, as with Nominalists in contrast to the via negativa, John of Damascus, some passages in Aquinas, and William Placher's comments on the domestication of transcendence. This laid seeds of trouble, but they

---

[21] Burns, *The Great Debate on Miracles*. Burns's analytic account is plausible; his constructive position seeks to rescue "miracles" from critical philosophy; not a course that I would follow.

6.2 The Way to Modern Science

did not fully germinate until the twentieth century.

Louis Dupré gives an account of the changes that extends to a lot more than just the new science, and it provides some context for the scientific changes. As he tells it, in the medieval worldview, God, man, and the world all had access to one another. It was possible for humans to make sense of both transcendence and the world easily and to understand themselves within those larger relationships. That synthesis was lost in the fifteenth and sixteenth centuries. Nominalism is usually credited with the major role in this development, to the benefit of science but not the humanities. The humanities (e.g. renaissance humanism then, romanticism later) came to live apart from the sciences, and that is an instance of the separation of man and transcendence from the world as nature.

Many trends affecting theology that did not appear until the twentieth century nevertheless started in the seventeenth. One is the idea that the natural sciences are the fount and source of all knowledge. In the separation that Louis Dupré chronicled, ideas about human existence that were at home with the sciences in the fifteenth and sixteenth centuries were banished to the humanities in the seventeenth. It was not until the twentieth century that some would try to reduce the humanities to the terms of the sciences. Science explains all, because only science produces reliable knowledge.

An issue different from colonizing the social sciences and abolishing the humanities is whether the natural sciences are based on any presuppositions. The presupposition of scientism is that real knowledge has to be empirically testable as scientific theories are. When this is noticed, the claim is seen to be a vacuous tautology: only science is scientific. The twentieth-century motive for such a claim is frustration with the state of the humanities. Out of Dupré's separation of man, transcendence, and the natural world has come frustration in philosophical anthropology and nihilism in face of a transcendence that has more or less evaporated. In between the rise of science in the seventeenth century and the rise of scientism in the twentieth some of the problems that scientific thinking bumped into when it was intruded into the humanities have been addressed, however incompletely. History and biblical criticism opened up in the nineteenth century and led to phenomenology in the twentieth, beginning a re-understanding of what it means to be human. We shall see them in chapter 7.

6.3 Darwin and Evolution

The seventeenth and eighteenth centuries brought to theology the challenge of physics; the nineteenth century brought challenge from biology. Both physics and biology, each in its different way, appeared to undermine the presence and action of God in the world. They did so not by contradicting established "theories" in theology but by forcing theology to make explicit what had never before been spelled out in concrete or quantitative detail. When theology spelled out what it supposedly thought, the results were disastrous — and in conflict with science. Science had started out as a devout project, with its trust in the orderliness of the natural world based in the biblical doctrine of the goodness of God and therefore in his reliability. When the conflicts appeared, science became opposed to "religion," and many have tried to hide or deny its parentage. But as we have seen, borrowing the history from William Placher (sec. 6.1 above), theology in the modern world became explicit only at the cost of betraying its central insights of earlier centuries. Until the Scholastics and the Reformers, God was everywhere (though not in a spatial sense) and incomprehensible. People didn't think they understood God. In the seventeenth century and following, people thought they could be quite precise (in a spatial sense) about what God did. This we have seen already.

The earlier confrontations between physics and theology were repeated in biology. The story is well known and well told in many histories.[22] After Darwin published *The Origin of Species* in 1859, there were clergy and scientists on *both* sides of the controversy, though the debates between Wilberforce and Huxley are the only ones remembered outside of academic histories. The theory was somewhat incomplete at first; the most conspicuous missing part was genetics, which had to await the work of Gregor Mendel and then the discovery of DNA. But it quickly became clear that the only possible foundation for theoretical biology and indeed the history of life on earth would have to take evolution as its naturalistic basis.

It would be fun (for those of us who are not biologists) to play the intellectual tourist and enjoy the history of evolution in its past and in its prospects for addressing unsolved problems in the future. That, alas, is not our task. The present inquiry tells the ways in which theology was debauched, in the modern world and sometimes long before. Evolution

---
[22] Depew and Weber, *Darwinism Evolving*. Bowler, *Evolution: The History of an Idea*.

6.3 Darwin and Evolution

exposed some of those ways.

The original naiveté in reading Genesis 1 and 2 rarely if ever noticed that the two creation accounts are mutually inconsistent, or if it did, I presume it had ways of papering over the apparent inconsistency. The import of those chapters was the creation of life (both good and related to its creator), not the details or order of events. Indeed, the Priestly account in Genesis 1 goes out of its way to cleanse the story of other gods,[23] trusting that its names for the biblical God could be heard to name a transcendent Other rather than yet one more among all the gods.[24]

So it was again after Darwin. Language that had before been taken to provide both sides of a Chalcedonian account in one, was forced to take sides, and it took the intramundane side (how could it not have?), and was then found to be incoherent when a better intramundane explanation (i. e., Darwin) became available. Transcendence was discovered to be lost, but it was lost long before, as Placher has shown. We cannot do what premodern theology could, namely, give a single account that does justice to both *fuseis* simultaneously present in one phenomenon without alteration or truncation. Yet the logic of such a phenomenon persists: the intramundane phenomenon calls forth transcendence whether or not it is acknowledged.

Astrophysicists have it easy: they can just show Hubble Telescope pictures, and the resultant awe both "speaks" for itself and keeps proper silence ($\mu\acute{v}\epsilon\iota\nu$) before sacred mystery. It does not incur the obligations of explaining its language. It doesn't even have to acknowledge or take sides among different awed responses to such pictures. (No wonder publishers love to put Hubble photos on the covers of theology books!)

So it is with evolution: the scientific story is just a chronicle of naturalistically explicable events in the time series that is life. That is not all it is, and everybody knows as much, whether it is spelled out or not. We know from the distributed ontology[25] that the material particulars of a story can be fitted into other stories retold at editorial pleasure.[26] Life on earth is not just a naturalistic time series, it is also a history, one that eventuates

---

[23] As when it names the sun and moon the greater light and lesser light instead of using proper names, because the available names were the names of nature-religious gods.

[24] Remember that the Priestly creation story was written *after* the biblical God had been taken by some in the history of the Monarchy as just one more god among all the rest, with idols of all of them resident in the Temple. The Priestly creation story was one reproach to that tradition. Ezekiel supplies another.

[25] *Living in Spin*, section 5.2.5, "Multiple Narratives, Multiple Acts."

[26] Hence both editorial freedom and editorial responsibility.

in the lives of the editors. We have a *stake* in the story, even though in its naturalistic aspects that never fully appears. (I think it is bracketed, but it is part of the ontological constitution of life.) Life may indeed be the sort of being that has a stake in its own being, but the articulation of that stake is carefully bracketed in evolutionary theory in order to show its naturalistic aspects. (What makes it naturalistic may be just the logic of this bracketing; naturalistic discourse excludes existential phenomenology by definition.) Nevertheless what was bracketed was not abolished, and everybody knows as much. Evolution may give us a naturalistic time series, but it also tells our own story. Not all evolutionary biologists have understood this, though it tells their own story as much as anyone else's. The logical issues appear in the role the term 'fitness' plays in the theory. I would contend, if I may be contentious, that fitness is an analogical category, meaning different things in different contexts.[27] It is miscellaneous, and it has the "same" meaning in different contexts only by analogy. There is no naturalistic definition that could capture all and only the features of "fitness" or the reasons for survival of some and not others. The only way the concept of "fitness" can be handled is by reference to the presuppositions of biology, namely, that life is the sort of being that has a stake in its own being.

"Fitness" plays a role that renders evolution a history in which moral aspects are intelligible. The term 'fitness' is an Aristotelian virtue term that has no business appearing in any naturalistic discourse.[28] It remains because people know that with it, evolutionary history is more than just a time series, it makes existential sense of evolution, and thereby gives meaning to human life in the sense of giving us a narrative that is humanly inhabitable. That is to say, Darwinism, even in its "atheistic" versions, makes a home for man in the universe, and that is the definition of theology. Many people don't like that theology. In it, those who survive deserve to survive[29] because of features inherent in themselves, features that they have no control over.[30] It is too reminiscent of a grotesque caricature of

---

[27] See *Where, Now, O Biologists*, chapter 6.

[28] The substitute name for the phenomenon in *Where, Now, O Biologists* was differential survival for miscellaneous naturalistic reasons, or differential survival manifest among available genetic limitations. See section 6.4, "DSMNR, DSMAAGL, and Synteresis," in *Where Now*.

[29] Deserving is never spelled out, and need not be, because everybody knows it is implicated in the theory of "fitness." A not-spelled-out policy of not spelling out is the diagnostic mark of self-deception, and we have yet to uncover what it covers up.

[30] The alternative, that organisms could better themselves by their own efforts (as with

predestination, but secularized. It can be used (as in "social darwinism") to legitimate the oppression of the weak by the powerful in society. In another interpretation (one that respects the naturalistic character of evolutionary biology), there is no moral dessert, and ultimate reality is inscrutable, contrary to any theodicy. This is not too bad theology, as William Placher and D. Z. Phillips have demonstrated.

In effect, the difficulties of a Chalcedonian method are not limited to Christian theology, they appear even for the sort of atheism that often travels with evolution, or better, often hides behind evolutionary theory. One who does better is Steven Weinberg, in *The First Three Minutes*. I don't share his theology but his method is exemplary. (And he is entitled to his theology, for that is a confessional commitment, not something empirical or open to disputation.) He spots his theology in premodern sources, and so his account has some historical integrity that even theologians don't always achieve.[31] He is able to distinguish empirical and naturalistic phenomena from his theological appraisal of them. Many who would like to pass off their theology as implicit in evolution do not do as well. Analogical concepts are not acknowledged as such, thereby evading responsibility for them.

Most of these considerations were not at all clear in the nineteenth century. They are postmodern, and the evolutionary controversies were all quite modern. The "God" everywhere assumed was still the naturalized and domesticated God of the seventeenth century, guilty as charged in Placher's indictment. The only way the then-traditional account of creation could make sense presupposed understanding divine action in a monophysite sense: God creates (and acts, in general) by interfering with the natural course of events. That monophysite theology is still very much with us, and the existential costs of giving it up are unbearable for many Christians.

6.4 Reform Judaism

The changes in rabbinic Judaism in the modern world are instructive for any who would understand the changes in Christianity, for they are par-

---

Lamarck's theory) was ruled out in Darwin's theory. Darwinian science was right, and questions about the theological overtones were never unraveled.

[31] The issue is with us everywhere; it has appeared in the efforts of theologians to evade responsibility for their confessional commitments, hiding behind "proofs" of the so-called "existence" of God or the correctness of biblical religion.

allel. One provides a narrative foil for the other, and both share common causes. Jacob Neusner tells the story.[32] The Judaism before 1787/1789, the American and French revolutions,[33] was continuous with the Judaism of the fourth century, the Yerushalmi, and the response to Constantine and the establishment of Christianity. It was the Judaism of the Dual Torah, which dealt with the problems posed by Christianity and its establishment. It presupposed the self-evident character of that Christianity in order to propose its own counter-self-evidence. After the American and French revolutions, in which civil polity was no longer erected on religious grounds, thus demonstrating the possibility of life without the received religious basis, Christianity lost its self-evident character, and with it, the inherited Judaism of the Dual Torah also lost its self-evident character. Some adjustments were necessary.

In brief forecast, for both Christianity and rabbinic Judaism, the innovators (Reform Judaism, Liberal Theology) came first. Then came the reactionary movements (Orthodox Judaism and various Christian biblical literalisms), each claiming to be continuous with the pre-crisis past. Last of all came the mediating positions (Conservative Judaism and the Christian Neo-Orthodox, among others). The claims of the reactionaries to be the unchanged continuations of their respective premodern traditions are spurious.[34] It is not that the reactionaries were without virtues; on the Jewish side, at least, the Orthodox have sustained their own faithful very well. Whatever may be said of Fundamentalists and Ultramontanists, Evangelicals and their Catholic counterparts have also sustained their faithful effectively. But biblical literalism comes at a great cost, as we shall see.

Reform Judaism did not begin with the American and French Revolutions as if they were a shock. Its precursors were in the eighteenth century as in Moses Mendelssohn, a philosopher of the Jewish Enlightenment, and in Neusner's account, its articulate spelling out was not until late in the nineteenth century. An example of Reform Judaism's recognition of its own identity came at a rabbinic conference in 1885 in Pittsburgh, Pennsylvania, not in Europe.[35] So it was a gradual process, as many in the history of ideas are. The causes were apparent only late in the nineteenth century, and institutional form also came only late. The Reform asked itself the character and purposes of Judaism in a changed world.

---

[32] Neusner, *Death and Birth of Judaism*.
[33] The dates are for the American Constitution and the start of the French Revolution.
[34] Neusner, *Death and Birth of Judaism*, 117–118.
[35] Neusner, *Death and Birth of Judaism*, 91–92 and 87.

Christian experience unfolded in parallel, though the issues were often different. Liberal theology paralleled Reform Judaism. The literalist reaction paralleled Orthodox Judaism. Ultramontanism came to institutional form as a reaction to liberal currents in the nineteenth-century French Catholic Church, themselves a consequence of rethinking in the aftermath of the French Revolution.[36] Protestant Fundamentalism came to self-recognition only in the twentieth century, with the Five Fundamentals at Princeton Seminary. Nineteenth-century Protestant literalism was a reaction to the biblical criticism of the mid-century, *not* originally to Darwin.[37] Creationism came in the twentieth century. What is often not noticed (but striking when it is) is that change came in response not to challenges from science but to changes in culture that may have been more diffuse than in the rabbinic case but were no less real. Today's regnant mythology attributes all the provocations to science, but the reality was more interesting. Schleiermacher and Hegel were the beginnings, after the Enlightenment and the new physics, but long before Darwin. They were responding to Kant and the Enlightenment as much as to physics.

Paralleling Conservative Judaism were the mediating positions: the Neo-Orthodox after World War I and many Catholic schools. The mediating positions were more numerous, nuanced, and complex than either the Liberals or the reactionaries. The watershed was in Liberal Theology.

6.5 Liberal Theology

Reform Judaism was paralleled a little later by Liberal Theology. Moses Mendelssohn (1729–1786) lived in the eighteenth century; Friedrich Schleiermacher straddled the turn to the nineteenth, contemporary to Hegel (1768–1834 and 1770–1831). The logic unfolded in much the same way in Christianity as it had within modern rabbinic Judaism. The Liberal innovation was met with a reactionary response that claimed to continue the inherited tradition, and eventually with mediating responses between the two. The reactionary claim of authority from the older tradition was, as with Orthodox Judaism, somewhat spurious. Among twentieth-century Protestants, the reactionaries became known as Fundamentalists, and they were opposed to "liberal" biblical scholarship long before they were opposed to

---

[36] For one account, see Weigel, *The Irony of Modern Catholic History*.
[37] For its logic in the twentieth century, see section 7.5.

evolutionary biology.[38] Among Catholics, the reactionaries are exemplified by Ultramontanists and Pius IX. Biblical literalism is still widespread.

Why did these changes occur when they did, at the beginning of the nineteenth century, instead of in the seventeenth, when the conceptual seeds were planted for a "conflict between science and religion"? Neusner's answer may be rephrased in the terms of the sociology of knowledge. Berger and Luckmann someplace remark that the ideas in a socially constructed world get their plausibility from social structures — they called them "plausibility structures" — that support those ideas.[39] What Jacob Neusner observed was that the plausibility structures for the inherited theological traditions were swept away by the French and American revolutions. The political changes demonstrated that neither of the Church and the State needed the other; each would have to stand on its own. The State was clearly capable of that, and the Church would have to adjust as best it could. On the Christian side, the changes in Liberal theology and its sequels were more than a little bit complicated.

What is surprising is how much continued from the older tradition. Some observations:

(1) Conspicuously, Liberal theology has kept the Marcionite instincts that it received from the tradition. It focused on Jesus, with little interest in the inheritance from the Exodus and Second Temple Judaism.

(2) The tasks of apologetics, justifying Christianity to the world, continued, though reshaped. Schleiermacher's *Speeches on Religion to its Cultured Despisers* is the classic work, and it attests that the plausibility of Christianity was already gone in significant parts of society before the start of the nineteenth century. Liberal theology gave up the solutions without giving up the problem of justification of religion. Its proposed solution was an evolutionary approach to the history of religions, told so as to culminate in Christianity. It was not terribly convincing. There were other approaches as well (some based on Hegel), but none were very effective as apologetics. They all confused the problem of arguing against outsiders with that of explanation to and catechesis of insiders. Both are problems of legitimation, a term taken from the sociology of knowledge. I think the

---

[38] Reactionary opposition to the new biblical criticism was deeper, broader, and earlier than opposition to evolution. For the late opposition to evolution, see Numbers, *The Creationists*, 4. For the character of conservative theological reaction, see Welch, *Protestant Thought*, both volumes. For the Catholic responses, see Welch, volume 2, 201.

[39] In the perspective of logic, it may be the ideas that support the social structures instead of vice versa, but that question may be left to sociologists.

problem with apologetics arises from a faulty assumption that biblical religion, especially of the Christian variety, *should* be justified (as in proven valid) to everybody. We have remarked the pathologies of proofs many times in this study. The Bible does not offer proofs, though many think it does. Commitment in and to biblical religion is a confessional choice, and there are many other possible choices if one wants to get out of biblical religion. Some of the Neo-Orthodox did better, but these issues are still open in our own time.

(3) Schleiermacher worked in an age when history itself was doubted, especially as a source of revelation. An earlier voice was Kant's *Religion Within the Limits of Reason Alone*, i.e., with only minimal reliance on history. And so Liberal theology sought to explain itself to itself as something growing out of present-day experience, without radical debts to history. The question of history was opened up in the nineteenth century, and what it means to live in history or to understand history has not been settled even in our own time.

(4) It bears mention in passing that Liberal theology attracted a reputation for an optimistic ethics and underestimating the problems of human sin.[40] How one could be optimistic about human sin after the twentieth century baffles me, but some are. Voices in the nineteenth century already protested; Dostoevsky for one example. Some have pegged Liberal theology as culture-Protestantism, which has some truth in it. When the liberal tradition was reminded of the problems of human evil, in our own time it has retreated into an ethic that is largely an instrument of class warfare rather than a broader theology of sin and evil. Those who live in the time of political correctness know what this means.

(5) In one respect, I think Liberal theology was an improvement on what came before. It moved the starting point from metaphysics to anthropology, an analysis of what it means to be human. It was only a beginning, but it developed greatly over the next two centuries. Religion begins in the heart, not in abstract reasoning. The language for which Liberal theology is most notorious is Schleiermacher's grounding of Christianity in a "feeling of absolute dependence," "*schlechthinige Abhängigkeitsgefühl*." Claude Welch deprecates the usual translation as "absolute dependence," preferring other adjectives (utter, simple, unqualified) but not changing the

---

[40] If one were to ask for an example, Niebuhr's comments in *The Kingdom of God in America*, 193 should suffice.

noun.[41] From my own perspective, I would prefer another phrasing, for dependence invites a question, dependence on *what* or *whom?* This will be explored further in *Unanswerable Questions*. We are "dependent" if you will, in the sense of being up against limitations that cannot be changed, even though we do not always know what the limitations are. But in addition to dependence, I would observe that we are always involved in interpersonal relations, and we interpersonate even after there are no more persons in this or any other world to interpersonate *to*. The difference is fussy, and even my own phrasing does not altogether satisfy me, but I think it is better. And as for feeling, this is not just a feeling, it is ontological; interpersonation is built into the being of persons. One can ignore it, but it is still there as part of being human. That said, people can interpersonate in many ways, not all characteristic of biblical religion.

As said, Liberal theology moved the starting point in theology to anthropology. Should anthropology be the *only* starting point for theology? No, not necessarily. Should it be one starting point? Yes, I think so. Should it be the ending point? No, not necessarily.

(6) Liberal theology revised monophysite theology of divine action greatly, but slowly. The process of dismantling an apologetic of miracles is not finished even in our own day. Though Spinoza began it, it flowered in the nineteenth century. The history of Liberal theology has been one of bargaining and accommodation. For one example, "We'll give you the miracles of Jesus, but we'll keep his ethics. You can have the Virgin Birth, but we'll hold on to the Resurrection."[42] Not quite. The miracle texts are important in the Gospels, and may not simply be written off. How to read them is quite another matter.[43]

The problems of literalism came to a head in nineteenth-century biblical scholarship, and that movement was the start of a return to a Chalcedonian method in theology *beyond* Christology. That is, historians asked questions about the intramundane origins of the events and the texts that gave them to us. They postponed questions about divine presence in those texts and events, because the logic of God present in history is different from the intramundane logic of historical events themselves. Divine presence is still not well understood, even to the small extent that it can be.

---

[41] Welch, *Protestant Thought in the Nineteenth Century*, Volume 1, 65, note 16.
[42] Berger, *The Sacred Canopy*, 159–160.
[43] See sections 3.2 and chapter 8, especially section 8.1.

6.6 The Birth of Biblical Criticism

Until the eighteenth century, the Bible was read more or less literally. The schema of the four senses of scripture from ancient hermeneutics rarely disturbed the literal meaning of biblical texts. Some biblical texts were obviously not meant literally, but any that could be read literally usually were. Problems and inconsistencies did appear, but there were usually ways to harmonize the texts. Nevertheless the problems of a literal reading grew.

In the nineteenth century, those problems all became conspicuous, and questioning unfolded with its own logic. We shall have more to say about that in section 6.7 and following, but for the moment we shall have to be content with citation of a few sources. The point that really does need to be made is that for all its failures in regard to transcendence, Liberal Theology and its culture enabled something that is rare in religious history. Critical study of the Bible was a form of *self*-criticism by (mostly) Christian scholars, and so in its way, it was a movement of great courage. The outcome was not at all clear and still is not, even today. This, for all its sometimes muddle-headedness, is biblical religion at its best: honestly self-critical, willing to proceed even without full answers to its questions, even willing to risk its own legitimacy. This is one model for biblical religion to follow now, and it continues a tradition that goes back to the prophets and the Pentateuch. It is an instance of the general openness to Exposure that is central to biblical religion.

Every beginning seminarian is expected to learn the critical tools of biblical scholarship, the principal results, and the history of the writing of the texts as well as the history told in the texts of the Common Documents. Typical are the Fortress Press guides to biblical scholarship, of which the first is *The Historical-Critical Method*, by Edgar Krentz. Two kinds of inquiries arose: questions about who wrote the texts and when, and questions about whether the texts were correct in all their (apparent) claims. Both had precedents before the nineteenth century. An early example of suspicion about the origins of a document was Lorenzo Valla's argument (1440) that the Donation of Constantine was a forgery. "His use of linguistic, legal, historical and political arguments makes him one of the founders of historical criticism."[44] That logic of questioning blossomed in the nineteenth century, when there emerged four stages in the editing of the

---

[44] Krentz, *The Historical Critical Method*, 8.

Pentateuch, a theory known as the Documentary Hypothesis ("JEDP"), in the work of Julius Wellhausen and others. Only then could it be recognized that Genesis 2–3 was taken over from Canaanite sources and adapted for the theology of the Yahwist, whereas Genesis 1 came from the Priestly editor's reworking of Babylonian cosmology, three or four centuries later. Ability to distinguish the conceptuality of the culture of origin from the theology expressed in those texts came later.[45]

A few points of interest along the way; even Krentz's brief history is too long to summarize here. Critical methods spread from the Bible to secular history and were often developed first to answer questions about the Bible (Krentz 22). It is a myth that critical methods were born for secular history and then turned on recalcitrant and backward theologians and the Bible. Biblical and secular historiography developed in tandem; sometimes the biblical scholars were ahead of secular historians. Late in the first half of the nineteenth century, Ferdinand Christian Bauer demonstrated an interest in Christian history for its own sake, rather than as a means to promote dogmatic or apologetic projects. "History is to be written to understand Christianity as an historical religion, not to extract eternal ideas from history. Investigation which was truly historical had arrived" (Krentz 26–27).

The problems in NT criticism were different, but the cultural and academic themes were much the same. Several histories (among many more) may be cited. Werner Georg Kümmel starts long before the nineteenth century and brings the story through two thirds of the twentieth century. David Laird Dungan provides another survey. Albert Schweitzer's *The Quest of the Historical Jesus* was the first of a least three such quests over the next two centuries.

In some ways, Krentz's introduction to critical history functions as an introduction for the whole series that it began. The actual history of the development of critical methods takes only two chapters and 32 pages, out of five chapters in all. The third chapter reflects on critical methods in their present form, but the fourth raises further questions, questions that I don't think even Krentz had answers to. When Krentz wrote, critical history had earned its right to continue, and it was secure against being abandoned or ejected from theological academia. It was also clear that it did not fit comfortably into everybody's theology even then, and what the

---

[45] See Hobbs on conceptuality and "understanding" in section 1.8 above.

6.6 The Birth of Biblical Criticism

future holds is (as always) uncertain. He was well aware that there are still today many who would be just as happy not to be troubled by critical history.

Krentz speaks of two alternatives: "Theology must either justify the use of historical criticism and define its nature or be willing to reformulate the Christian faith in terms of a positivist truth that historicism alone will validate" (p. 61). The first alternative is the better one, for the second, historicism, leaves unanswered too many questions. In particular, it is too similar to attempts to "prove" the validity of Christianity from a quest for objectivity that turns out on further investigation to protect concealed choices about the history. Historical-critical research often also has tacitly presupposed that it is possible to tell the story of the past isolated from the tellers in the present. That is, it is possible to isolate origins and use the origins to criticize the later development. Robert Barron demurs that "The Catholic instinct is not so much to assess the development by the origin as to appreciate the development as the full flowering of the origin."[46] In my words, not his, the events of the past are constituted by historical narratives that are unfinished and so incompletely accessible to us even now.[47]

It is odd that neither Edgar Krentz nor Van Harvey worked with H. Richard Niebuhr's distinction between "external" and "internal" history, because they both knew Niebuhr's work. The distinction can be stated in its simplest form as that the two kinds of history ask different questions, to which different kinds of explanation are appropriate.[48] They may not contradict or interfere, but each has its own integrity.[49]

In retrospect, scholars and theologians have rarely escaped from the assumptions of a monophysite theology of divine action. That was the common assumption in debates between Deists and their "orthodox" opponents, that divine action interferes with the ways of nature, and that such interference can stand as a sort of proof of divine presence and action. That characterization of divine action was accepted by the "orthodox," and rejected by the Deists, but they both agreed about what divine action is and

---

[46] Barron, *The Priority of Christ*, 43.

[47] See *Living in Spin*, chapter 5.

[48] The distinction is elaborated in detail in *The Meaning of Revelation*.

[49] In passing, I would demur from the thesis that external history comes first, and internal (confessional) history has to work with what external history gives it. External history of human lives and actions has to presuppose that there is an internal history, whose internal and existential aspects it mostly brackets. But that is a problem for much later than the nineteenth century.

disagreed only about whether it happens or not. They did not have what I am advocating here, a Chalcedonian understanding of divine action, in which transcendence is not to be explained in the same way as intramundane processes. If they had had such a perspective, their work would have gone faster and more happily. It is a tribute to their courage that they proceeded anyway, without the resources that could have made theological sense of it. Indeed, it was the slow realization that the results of critical history are incompatible with a monophysite theology of divine action that leaves us today in need of forging a Chalcedonian theology of divine action. In other words, "orthodox" theology of divine action was monophysite in the nineteenth century, and we still don't have a very robust Chalcedonian improvement on it.

To look well ahead of the nineteenth century problematic, Krentz in his last pages observes that the challenges to critical history come today (post-1945) not from biblical literalists, but from those who doubt whether adequate historical knowledge is possible and are uncertain how to get it or use it.[50]

The chosen central problem in NT criticism was the recovery of a historical Jesus.[51] I don't think most scholars were very clear about whether they were trying just to *explain* their Christian faith or whether they were trying to *justify* it. The difference is that the first is a confessional commitment, but in the second, the supposedly "objective" history is made to take the responsibility for the believers' faith.

What began in critical history grew into much more in historiography and the philosophy of history. Those questions came later, at the end of the nineteenth century and well into the twentieth. We come to those problems in the sections on history.

6.7 The Discovery of History

History in its simple sense was not discovered in the modern world, for there had always been some knowledge of history, and people read it to draw lessons for their own time. It was, as Collingwood said, naive and

---

[50] See Krentz *The Historical-Critical Method*, 84–85 and the comments on Peter Stuhlmacher and those who have come after him. I would observe that this kind of challenge to critical history has grown since Krentz wrote in 1975.

[51] In passing, this was a Marcionite approach; interest in the Common Documents was historical rather than motivated in faith. That changed, but slowly.

uncritical before about the turn of the nineteenth century. Biblical religion was always historical, in the sense that it was about particular events in history that could not be explained in terms of nature. It told a story, and in that it was not unique: royal houses kept chronicles (some are cited in the Common Documents) and there were historians in the Greco-Roman world. Herodotus and Thucydides and the Latin historians can stand as examples.[52] But biblical history was more than just chronicles or secular history. It was salvation history, a way to use history to make sense of man's place in the universe and as a way to confront transcendence. More to the point, it was the salvation history of a very particular people. But none of that was spelled out in any theoretical way in the Common Documents, the New Testament, the Fathers, or the Talmuds. That literature brought man, God, and the world together with a naiveté and innocence we would be happy to recover. That, alas, is neither possible nor fitting.

There was a change in the character of historical thinking roughly at the beginning of the nineteenth century. It became interesting in ways that it had not been before, and historians asked questions about their work that rarely were asked earlier. Several kinds of questions stand out. As R. G. Collingwood observed in *The Idea of History*, historians systematically asked themselves whether they should believe the documents and other evidence they worked with, and so history became critical.[53] Collingwood saw more than just this, however, and his observations are often dismissed as "idealism" because they are unintuitive (to "realists") and sometimes difficult to work with. He said that the historian works with the present; the past is gone and inaccessible, though it has left traces in the present. What the historian works with is *thought*: he rethinks the thoughts of those in the past whom he studies. The purpose, Collingwood said, was for "self-knowledge": what it means to be a human being in history (p. 10).

History as self-knowledge, beyond mere criticism of sources, was a candid example of something quite postmodern: the history that we have is (in part) the result of questions that arise in our own time, and the results fit into our own time, whoever the "we" happens to be. This has appeared in various forms besides Collingwood's, especially as historical thinking drifted into a postmodern approach. Since it has intruded the historian into the results of the historian's work, it has raised anxieties from time to time,

---

[52] Collingwood, *The Idea of History*, Part I gives examples from the Greco-Roman world, and later Parts supply the historiography since then.

[53] The thesis was announced in Collingwood, *The Idea of History*, 9–10, and developed in the course of the argument.

among those who want something "objective." That, however, is to get ahead of our story and look at where it is headed.

Begin somewhat earlier. Collingwood started with Greco-Roman historians, but the eighteenth century is adequate for present purposes. Some merely wanted more detail about history. One could cite David Hume's history of England or Gibbon on the fall of the Roman Empire. Early in the nineteenth century history became an object of professional study. That was the work of Wilhelm von Humboldt, who was called to Berlin in 1809 to "reorganize the Prussian system of education."[54] Out of this grew the University of Berlin. In Iggers' telling, German history in the nineteenth century began as an optimistic project to construct a kind of historical knowledge comparable in its power and certainty to the natural knowledge of the physical sciences. It was not to be; apart from particular histories, the prime lesson learned was that historical knowledge is not like the natural sciences.

Along the way, Iggers' account corroborates Collingwood's observations about the location of the historian's questions in the present. The German historians' questions about the past were never far from their questions about the German constitution. The present raised questions about how German society and institutions *should* be structured, and those questions were to be answered on the basis of the history of the past.

Collingwood covers much of the same ground, expanded to include historians in Italy, England, and France, but his structure is different. Instead of the rise and fall of historicism, Collingwood measures each figure he surveys for his progress toward what he (RGC) called "scientific history," and usually for that figure's ability to avoid being drawn into psychologism. Curiously, Collingwood did not include Troeltsch or Troeltsch's *Der Historismus und seine Probleme*, which the Oxford libraries had in 1923.[55]

Along the way, Troeltsch's *Historismus* collects in a section on the formal logic of history eleven categories of historical thinking. They are bracketed by "individual totality" and "development"; in other words, questioning begins with identifying *what* are the phenomena one studies in history. The last, development, takes up half the space, as I suppose it should in any anatomy of historical reasoning. Yet Troeltsch remained

---

[54] Iggers, *The German Conception of History*, 52.

[55] Stephen Arnold at the Bodleian Library, email, 2010/06/07. Mark Chambers, who has studied Troeltsch's work in detail, also did not know why Collingwood omitted Troeltsch.

exploratory to the end.[56]

By the end of the century, in the work of Troeltsch and Dilthey, the quest for certainty in historical knowledge, known as historicism, was in crisis. That crisis still elicits questioning.[57] Charles Bambach summarizes:

> The "crisis" of historicism in this sense is really nothing other than the coming to self-consciousness of the temporal, historical, cultural, and institutional character of scientific inquiry itself — a topic that we now conveniently label "post-modern." But in opening up the metaphysical contradictions at work in the scientific demand for objective truth, historicism simultaneously reveals the contradictions at the heart of the modernist vision ... [58]

Criticism in historiography arose at many levels, and in later years (the twentieth century) it became criticism of narratives. For one example, American historians still debate at length the causes of the American Revolution and the Civil War. For another, historians today rethink the causes of the Great War of 1914–1918. This is an instance of the narrative of human actions as explored in *Living in Spin*.[59] Questioning has to answer what to include, what to leave out, and how to characterize what gets included, and above all, questioning arises in the present. These features of historical thinking have come out only slowly, over the course of two centuries. Action in history arises because some contingency affects someone's interests and is narratable. The constitution of actions in history is thus very different from that of motions (trajectories, really) in physics. The "motions" in actions are selected editorially and arise within narratives. Trajectories, if any, come last and are not always available at all.

Eventually, historians came to reflect on the kind of knowledge they could hope for. An initial trust that they could recover the *trajectories* of events in the past was disappointed. It was replaced by a hope to recover the *meanings* of events, with some cautious inferences about the *motions* of past events.[60] History differs from physics: The Jet Propulsion Laboratory

---

[56] He died prematurely in 1922, so his work was never really finished.

[57] Megill, "Why was there a crisis of historicism?" *History and Theory* 36 no. 3 (1997) 416–430.

[58] Bambach, *Heidegger, Dilthey, and the Crisis of Historicism*, 124.

[59] See my *Living in Spin*, 68, 126–127 and passim.

[60] The terms are from *Living in Spin*. See chapter 6, and especially section 6.1.

publishes the positions of the planets long ago, to great precision, but those are trajectories, and that is not history, it is orbital mechanics. Trajectories by themselves are meaningless. The natural sciences have been the sirens attracting historians away from historical thinking, because the sciences offered certainty, detail, and precision of a kind that is not available in historiography. I would say that seeking scientific precision in history is a category error; history just doesn't work that way. But that is to get way ahead of our story, to the twenty-first century. We are still in the nineteenth.

Along the way, as Collingwood tells it, some came to interpret history as self-knowledge of man in the present.[61] We are creatures constituted by our pasts, as can be seen in the Short Historical Creed in Dt. 26.[62] That, of course, opens the possibility that one could choose some *other* history in one's own self-definition; but that problem is post-modern, not modern.

Later on, questions arose in the twentieth century. Is there a "mechanics" of history? Is it predictable or calculable? How does causation in history work? What about Hegel? When we know something about past history, what is it exactly that we really know? Is history an evolutionary process, in which the surviving people, ideas, and institutions are by the fact of survival better than those they displaced? As in biological evolution, read as social darwinism (a morally pretentious reading)? And by what assumption do things get better with time? Many have viewed history as a story of decline, not progress, with reverence for a golden age in the past rather than anticipation of progress in the future.

---

[61] Collingwood, *The Idea of History*, 10.
[62] See section 2.5 above.

Chapter 7

Postmodernity

Modern science, especially Newtonian physics and Darwinian biology, promised a world with a certain and solid basis, upon which answers to all remaining questions could be built. In a transition that coincided roughly with the turn from the nineteenth to the twentieth centuries, the foundations turned out to be more interesting, more open, and less solid or certain. Change began in the nineteenth century, as we have already seen. The import for history was a re-understanding of its basis, methods, results, and outlook. It was a new world. Much that was certain was lost, and we are not entirely sure how to handle our uncertainties.

It is often said of Kant and Schleiermacher that they moved the starting point of philosophy and theology from the cosmos to human understanding. That is fair enough, but the later fruit vastly exceeded the beginnings. The changes that originally were fairly narrow in scope burst out in many fields in the postmodern period. Philosophy (many names could be cited), the Neo-orthodox in theology, the understanding of language and logic, hermeneutics and phenomenology, and the sociology of knowledge all blossomed handsomely. There were reactionaries also, among Cartesians, biblical literalists, and Analytic philosophy of religion. The new developments, taken together, have put us in a new world. They have shown us whole new disciplines each with its own ways of interpreting the world. They are also unfinished. These developments have prepared our world for the perplexities in theology that we live with today. Some of this we saw at the beginning, in chapter 1, because it seemed appropriate to spell out the presuppositions of the present study, especially where they differ from the typical in today's secular culture. More that came in the twentieth century follows in the present chapter.

Bruce Wilshire lamented that twentieth-century philosophy began on the doorstep of major opportunity and then turned back. The Wunderjahr was 1927, the year of quantum mechanics,[1] *Being and Time, Process and Reality*, and one could go on.[2] The years just before and after, in the 1920s and 1930s, provided even more breakthroughs. Wilshire's appraisal is simple enough: Twentieth-century philosophy stood on the threshold of a world unimaginable in any philosophy in the platonist tradition — and turned back. The sciences have done better, but the humanities have been disappointing.

We continue with issues that were born in modernity, the seventeenth to nineteenth centuries, but transformed in postmodernity, with a transition spread out in the nineteenth and twentieth centuries. As before, the apportionment is somewhat arbitrary. Some think they have identified the defining marks of postmodernity, but that is more than I can say. What follows are just a few features needed for the present story. There were many changes, not all at once, and probably not all related. There is a thread that runs through them: the so-called Copernican revolution in Kant's shift from starting with the cosmos to starting with man, specifically human *interpretation*. Schleiermacher was not the only one; see also Kierkegaard, eventually the historians, Heidegger, hermeneutics and phenomenology. It was typical of the nineteenth century. It should be noted, however, that a starting place, a point of departure, need not be where an inquiry ends and comes to rest. This chapter includes only a few steps on the way to today's perplexities in theology; a complete history would be larger than this book.

We deal first with a little of the philosophy that led to issues in twentieth-century theology: Kierkegaard, Heidegger, and then the Neo-orthodox. Some disciplines opened up the issues in their own characteristic ways: language, sociology, hermeneutics, and the history of religions. Then we come to the opponents of these changes: Cartesians, biblical literalism, and the quest for proofs in analytic philosophy of religion. Lastly, a summary collecting the results.

---

[1] Schrödinger and Heisenberg published in 1927, and so consolidated earlier work by Planck, Einstein, and Bohr. 1927 was not the beginning, but things began to come together then.

[2] Wilshire, "Fifty Years of Academic Philosophy."

7.1 Kierkegaard and Heidegger

Kant's turn to the subject in the first Critique was focused on what he called "pure reason," or in more concrete terms, the presuppositions of mathematical physics: time, space, causality, and the other categories at the beginning of scientific reasoning. Some in the nineteenth century began their anthropology not with scientific reason but with the human self in its relation to itself and to others. Søren Kierkegaard borrowed language from Hegel and declared the self a relation that relates itself to itself — but one that is constituted as such by an Other.[3] As things unfolded, he focused on anxiety for a part of his inquiry. Heidegger took it as the phenomenon that best discloses the structure of human being. Heidegger built on Kierkegaard, but the later thinker departed from the earlier and went his own way in regard to anxiety.[4] We can learn from both of them, if we proceed carefully.

Anxiety is about whether the self will be or become what it can or should be. That may begin with its mere survival (be-ing at all), but most of the time it presupposes some conception of what the self could or should become, and so anxiety is also an issue of success or failure. Kierkegaard and Heidegger develop this in quite different ways. For the curmudgeon of Copenhagen, it is (in *The Concept of Anxiety*) the way into a relationship with God (since the self's relation to itself is constituted by God), and also the way into an understanding of original sin. It opens the way to two despairs — self-assertion (without God), and giving up (still without God). Faith (including hope and trust) consists in accepting the self's being as a gift from God. As such, faith is a choice, and the self that results is also a choice.[5] I would say that selfhood is a gift that we never fully understand but that may be more than Kierkegaard says. What Kierkegaard does emphasize (and Heidegger does not) is the presence of other people:

> ... what is essential to human existence: that man is *indi-*

---

[3] The definition is in the opening of *Sickness Unto Death*. See Lowrie, trans., *Fear and Trembling and The Sickness Unto Death*, 146. See also *The Sickness Unto Death*. Trans. Hong and Hong, 13–14. The phrasing is adapted from Hegel's *Phenomenology of Spirit* (Trans. A. V. Miller), 14.

[4] Dan Magurshak, "The Concept of Anxiety," in Robert L. Perkins, ed., *International Kierkegaard Commentary*, Volume 8: *The Concept of Anxiety*, 167–195, esp. 169. Heidegger did not really understand Kierkegaard. As usual, Heidegger is interesting but never a reliable secondary source.

[5] To be repetitious, that is the theme of the present book. Choice — and responsibility — are in everything.

viduum and as such simultaneously himself and the whole race, and in such a way that the whole race participates in the individual and the individual in the whole race.*

The footnote:

> If a particular individual could fall away entirely from the race, his falling away would require a different qualification of the race. Whereas if an animal should fall away from the species, the species itself would remain entirely unaffected.[6]

This is something that Heidegger never gives us in *Being and Time*. Other people appear in a negative role as the "they" but never in any positive role.[7] They are missing in his definition of human being on page 12. The German has slang, "in seinem Sein *um* dieses Sein selbst geht," which conceals what is left out. The English translations, human being "is an issue for itself" (Macquarrie and Robinson), or human being "is of concern to itself" (Joan Stambaugh), make it possible to see what is left out. I am not the only one for whom my self is an issue. To paraphrase, I am not the only one who has *stakes* in my self and selfhood; other people do also, as I have stakes in their being. What Heidegger *does* give us is that this (suitably corrected) is the mode of being of human being. It is primordially constitutive of human being. In effect, being is not just matter, it is also matter*ing*, and it is the mattering that ontologically holds the matter of a thing together as *one* thing.

Heidegger does not jump immediately to anxiety; anxiety emerges only later, after considerable work. Being human is being-in-the-world, and that means an understanding of the world and the self's place in it. Heidegger distinguished four senses of 'world.'[8] He usually intends his third meaning, the world as a context for human living, before any philosophical reflection on it. In this sense, human selfhood and the world as it is for humans arise together.

Interpreting the world is a matter of understanding, originally tacit and later (maybe) spelled out. It is worth tarrying briefly over the worldhood of the world. We have prelinguistic involvements in the world and with

---

[6] Kierkegaard, *The Concept of Anxiety* (Trans. Thomte), 28.

[7] Being-with other people appears in section 26, but it is never developed outside of that section and so does not have the influence it should have.

[8] Macquarrie and Robinson trans., 92–93; German, 65.

people and things in it, but the moment we attempt to articulate those involvements, we are in language.[9] It is an interpreted world, which is to say that it and things in it are human-relative. Everything we know about the world comes to us through our own interpretation. Attempts to get around our interpretations merely replace one interpretation with another. This does *not* mean that everything in the world is zuhanden, to use Heidegger's language. The vorhanden is an aspect of virtually everything, the substrate of all material things. It is not useful to humans, but it is nevertheless part of the context for human living, and in that sense it is human-relative. That is not to say that the world cares (or even knows) about us, but we do care about the world. It makes a difference to us, whether it knows or not.

A human's place in the world puts the focus on the human being and its prospects — in other words, anxiety and its issues. Will the human being succeed in becoming what it can be? And what has to happen for a human being to succeed? Heidegger's answers are quite different from Kierkegaard's.

We have enough at this point to see what their inquiries have given us. To be human involves choices. It is also a matter of interpretation, and as such, it is ambiguous. People differ about what constitutes living well.

7.2 The Neo-orthodox

The legacy of nineteenth-century biblical criticism and the Liberal failure of transcendence provoked a crisis early in the twentieth century. Before World War I, Ernst Troeltsch knew that the project of historicism could not succeed, and he did not live long enough to explore much beyond that impasse. Critical scholarship had made a literal reading of the Common Documents impossible in places that inevitably left both theologians and laity uncomfortable. How to explain the dependence of the world on God (creation) was no longer clear, and science having destroyed biblical creation stories did little to provide theological replacements, though many have cast the sciences (especially evolution) in the theological role of just such a replacement. In the New Testament, as Albert Schweitzer recounted, a series of christologies had all failed, leaving theologians again somewhat lonely.

The failure of transcendence was harder to recognize at the time, though the spread of atheism in its place was clear enough, soon followed

---

[9] Heidegger, *Being and Time*, sections 31–33.

by "secularism," or wholesale apostasy in European society. Inherited versions of transcendence survived (and still survive) well enough, but they entailed problems with the natural sciences. I contend that these problems stemmed from a monophysite theology of divine action. That is, the only way people in the mainstream of culture can now understand divine action is by some sort of interference with natural causes. This is just as Robert Sokolowski observed in the more limited problem of Christology. The Christological problem and the problem of divine action in the world both depend on the prior question of divine transcendence:

> [T]he Christian distinction between God and the world serves to permit the other Christian mysteries to be thought as mysteries and not as incoherences.[10]

Having domesticated real transcendence, Christian mysteries were converted into puzzles. Some were "solved"; some were shown just to be incoherent. The only things left were mere natural phenomena.

The two sources of crisis came to a head in World War I. That war was not a theological conflict, but it did serve as a clearing, an opening in which the root theological problems began to be visible. They have not entirely been solved a century later, but twentieth century theology made enough progress so that one could say today that we have not fully appreciated the resources bequeathed to us in the twenty-first century. We have seen a little of the structure of life in history, and we shall see more. One of the functions of transcendence is to enable people to come to terms with disappointment and Limitation. Without some kind of transcendence, all that is left is a war of each against all, seeking to escape disappointment and Limitation. When claims of transcendence are in bad faith, merely serving to mask will to power, as they were in World War I, the resulting disillusionment was insufferable. The self-destruction of Europe in the first half of the twentieth century was followed by its apostasy in the second half. The shock of World War I was a clearing that forced realization that there was a problem with transcendence. It did not show the way to a solution.

Karl Barth's commentary on Romans was the beginning of the necessary rethinking. With it began a theological conversation of many names, "Neo-orthodox" theology one among them. The movement was mostly Protestant but Catholics had to deal with the same issues — history and

---

[10] Sokolowski, *The God of Faith and Reason*, 37.

7.2 The Neo-orthodox

transcendence. Fergus Kerr recounts the story, centrally of how the Dominicans and the Jesuits fought for and won permission to think historically.[11]

The Neo-orthodox didn't deal successfully with philosophical issues, metaphysics, the character and reality of transcendence. They certainly tried. In the end, they (or their heirs) were sucked back into Liberal Theology, in effect, into a monophysite theology of divine action and presence, but monophysite of the intramundane, without real transcendence. Former Barthians generally revert to Liberal theology. Why? I think one reason, to get way ahead of our story, is that it is always possible to reassert monophysite presuppositions in the questions one asks. Sometimes those questions are legitimate; sometimes the best response is to call out the category errors implicit in them. The result today, unwilling to deal with transcendence, is Liberal theology, both Catholic and Protestant. Without any transcendence, it is left with defending power relationships in society: both the so-called sexual revolution and the establishment of liberal politics in society.

There is a very brief but useful typology of ways to construe theological language in David Burrell's *Knowing the Unknowable God*.[12] Along the way, Karl Barth puts in a cameo appearance. One can, Burrell says, treat religious language about transcendence as univocal, analogical, or as equivocal. The hazards of univocal language are briefly noted (there is more elsewhere): the God gets sucked into the world, on the world's terms, a move whose costs have been noted by many. Univocation undermines or abolishes real transcendence. Most of the book is about a Thomistic understanding of analogy, a kind of equivocation, but not equivocation *simply*.[13] On the way, simple equivocation is ascribed to Maimonides and Barth, "but," Burrell continues (p. 17), "one always feels in such cases that one's religious self holds one's mind captive." Hence the need for some kind of analogy, some way of bridging the apparent gap in meaning between intramundane distinctions and the distinction implicit in transcendence.

What goes for Barth applies also to most of the other Neo-orthodox. That tradition is older than the twentieth century; it gets reinvented from time to time. Gregory Rocca adds pseudo-Dionysius and John of Damas-

---

[11] Kerr, *Twentieth-Century Catholic Theologians*.
[12] Burrell, *Knowing the Unknowable God*, 17
[13] Some of this we saw in Placher's discussion of Aquinas and Cajetan above.

cus, and Burrell also mentions Damascene.[14]

Part of the problem lies in the way transcendence shows itself in the world. It is not cleanly distinguishable from the intramundane phenomena in which it is visible. It is not a component, one among other components. The Chalcedonian presence of two *fuseis* in one phenomenon doesn't work that way. It starts from its visible, intramundane aspects, and in them encounters transcendence. I see a rock or a sunset; why? Why is there a world at all? Why beauty? Why pain and suffering? These questions in some of their meanings are unanswerable, and that way lies transcendence. But that presupposes the intramundane aspect of the phenomenon, and that is always a social construction.

Social constructions come in many varieties, they are fallible, and we would like to deal responsibly with that fallibility. What can be learned from one culture and age for applications in another? Rudolf Bultmann also met the issue. Sometimes, as he emphasized, a worldview is mythological.[15] For him, mythology was a technical concept with a theory of some subtlety and depth. He proposed to "demythologize" the message in the Gospels, and that provoked outcry and protest, a fair amount of misunderstanding, and general neglect of Bultmann's own philosophical and conceptual presuppositions.[16]

Rather than try to follow Bultmann to his sources, let us import instead something a little more general as a way of extending Bultmann's instinct. Edward Hobbs distinguished between what he called "conceptuality" and what he called "understanding."[17] Both terms are vague enough to be problematic, but with a little help the ideas can be made precise enough to serve. Conceptuality is the repertoire of concepts with which a culture meets the world. An understanding of life is expressed in a conceptuality, but it is not exactly the same thing. 'Understanding' is not the term I would have chosen; it has too many other meanings (as Hobbs himself noted). Some of the other meanings are necessary here, making confusion inevitable. My own choice, in this book and elsewhere, is "basic life orientation" — almost as vague, with meaning to be filled in as needed, but suggestive enough to be useful. Hobbs's "understanding" is a basic life orientation inasmuch as it is (in his words) "the basis for action." The relationship between con-

---

[14] Gregory Rocca, *Speaking the Unknowable God*, 355. John of Damascus appears on p. 12 of Burrell.

[15] We return to Bultmann in ch. 8, p. 166.

[16] For a guide to those presuppositions, see Johnson, *The Origins of Demythologizing*.

[17] See section 1.8 above.

ceptuality and understanding or basic life orientation is analogous to that between a language and what one says in that language. Translation into other languages is sometimes possible.

At this point, we have two approaches to the problem of understanding[18] texts and actions from another time or another culture, Bultmann's and Hobbs's. Yet another would be Hans-Georg Gadamer's, in *Truth and Method*, where he speaks of the "fusion of horizons" by which an interpreter from within a present horizon makes sense of the past horizon of some other culture and its historical artifacts. The fact that the phenomenon of interpretation can be explained in many different ways should caution us that none of them may be calculated from the others, nor can the problem be reduced to the terms of an analytic system. Perhaps Gadamer's beginning with taste and culture can make the point also: we are not in the land of a transcendental deduction but of *familiarity* with culture, past and present. Given familiarity, the things that matter will become conspicuous and show themselves, but they do so in terms of a conceptuality that is pre-given (if changeable). It is also usually unnoticed because it has to be taken for granted in order to get started in thinking about life and the world at all. Hobbs accordingly likened a conceptuality to a language. Conceptuality becomes conspicuous when viewed "from the outside" — that is, from some *other* conceptuality. Then it becomes possible to ask (and sometimes even to answer) questions about someone's basic life orientation.[19]

Paul Tillich supplied yet another approach to the problem of life orientation. In his language, to find someone's gods, seek that person's *ultimate concerns*, a move central to his theology. Tillich's re-posing of the question of God came as a surprise. For many, it opened up ways to think about God that got around what had been stalemates and impasses before. There are parallels in H. Richard Niebuhr also,[20] and given Niebuhr's reading of Barth, probably in Barth as well, but my knowledge of Barth is not sufficient to be very helpful.

The import is that the Neo-orthodox reopened longstanding questions from a new perspective. The fact that they and their students petered out

---

[18] The more common meaning of 'understand' is indispensable, which is why we replace the term with 'basic life orientation' when we speak of what gives coherence to a human life and human action.

[19] This presupposes a workable concept of basic life orientation. Seeking precision in such a concept would be a mistake, but depth might be possible. It is a narrative concept, not something calculative.

[20] See especially *Radical Monotheism* and *Faith on Earth*.

should not detract from their achievement. Their unfinished tasks remain. They saw the need to deal with suffering and evil at a level more serious than either Liberal Theology or Analytic philosophy of religion could. The Neo-orthodox also saw some of the subtlety of what it means to be a historical being, to live in history. That was only the beginning. There is more to hermeneutics than just history, and it turns up in the groundwork of many fields.

It may help to tell a story from my own experience. Let me be brief. My professors were among the last students of the Neo-orthodox, and Edward Hobbs was my New Testament teacher. One day in a beginners' class, when critical history was new, another student asked the inevitable question about miracles. Hobbs explained that the difference between Israelite religion and Canaanite religion was not that one provided genuine miracles and the other(s) provided none or only fraudulent "miracles." For modern readers and Canaanite religion alike, the purpose of "miracles" is to get the believer out of the pains of life, to deliver success in life, more or less on the believer's definition of success. Biblical religion was not like that, though there are plenty of traces of it in the biblical texts. The difference was that in biblical religion, the deity provides good in all of life, pains included, not just in the "good" parts of life. This was the beginning of my own definition of biblical religion as the basic life orientation that affirms all of life in this historical world as good, in full view of its pains. Hobbs told a little of how he came to his own formulation.[21] Some roots were in linguistics, not obviously a source for theology, but that progression of thought was by way of many analogies. Other roots were in the Bible, in many places, not all spelled out explicitly. One that stood out was Karl Barth's commentary on Romans, for in Barth's reading, when God appears to say No, underneath the No lies a deeper Yes.[22] Hence the analogy to syntactic transformations.[23] The development into a transfor-

---

[21] Hobbs, "An Alternate Model from a Theological Perspective," in Otto, *The Family in Search of a Future*. For an extended development of the central thesis, see Porter and Hobbs, "The Trinity and the Indo-European Tripartite Worldview," I did most of the editing, but the ideas were mostly Hobbs's.

[22] See Barth, *The Epistle to the Romans*. 'Yes' and 'No' are not normally indexed, but here are some instances in this translation: 41–42, 61, 62, 108, 110, 125, 137, 141, 153, 169, 176, 188, 201, 204, 208, 212–213, 216, 226, 229, 231, 232, 234, 250, 272, 278; No becomes Yes: 14, 48, 123, 142, 156, 177–178, 186, 198, 203, 251, 253, 256. More emphasis on pp. 252–256, 198.

[23] Hobbs was never a Barthian, but he learned from Barth at this point. His own chosen

mation of the cardinal pains of life (Exposure, Limitation, and Need) into blessings grew out of this line of inquiry.

Something of the power of this idea should be appreciated. Are we saved *from* Exposure, Limitation, and Need, or are we saved *in* them, even though we want to be let out of them? Some pains in life can be avoided honorably, but not all. If we are saved in them, it becomes possible to affirm all of human life in this historical world in full view of its pains. It becomes possible to answer the question, "Where does your proposed ultimate reality show itself in this world?" It is not necessary to modify this world, or to interfere with natural processes, or to write off as barren the pains of life. This will not be easy; the pains can mount to affliction. Embracing life as good does not mean that no acts are wrong; some are very wrong. Embracing life as good cannot be done without some form of grace, but with grace it can be done. As I sat tipped against the back wall when I first heard Edward Hobbs explain this, it incidentally became clear that all problems between science and theology were dissolved; theology has nothing to say that could interfere with the natural sciences. Those problems were replaced with other and more interesting problems, and the present work is an attempt to explore some of them.

We have come to the end of the historical part of this chapter, and we turn next to postmodern changes in several disciplines and their effects on theology.

7.3 The Many Faces of Interpretation

Where the modern period sought certainty and simplicity, the postmodern has (so far) dismantled that, and given us interpretation, human choice, ambiguity, and fallibility. Let me consider in this section two aspects of interpretation: a revised understanding of language and the inquiry into interpretation itself, i.e., hermeneutics.

In comparison to the twentieth century, the previous understanding of language seems simple: words name things, and sentences express propositions about things. The model for grammar was Latin. That may be criminally over-simplified, but it is what our time remembers of the past. I suspect the past was richer than that, and perhaps more of the premodern understanding of language will someday be recovered. In any case,

---

Neo-orthodox sources were more often Rudolf Bultmann and H. Richard Niebuhr.

many things have changed. Aristotle's logic has been replaced by Fregean first-order predicate calculus. The Latin model was replaced by linguistic disputes and theories, with Noam Chomsky close to the center of them. Nominalism is everywhere available, and this may be a legacy from the modern period, freshly spelled out and elaborated: words name things. But philosophy of language began to probe beyond that. Ludwig Wittgenstein saw that language games are not so simple as the nominalist tradition has it. John Searle found ways in which language goes well beyond propositions: we do many more things with language than just make statements. In the spirit of Wittgenstein and Heidegger, we could say we do many more things *in* language than just make statements, issue commands, make promises, declare social arrangements, express feelings (to name Searle's list). A true postmodern would probably say that Searle remained in the spirit of the modern: language is still close to calculation, with a structure close to mathematics; he just expanded the range of syntactic and semantic structures beyond mere statements.

Searle's approach was inspired by mathematical instincts but language can go far beyond mathematics. Its riches are elusive but some examples can be found. Irony is my favorite: a text tells more than it appears to because readers know more about being in the world than the text superficially acknowledges. It is in language that linguistic beings have a world, instead of just an environment.[24] Language as narrative always gives us more than can be reduced to propositions. And where syntax outruns semantics, we are on the way to unanswerable questions.

Hermeneutics called attention to itself in the development of Continental philosophy. One lesson from the re-understanding of language was the degree of human involvement in the world we know in language, and so of human interpretation. The same lesson was offered in other ways from philosophy and biblical scholarship. Modern texts on hermeneutics go back to Schleiermacher, but the real blossoming came a century later. Historicism failed and what was left was interpretation in historiography: hermeneutics. Heidegger in *Being and Time* provided one entry point.

His student Hans-Georg Gadamer developed this into an explicit hermeneutic in *Truth and Method*. We shall see more of the hermeneutical circle when we come to its application in interpreting the Gospel of Mark, in section 8.1. In the meantime, several points should be observed.

---

[24] Heidegger attends to the distinction in *The Fundamental Concepts of Metaphysics*.

7.3 The Many Faces of Interpretation

First, interpretation begins with prior presuppositions, a starting point that is simply assumed. (It may not even be fully spelled out.) Gadamer called this prejudice and argued that there is no such thing as reasoning without prejudice. One may or may not know one's prejudices; rarely if ever do we know *all* our presuppositions. Second, the whole of which a text is a part only starts as the whole document; that whole is nested within a larger context, and Gadamer acknowledged that. What he did not emphasize is that there are many larger contexts,[25] and which ones matter are at the disposal of the interpreter — a matter of choice and ambiguity. Third, this is not circular reasoning. Heidegger already in *Being and Time* anticipated that charge, but Gadamer is clearer. It is an iterative process, differing from mathematical iterative processes chiefly in that it is not quantitative.

A hermeneutical circle is not vicious. It can *become* vicious if it is mistaken for or treated as a *proof*. Any hermeneutical circle, when spelled out, is only an explanation. (It may simply be presupposed.) This suite of distinctions has widespread consequences for philosophical theology in our time, for hermeneutical circles in philosophy and theology are frequently mistaken for proofs. A further consequence is that wherever there is human interpretation and chosen presuppositions, there is also ambiguity and most likely disagreement as well.

Many who started out as platonists were disappointed when postmodern thinking dismantled the certainties of their earlier worldview. They bought into nihilistic relativism, in which there is (supposedly) only power and no truth. (There may be no *platonist* absolute truth, but that does not mean there is no truth.) A concept of historical religion, a responsible liberty of interpretation, and tradition-bound rationality could have saved them from this despair. Instead, the platonism, nominalism, nihilism cycle has bewitched those who are still in quest of a kind of certainty that platonisms first offered.[26] If one can trust that Exposure can bring something good, then being found wrong is not a catastrophe; or, as the Thomists say, truth proceeds more readily from error than from confusion. Openness to being found wrong is not a universal virtue.[27] We saw the origins of an interest in Exposure when we came to Edward Hobbs among the Neo-orthodox.

---

[25] We shall see an instance of this in the Gospel of Mark, in section 8.1.

[26] For the cycle, see *Living in Spin*, section 8.4, "Escaping the Platonism Cycle."

[27] Alasdair C. MacIntyre, "Epistemological Crises," in Hauerwas and Jones, *Why Narrative?* Originally in *Monist* 60 no. 4 (1977/10) 453–472.

With these changes in disciplinary paradigms, we return to some history: movements that opposed the changes we have seen.

7.4 Analytic Philosophy and its Kin

One of the changes around the beginning of the twentieth century was the discovery of the predicate calculus, set theory, and related ideas in mathematics. An application begs to use these as a basis for all of mathematics, and that effort was often successful. Whitehead and Russell's *Principia Mathematica* is exemplary. The successes of this project in mathematics presented an obvious temptation to extend it to all knowledge, in spirit if not always literally. It resulted in the many forms of Analytic philosophy (logical positivism among them). The limits of that project became apparent in Gadamer's work, among others, but that was a half-century later.

The present stage of this research tradition would probably be "artificial intelligence," in which scientists attempt to simulate human personhood on a computer. If successful, this research tradition would thereby achieve a philosophical anthropology, one of the central and necessary parts of any philosophical worldview. Indeed, it is less formally known as the computational model of mind. The term 'artificial intelligence' has many meanings, and in one, it simply means calculating something that humans reason to in other ways. In another, it means "reasoning about the world." But computers are just tools; only persons qualify as being-in-the-world, in Heidegger's sense of that term. AI has a not-spelled-out policy of not spelling out that it is not artificial personhood, artificial Dasein.

With regard to AI, there are two kinds of people: those who read Heidegger and those who do not. They are not on the same page, both figuratively and literally. They do not make sense to each other. For the non-Heidegger readers, the computational model of mind is self-evidently obvious and it just needs to be fleshed out. For those who know Heidegger's work, understanding the world presupposes being a personal being with stakes in itself and the world as they were uncovered in the phenomenology of Heidegger, Gadamer, and others like them. A computer is just a tool (zuhanden in Heidegger's terms), and to treat something zuhanden as personal is a category error. An AI could produce a *representation* of a person or of a person's reasoning but that would not make it a person. The error is akin to the colloquial proverb, "the map is not the territory."

All this fits into a quest for control in our attempts to understand our-

7.4 Analytic Philosophy and its Kin

selves. Hubert Dreyfus summarized this tradition:

> Thus both philosophy and technology, in their appeal to primitives continue to posit what Plato sought: a world in which the possibility of clarity, certainty, and control is guaranteed....[28]

Cartesian philosophy and its latter-day children, in carrying on the Platonist quest for control, at least conceptual control, is implacably opposed to ambiguity and uncertainty, to living with limits to our knowledge, opposed to living in a world that has ambiguity and uncertainty built in.

"Clear and distinct ideas" was the slogan under which a formerly Aristotelian instinct became naive and was allowed to run amok. It reduces all to calculations, divides the world into systems, and assumes a naturalistic ontology. There is no generally accepted definition of naturalism that I am aware of. I think people just say, "I know it when I see it." When Lester Embree tried to define phenomenology, he said "not naturalism."[29] If I were to try to define naturalism, what follows is based on physics as an exemplary model that goes beyond just Descartes' "clear and distinct ideas." Physics is about *systems* that have well-defined *states* that are a function of *time*: systems, states, and trajectories of material substrates. A system is demarcated from the rest of the world; you can tell what's inside it and what's not. The other natural sciences bear some analogy to physics. That, of course is a matter of judgement, and so the root problem has been dodged, but it's the best I can do now.

When I chose the term "distributed ontology" for the concept of human action in *Living in Spin* I was unaware that it had already been used in AI but in a different sense: AI researchers speak casually of a "distributed *system*," but that strikes me as a contradiction in terms. If something has a distributed ontology, it is not a system at all. Something is distributed in the sense that it breaks the naturalistic criterion of having a clear separation from the world and other concepts.

---

[28] Dreyfus, *What Computers Can't Do*, 211-212. In the third edition, *What Computers Still Can't Do*, 212.

[29] Embree, ed., *Encyclopedia of Phenomenology*, 1. Phenomenology is also not interested in grand speculative systems, or "unobservable matters."

7.5 Biblical Literalism

It is said that Christians were biblical literalists from the beginning. That is not as true as it might seem; the early Fathers knew well enough that literal meanings were not always credible. But on the whole, an intelligent naive reading was usually possible. The cosmologies in Genesis 1–2 were accepted for lack of something better, and they were harmonized without worry about the contradictions between them. The flat earth with waters above and below it was quietly ignored (again without much worry) because Ptolemaic geocentric astronomy and a spherical earth were well known and not problematic. Even Galileo was eventually assimilated, though the story is more complicated than its common simplifications.[30] All of this qualifies as a relatively innocent naiveté: critical thinking about the Bible was domesticated; it fit into the world of the faithful without serious tensions.

The nineteenth century was different, and the history parallels at a distance the sequence in rabbinic Judaism. First came the liberal challenges, then a reactionary response, and last the mediating positions. When critical reading of the Bible emerged in the nineteenth century, the naive naiveté of the tradition became the tenacious naiveté that we know as biblical literalism. Critical hermeneutics cannot conceal itself, and so human responsibility in the reading of the sacred texts had to be acknowledged. Those for whom this produced too much anxiety retreated to an entrenched literalism. Some texts at issue:

> Genesis 1–3 (creationism)
> the Exodus
> selected legal texts
> Resurrection texts after Paul and Mark[31]
> the Gospel miracles
> the Virgin Birth

The same phenomenon appears in modern issues of authority:

> the Deposit of Faith, never changing
> Papal infallibility

---

[30] For an uncommon perspective on Galileo's place in Italian mathematics, see Amir, *Infinitesimals*, which claims that organized Jesuit resistance to infinitesimals drove serious mathematics out of Italy and into Northern Europe.

[31] 1 Cor. 15.35 and Mark 16.8, to be precise.

the Five Fundamentals
scriptural inerrancy

What does literalism do for those who profess it? It objectivates the meaning of biblical texts, usually miracle texts, and thereby gets literalists out of responsibility for their faith, because it itself takes that responsibility.[32] It gets them out of the anxiety that would come with a candid confessional commitment to the Faith. It provides a kind of spiritual strength that in its extreme forms gets called fanaticism, and it reasons from a tenacious naiveté. In mild forms, with a naive naiveté, it just simplifies issues and enables its adherents to get on with life in the faith. Naive naiveté is an instance of pre-critical (and pre-scientific) thinking. Tenacious naiveté is held *in defiance of* of critical thinking, not *before* critical thinking.

The phenomenon of literalism appears at the center of the changes in theology in and since the modern period. One recent example illustrates the issues well, though unintentionally. In 2018, the Church of England sent the Very Rev. John Shepherd, an Australian, as an envoy to Rome to represent the Anglican Communion to the Vatican. Shepherd in 2008 had pleaded in a broadcast sermon for the church to lead people out of a literalist reading of the Resurrection texts. We shall see that issue in more detail below, in chapter 8. Tyler O'Neil, an American journalist and layman, protested in outrage that Shepherd was not "orthodox" and didn't "believe in the Resurrection." That asserts by presupposition a reading of the Resurrection texts that is never acknowledged as one choice among others, but there is more, and the real issue comes out in O'Neil's remarks:

> Furthermore, doubting the Resurrection "ties directly to a key question: is the Bible trustworthy?" Walton added. "The Gospel writers and the creeds clearly state that Jesus died, was resurrected, and ascended into heaven. If we cannot trust scripture on this important claim, then our faith has nothing to stand upon."[33]

---

[32] It also makes conceivable the immanent presence of transcendence, a meaning that Rudolf Bultmann used as one definition of myth. It might be classed as one species of analogy, if its analogical character is not forgotten.

[33] Tyler O'Neil, "The Church of England's Vatican Envoy Doesn't Believe in the Resurrection of Jesus." *PJMedia* 2019-01-14.

This issue we shall see again, namely the quest for objective certainty in proofs. The key phrase is "then our faith has nothing to stand upon." On the contrary, there is no basis for faith; faith is the basis for everything else, and it is a chosen starting point, not something reasoned *to*. Faith is *rooted* in history, but it is not derived by reason or inference from history. The logical differences are crucial. Inference presupposes a starting point in premises chosen someplace *else*. Biblical literalists never spell out those choices, but they can be guessed with fair confidence: For hard-core literalists, biblical faith is supposed to get them *out* of the pains of life, rather than bringing them some sort of salvation *in* the pains of life; we shall see more of this in chapter 8. O'Neil's complaint is a fairly candid and explicit confession of objectivation and of what it does: it takes the responsibility for the faith of the believer, thus getting the believer out of responsibility for his own faith. A more candid guilty plea to the charges in *The Sacred Canopy* would be hard to imagine.

Returning to O'Neil's phrasing, the word "trustworthy" begs too many questions. It asserts by innuendo a Rankean historicist hermeneutic, in which the biblical text gives us "just the facts," in a way that can be relied upon and interpreted without irony — thus evading the existential challenges to the reader that come with irony. But why is the Bible forbidden to speak in literary genres (such as special effects, or irony) that we know well and find quite expressive? Special effects work like Bultmann's "myth," on his definition; see p. 166 for more. Irony can say things about (and to) human personhood that quite escape propositional logic.

If you deny literalist readings of the Bible, you will be met with an anxiety tantrum disguised as "logic." Assertion by presupposition without spelling out the presuppositions is characteristic of literalism. Literalism cannot tolerate having its presuppositions spelled out. A not-spelled-out policy of not spelling out what one is doing is the pivot of self deception,[34] and it protects some failed engagement with life. In this case, it hides the evasion of responsibility by the believer for his choices of basic life orientation, exactly as *Sacred Canopy* argued. In summary, literalist hermeneutics is an example of objectivation because it turns the interpersonal counterpart of faith into an *object* of faith. It is not an object at all.

All this said, how is it that the literalists in the Catholic Church are

---

[34] Herbert Fingarette, *Self Deception*, chapter 3.

some of the most vigorous faithful? Consider one issue, abortion. Not everyone prolife is a biblical literalist, and not every literalist is seriously prolife, but people who are prolife tend to be occasionally literalist also, in part because the Church's teachers have not given them anything better. It is the default catechesis in our time. A Catholic Old Testament professor far more familiar with mores in the Church than I am once said to me that most Catholics are biblical literalists but not Fundamentalists. She did not explain to me what she meant by the difference, so we must proceed with caution.

Restate the lesson that we saw above in Edward Hobbs's trio of the cardinal pains of life, Exposure, Limitation and Need: We are put to a question — whether to be prolife when life hurts. Biblical religion answers in the affirmative. People who are seriously prolife (in the common sense) know that if abortion is tolerated (and with it usually contraceptives, cf. section 9.6) the entire commitment to being prolife when life hurts is undermined. Serious exceptions to the principle work by modus tollens to invalidate the principle itself.

So let me apply this reasoning to another issue, critical history, historical and cultural relativity, and religious pluralism. Focus especially on critical history, for it is the academic discipline that has demanded revision of our explanations of the faith. You who are seriously prolife are the life and soul of the Church; but can you be prolife when the disappointments of life come in the form of critical history instead of unwelcome pregnancies? It can be done. You might fairly ask in reply, "Can anyone show us how? We want to be consistently prolife, even in doing our theology, but we are not biblical scholars or philosophers." To that we come in the later chapters of this book. Many lessons could be drawn, but one does not go without saying: the typical Christian is in a state of incomplete conversion, and the pilgrimage of life is a process of completing that *conversio morum*.

7.6 Pathologies of Proofs

With the twentieth century came a big expansion of a modern problem, that of proving the so-called "existence" of God. The roots go back to Anselm (cf. sec. 5.2), with a little before Anselm, but not much. In part, this was because of something not postmodern at all, the flowering of analytic philosophy and its attempts to reduce all truth to propositions with the newly fashioned tools of predicate logic. That logic was not as all-encompassing as it at first appeared. The growth of analytic philosophy was a return from the postmodern to the modern, and the retreat to analytic terms is still with us.

The problems with proofs are of three sorts: problems in logic, in semantics, and in misunderstanding what proofs do and what should be done instead. They are intertwined. Virtually all the proofs of the "existence" of God have been disputed by atheists, credibly exposing errors of logic. Errors in logic may safely be left to the pertinent technical literature, since the present inquiry has more serious objections to proofs.

Trying to prove the "existence" of God asserts by presupposition that the things it speaks of are susceptible to the kind of reason found in proofs. They make God one being among other beings, a being of which "it exists" (or not) makes sense. If "exists" means something else, that is rarely clarified. Perhaps "exists" just means "makes sense"? That is not something that can be proven, though it can be explained.

Given the nature of such "proofs," they are always circular in an unattractive way, and that is never seen by their advocates. To try to prove one's starting point is incoherent: it simply moves the starting point to something else and then hides the new starting point. And part of the semantics of "God" is that the term indicates something of ultimate reality. Ultimate reality can only be assumed; it is intrinsically axiomatic, postulated, not proven. People manage quite well to quarrel about what to postulate, but that merely reiterates that they disagree about ultimate reality. To believe proofs is to believe *in* proofs, or to believe in the assumed premises of the proffered proofs.

In his introduction to *The Existence of God*, John Hick admits the impropriety of trying to prove the "existence" of God. The voice is Paul Tillich's:

> Thus the question of the existence of God can neither be asked nor answered. If asked, it is a question about that which by its very nature is above existence, and therefore the answer — whether negative or affirmative — implicitly denies the nature of God. It is as atheistic to affirm the existence of God as it is to deny it. God is being-itself, not *a* being.[35]

---

[35] Hick, *The Existence of God*, 2, quoting Tillich, *Systematic Theology*, vol. I, 237. In his last assertion, that God is being-itself, Tillich follows many before him. That is not the only way to avoid the mistake of taking God as *a* being among other beings. Treating God as being itself would not be my own course, though many others have taken it.

John Hick, in his own words, in his editorial preface: "religious faith is not, in my view, dependent upon philosophical arguments." Hick's introduction is well aware of the logical oddness of proofs of the so-called "existence" of God, and he cites others who agree. Nevertheless, having undermined the project of his book, Hick then suavely ignores his own admission and goes on with an anthology of "proofs." Those who know they don't need proofs yet traffic in them anyway are, I think, somewhat puzzling.

Tillich spoke from a minority, one centered in German-speaking theology. The Anglophone tradition in the twentieth century did a brisk trade in proofs. Logical positivism and its relatives dismissed religious language as nonsensical, as with A. J. Ayer. British and American philosophers and theologians responded by trying to give logical positivism what logical positivism demanded — demonstrations, or in other words, proofs. This has logical problems, both from the inside and from the outside. Some history may help, but first, the illogic.

From the outside, the demand for proofs was implicitly a demand to shift the conception of ultimate reality to something more congenial to the logical positivists and the modern tradition that they stood in. Once conceded, the shift to "atheist" presuppositions could be cashed at leisure. That has been the history of modern atheism in the history of modern proofs of the so-called "existence" of God. From the inside, the reader may enjoy the illogic as it appears in *Sickness Unto Death*. To try to prove that one is in love is to let on that one is pretending.[36] Once again, the truth may come out slowly, over the centuries. Now for a little history.

The English-speaking theological and philosophical world did not keep up with the Germans, and the Germans were still sorting out their own inheritance from nineteenth-century Liberal theology. That was the work of Neo-orthodox theology and its companions in biblical criticism. The French in a parallel way were re-understanding their own Catholic inheritance and its engagements with history.[37] But in those days, Catholics and Protestants did not speak to each other. Mid-century, proofs and disproofs abounded, even among those who knew better: they knew that faith does not come from proofs but "from the heart." The Neo-Orthodox were not fooled, but their tradition died out. Liberal Theology came back, and with it "postmodernism." Analytic philosophy of religion, by contrast, has

---

[36] My summary, not Kierkegaard's words. Best not to comment more. *Sickness Unto Death*, Hong and Hong trans., 103–104.

[37] Kerr, *Twentieth Century Catholic Theologians*.

continued as a hardy academic subculture. Alvin Plantinga in America and Richard Swinburne in Britain are typical exemplars of such philosophy. Plantinga at one point collected two dozen arguments for the "existence" of God.[38]

C. S. Lewis affords an example of the influences of that day. He was not a philosopher but he was philosophically literate.[39] I think he felt obliged to describe his own conversion in philosophical terms in order to make it intelligible, but the account in *Surprised by Joy* is about the conversion of the heart, not logical or philosophical rigor. Lewis is quite explicit about that: in the end, it was a *choice*, not an inference.[40] It is a puzzle to me why so many who like analytic philosophy of religion love Lewis so much. Perhaps Lewis offers them something they cannot get from their philosophy, something which I have cavalierly called "heart" and which Lewis located in the heart in "Men Without Chests." Proofs are a poor substitute for the life of the heart. Many readers have taken Lewis's accounts as proofs of Christianity, though I think their real function was as mere explanation: They make a Christian choice *intelligible*, and thereby make it *possible*; but it still remains a choice, not an inference. Lewis saw that, where analytic philosophers often do not.

The twentieth century was the age of logical positivism, one in which proofs made sense and were thought necessary. People did not see through them or recognize proofs as category errors. When proofs were exhausted, by late in that century, academics simply gave up and became postmodern nihilists instead of recovering resources from the tradition that could have avoided the problem entirely. The culture has to a great extent followed its academics.

What Lewis gave us has its roots in the sixteenth century and earlier — but that lost age is in its strange way more accessible and intuitively sensible than the problems of our own time. The richness of Lewis's world was rooted in literature, not philosophy. As the reader may have noticed, the present book is an attempt to bring older resources in theology to present problems — without retreating into the past. In our own problems, we

---

[38] Plantinga, "Two Dozen or so theistic arguments."

[39] He pays his respects to philosophy in *Surprised by Joy* and probably in other places as well. Nevertheless, the satires of his philosophical neighbors are hilarious. See *The Silver Chair*, about lamps and cats, suns and lions, with Plato's Cave in the background, for those still awake.

[40] Lewis, *Surprised by Joy*, 224, in ch. XIV, "Checkmate," has 'choice' or its equivalent at least 7 times.

7.6 Pathologies of Proofs

have both recovered and re-understood past problems, often problems that were poorly solved, but whose solutions were nevertheless seen long ago.

I think the logic of proofs can be reconstructed with a little confidence. To try to prove (or equally, disprove) the so-called "existence" of God is to take 'God' as referring to something that *could* exist.[41] That makes him a being *within* the collection of beings. Denials are not convincing: to put him outside the world doesn't work, since the world can simply be expanded to include him. To try to fix that illogic is incoherent and impossible, though the effort could function quite well as a smoke-screen to conceal what is really going on. What such talk does is make God (and ultimate reality) susceptible to propositional reason, which safely protects the one doing so from having to face anything refractory to human reason. This is to say that such talk protects one from anxiety, because it makes unthinkable aspects of the world that could cause anxiety.

Anxiety is taken in the sense of Heidegger's introduction to Chapter VI, Division I, "a distinctive way in which Dasein is disclosed."[42]

In the perspective of the distributed ontology of action, human and otherwise, it could be observed that "proofs" of the "existence" of God are ambiguous in what they do. Explanation can be taken (or mistaken) for proof. Catechesis of the immature faithful can be mistaken for proof. Proof can function as a warning to the faithful against those nonbelievers, whoever they are. The ambiguous function of greatest interest is that proofs function as a way to prevent awareness of anxiety.[43]

Every proof starts from presuppositions of some sort, and it is impossible to reason without presuppositions.[44] This is the root of circularity.

---

[41] 'Could' here means 'makes sense'; it is neutral with regard to ontological arguments about the existence of God, claiming that God exists *necessarily*.

[42] See Heidegger, *Being and Time*, 228 (Macquarrie and Robinson), 184 (German pagination). See also Magurshak, "The Concept of Anxiety." We have little interest in anxiety as a psychological state. It is relevant as a window into the ontological structure of human being. In this, we follow the tradition of Kierkegaard and Heidegger (if it can be called a tradition, since they did not entirely agree).

[43] Anxiety in Heidegger is an ontological condition whether or not it is psychological. It would be confusing to render it as creaturehood, but as an ontological condition (and for Christian readers) it is one feature of creaturehood. It was central for Kierkegaard before Heidegger took it up.

[44] This can often be demonstrated by identifying the presuppositions and finding someone who does not agree with them, thus showing that they are a choice. The fact that alternative choices have no plausibility for the pertinent readership does not make them any less choices.

If what follows from those presuppositions is treated as merely an explanation, and not a proof, then the circularity is merely hermeneutical. If the reasoning is treated as a proof, then the circularity is vicious. The ambiguity can never entirely be eliminated. After all, Anselm's so-called "argument" was a confession of faith trying to explain itself, but it has usually been taken as a proof, even among those not convinced by it. An author may label his thoughts candidly and clearly, but he still has little control over how his readers take them.

There is more to the larger problematic of which proofs are an unattractive part. Proof is impossible, but that does not mean we are in a situation of liberty and arbitrary choice. For one person's choices do make demands on other people, whether he wants to make demands of them or not. If I were to believe that the moon is made of green cheese and get enough other people to go along with me, it would make a kind of demand on you, whether you or I like it or not. We have ways of fending off such implausible demands, but they nevertheless remain demands. This is part of human interinvolvement with one another: it is built-in, an inescapable part of human existence.

The Church faces some choices at this point, choices of strategy, choices of logic in explaining the Gospel to its own and to the world. We have seen them all along. The difference between proof of the validity of biblical religion (in either of its variants) and a confessional stance is one. "Proofs" fit well with a triumphalist stance in which the Church claims an authority over all men — and thus claims a sacred canopy. We do make claims on all men, simply because we exist, but not all claims have the same logic. A confessional stance is consistent with Joshua 24 but not with the claim, widespread in the last century or two, that unaided reason can "prove" the "existence" of the biblical God. When confronted by history with the inescapable plurality of human religions, some Catholics responded by crafting an "inclusive triumphalism," in which those not Christian were "baptized" without their knowledge or consent.[45] Buddhists don't particularly like being misconstrued as anonymous Christians, and there are better ways to explore religious differences with integrity and respect.

One thing that is not obvious should be noted: the future is open, and

---

[45] White tells a little of the story in "Catholicism in an Age of Discontent." White recounts some of the opening of French theology after the age of Vatican I and Leonine Thomism. The challenge of pluralism and confessionality was not met as well as one might have wished.

what will happen to biblical religion, especially of the Christian variety, is not clear. It shaped European culture (which now stretches far beyond Europe), and it was the cradle for a kind of freedom and order seldom if ever seen elsewhere. It brought hope to its people, in the sense of affirming human life in this world as good, even in full view of all its pains. What Western civilization will do at this point is unclear. Continued apostasy — at least formal apostasy — is one possibility, in which the culture turns away from biblical religion in any kind of formal acknowledgment, whether or not it turns away from affirmation of human life in this historical world as good in full view of its pains. In this circumstance, the place of the Church would be like that of ancient Israel, dissenters in the world of Canaanite pagan religions, a confessional stance. On the other hand, the Church may provide, and the culture may accept, a conscious way to continue the inheritance of world-affirming historical religion without the burden of "proofs," sacred canopies, and all the other pathologies that we also inherit.

7.7 Revisiting Sociology of Knowledge

Around the turn from the nineteenth to the twentieth century, the foundations for sociology were laid in the work of Durkheim and Weber and others after them. Sociology deals with human phenomena under the aspect of sociality. Knowledge is one of them, and the sociology of knowledge attempts to explain the social sources, production, distribution, consumption, and uses of knowledge.

One of the fundamental presuppositions of the sociology of knowledge is that knowledge is knowledge of a *world*,[46] and to the extent that it is comprehensive, coherent, and integrated, it is *religious*, for it does the work of religion.[47]

This is to take religion as basic life orientation, not as belief in the supernatural. Not everybody believes in the supernatural, but everybody has a basic life orientation (BLO), and everybody has some sort of ultimate reality (u-r). Obviously, people disagree about both basic life orientation and ultimate reality, and the sociologist of knowledge, like a Wittgensteinian

---

[46] Heidegger defined human being as the sort of being that has a world, as we saw briefly in section 7.1. He asked questions about worldhood somewhat different from our immediate concerns in sociology.

[47] This theme is developed more in *Sacred Canopy* than in *Social Construction*.

fideist, cannot from premises *in sociology alone* judge or criticize. He can only say, these ideas were embodied in social institutions, and they have such-and-such a structure. For example, a sociologist or a Wittgensteinian has no basis for choosing between phlogiston and oxygen, but a chemist has no trouble, no trouble at all.

Many took *The Social Construction of Reality* to license nihilism, nothing means anything, there is no truth, only power. In *Adventures*,[48] Berger repudiated the nihilist interpretation of *Social Construction* and dealt with the problem in more detail in *In Praise of Doubt*.[49] I think that the problem and its solution can be stated fairly simply, at least from my own perspective, whether or not Peter Berger would have agreed.

The truth that died in "postmodernism" would be a platonist objective and absolute truth (possibly a naive realism), the loss of which often issues in nihilistic despair.[50] Sociology of knowledge relativizes other knowledge simply; its relation to itself is more complicated. It is not a claim that "all knowledge is relative to power, therefore there is no real knowledge." *That* cheap cynicism presupposes that knowledge has to be platonist to qualify as knowledge.

As said before, sociology studies the production of knowledge, some of which (but not all) may implicate power. Just as Gadamer argued that there is no reasoning without prejudice (i.e., presuppositions), someone could argue just as well that there is no social life without power. The remedy in both cases is the same. In the hermeneutical circle, presuppositions can be criticized and corrected. A community's leadership (power) can also be criticized and corrected. Some social structures and institutions of knowledge are open to being corrected, some are not.

There are several stages in the logic of criticism of knowledge. In the first stage, we accept the premise of sociology, that all knowledge is a social construction. A question follows immediately: Why are some social constructions better than others? And which ones? Questioning does not require a platonist absolute or objective truth.

Criticism takes the form of noting that, as in the sciences, in a dispute between two paradigms, one paradigm can explain the successes and failures of the other better than the other itself can. It is then rational to choose between paradigms, even though there is no neutral standpoint from which

---

[48] Berger, *Adventures of an Accidental Sociologist*.

[49] Berger and Zijderveld, *In Praise of Doubt*.

[50] A Kierkegaardian would say the original platonist outlook was itself a form of the despair of self-assertion, and its failure logically led to a despair of giving up.

7.7 Revisiting Sociology of Knowledge

to make the choice. Then comes another question, whether the individual, or society, or professional community is open to a paradigm shift. Some are.

In effect, the issue is whether to embrace Exposure as bearing blessing — or not. If one is open to Exposure etc., then all problems can be solved. If one has closed off Exposure, then all social constructions, including human lives, are vulnerable to catastrophic overthrow and need to be defended accordingly. This observation is not native to sociology, and it appears outside of Edward Hobbs's work; here is Alasdair MacIntyre:

> What can liberate rationality from this identification[51] is precisely an acknowledgement, only possible from within a certain kind of tradition, that rationality requires a readiness on our part to accept, and indeed to welcome, a possible future defeat of the forms of theory and practice in which it has up till now been taken to be embodied within our own tradition, at the hands of some alien and perhaps even as yet largely unintelligible tradition of thought and practice; and this is an acknowledgement of which the traditions that we inherit have too seldom been capable.[52]

This is normal procedure in the natural sciences. Paradigm shifts are welcomed, but not too quickly, since so many proposed shifts don't pan out. Theology and philosophy have not always been quick to adopt the same attitude toward changes in history.[53] Twentieth-century science produced examples of paradigm change enough so that the problem was explored philosophically in some detail. It is called "tradition-bound rationality," and it supplied rational grounds for changing a paradigm without any neutral or absolute position from which to judge competing paradigms. That does not by itself solve all problems in philosophical theology, but without it, one can solve none. This is one implication of sociology of knowledge for theology. We do not have (and do not need) platonist absolute truth. We are on a pilgrimage through history in company with a transcendent Other as Merold Westphal said in *God, Guilt, and Death*.[54]

---

[51] MacIntyre speaks of an Enlightenment view that can conceive of contending rationalities only as expressions of contending wills to power.
[52] MacIntyre, "Relativism, Power, and Philosophy," 19–20.
[53] Porter, "The Barbour-Smith-Gilkey Paradox."
[54] Westphal, *God, Guilt, and Death*, sections 11b and 11c.

The sociology of knowledge is typical of changes in the twentieth century. The earlier confidence of objective realism has been shaken and in some quarters given up. The natural sciences have demonstrated that it is possible to live without eternal objective truth, and both theology and Catholic culture have not assimilated this very well.[55]

7.8 Postmodernism So Far

To collect some themes of the postmodern period, consider hermeneutics, ambiguity, choice, responsibility, and fallibility. There were reactions to all of them. Hermeneutics: things are a matter of interpretation, not naive realism in which language is a clean, transparent window onto the world.[56] Interpretation brings with it ambiguity, for there are often multiple possible interpretations of something or someone in the world. With ambiguity comes choice, and with choice, responsibility. Human actions are fallible and often mistaken or wrong. One remedy is to look for blessing in Exposure, Limitation, and Need, especially Exposure. That remedy is not always welcome. For some, the ultimate goal is to escape from Exposure. We call that "stonewalling."

There has been resistance in many ways. Ambiguity, choice, and responsibility have been simply denied, and the quest is still with us for a platonist or naive realist ahistorical absolute truth. Among the movements that could be cited as instances of resistance to the postmodern are biblical literalism, Analytic philosophy of religion, proofs of the so-called "existence" of God and of the validity of Christianity. The theme is often an attempt to objectivate the Christian faith. More recently, some who actually call themselves "postmodern" have questioned whether there can be any truth at all rather than just will to power. That strikes me as itself presupposing some sort of truth beyond power, for it appeals against abuse of power to some sort of truth. It cannot consider the possibility of a mode of truth beyond the platonist tradition. Instead of a quest for absolute platonist truth, I think we are living in a pilgrimage in history, but culture today thinks that means technological progress, not something existential. The postmodern world is still barren of transcendence; what was lost in

---

[55] This is only one reason why so many today think that Christianity has problems with the sciences; "miracles" are another, and we shall see more in the next chapter.

[56] This is not as new as it might seem; the precursor was the agent intellect in Scholastic philosophy.

7.8 Postmodernism So Far

domesticating transcendence has not been recovered. Some examples may illustrate.

Our culture is still conflicted about the naturalism of the sciences. Some think they can cut exceptions to natural laws in order to make room for transcendence. Some think they can deny any form of transcendence in order to protect the integrity of scientific naturalism. Both are unwittingly repeating the logic of the Christological controversies that were eventually regulated in the Definition of Chalcedon. Because they do not know what they are doing, they cannot conceive of real truth outside of the natural sciences. Even the comic strips (think *Far Side*) can be enjoyed but cannot be recognized as transcendence present and visible in the immanent.

The loss of Chalcedonian thinking appears in other places as well. Scholars have begun to argue that the early Church was the product of will to power.[57] The tacit alternative was that the Church was *just* the design and creation of God himself and so was entitled to an obedience from everybody. This sometimes gets called "triumphalism." The alternative is that Christianity (like rabbinic Judaism) was a daughter religion born out of the ashes of Second Temple Judaism, in a fallible human movement that still has enough theological coherence to be viable today. The same un-Chalcedonian mistake lies at the root of the problems: failure to see transcendence in the human creation of the early Church without doing violence to that immanent history in order to make room for transcendence.

Sociology of knowledge has shown us our anxiety in the face of potential meaninglessness; theology then shows us our turn to objectivation (in monophysite thinking) and evasion of responsibility for our faith.

---

[57] To be fair, this is explicit in the Gospels themselves, as Theodore J. Weeden Sr. argued some years ago.

Chapter 8

Some Applications

8.1 Returning to Miracles

The review of the New Testament and its problems[1] left us only a foretaste of an unfinished inquiry. It is time to redeem its promises. We have resources in the twentieth century that were not naively available to a reading of the early Christian centuries. The nineteenth-century quest for historical facts "as they actually were" encountered enough problems to elicit an interest in hermeneutics, on the possibility that we do not have "facts" uninterpreted, and need to become aware of our own interpretive acts. Hermeneutics also led (in biblical scholarship) to an awareness that there are many genres of texts in the Bible. We shall see other assumptions questioned as we go along.

Miracles and especially the Resurrection are one focus of problems bequeathed to theology by the modern period and only partially re-understood in the postmodern period. Why? Because the transition from the Scholastics to the modern period effectively lost a Chalcedonian understanding of divine action in the world, replacing it with something distinctly monophysite: God acts by directing events in ways contrary to natural law, but effectively still by causes just like natural causes. The problem eventually puts us to the question, how to read the miracle texts, and how to read the Resurrection texts in particular. The vast literature on the problem attests the depth of theological neuralgia at this point as well as the scarcity of remedies for it. It is only when a reading of a text has problems that people eventually return to the more basic question of what kind of

---

[1] Section 3.2, p. 42.

8.1 Returning to Miracles

text it is: the question of where to enter the hermeneutical circle and on what assumptions.

That's not how it began. Coming into the twentieth century, people took the miracle and Resurrection texts "literally" and either accepted them "literally" (without inquiring too deeply what that might mean), or they dismissed the texts as absurd and impossible, with whatever insults or condescension fitted the authors' tastes. Some invoked Hume; more careful minds read Troeltsch. In the twentieth century, people started to ask how to read the texts with a new kind of seriousness.

These are examples of the principal habits of mind that this book argues against. They assumed they could start with Jesus, instead of with the prior history of religions, the Exodus and the emergence of world-affirming historical religion. They never quite gave up the assumption that God acts by interfering with the natural course of events; the idea that grace could appear in a natural and historical world without interfering with nature[2] was still unthinkable. And they wanted to find something in events of history that would take the responsibility for their own faith, thus relieving them of it, and also providing answers for the hecklers' perennial chant, "Where, now, O Israel, is your God?" Above all, the assumption in coming to the miracle texts and the Resurrection was that these texts are reports of events. Nothing else was conceivable. Some could write them off as part of the conceptuality of a bygone age, an age with outmoded ideas of what sort of things can happen and what sort of things cannot happen. There are examples aplenty of that issue in present-day cultures and subcultures where science and "scientific" history[3] are unknown or not accepted. But the issue itself presupposes that we are dealing with reports of events in the texts. That the issue needed to be redrawn was rarely suspected. It emerged only slowly. To examine a literal interpretation of the texts would risk questions about what they really entail. The other common alternative is to dismiss them as false (on a literal reading) and either become Liberals or just give up on Christianity. These are not the only possibilities, as we shall see. They all presuppose reading the Resurrection texts as reports of an event, and the conversation among NT scholars has slowly weaned itself from that assumption. We begin below with a different assumption: the texts are invitations to faith, not literal reports of events. Events can be inferred only incompletely and cautiously.

---

[2] Aquinas, to the effect that "gratia non tollat naturam" is cited on p. 12 above.

[3] The historicism of (for one example) von Ranke, followed by modern critical history.

In the twentieth century, the question was broadened some, but only some. Reginald Fuller, in *The Formation of the Resurrection Narratives*, reminded people that the Resurrection texts can be dated, and that they show a development over time from the earliest to the latest. In a second kind of questioning in the twentieth century, many asked whether the Resurrection was an "historical" event or whether it could be verified, proved or disproved by historians. Not all thought of it that way; some began to suspect that the Resurrection was not an ordinary historical event that could be reached by ordinary historical reasoning. What they never entirely escaped from was the assumption that the texts are to be read as reports of "actual" events. Scholars tried to fit an interpretation of the texts as giving us something trans-historical into the received assumption that the texts are reports of a historical event. How that might work was never successfully spelled out, probably because it was an attempt to understand the tasks of one paradigm in the terms of another.

Scholars still clung to the assumption that the texts directly answer (and were intended to answer) the sort of questions characteristic of nineteenth-century historicism: Rankean history, telling events "as they actually happened." Only later did any suspect the possibility that the NT writers did not share the presuppositions and intentions of modern historicism. (The Gospels also are not biographies or histories, both of which genres were known in the ancient world.)

Gradually, the defenders of a literal reading dug in against their critics. They pleaded that their opponents owed them at least the possibility of what was in dispute — it would be circular (and unfair) to rule out apriori the historicity of the events reported in the Resurrection texts.

To this, let me tell you a story. I have a window in my house, a far-see window,[4] through which I can see and watch events far away. Wonderful things happen in it. An old, bald muscle-builder comes up out of the drain in a kitchen sink, in a burst of sparkles, and voilà! The kitchen is clean. We know these things have happened because we have pictures of them happening. I myself saw it happen. You doubt me? Why do you question apriori the possibility that these things are factual? If you won't believe my miracles, why should I believe your miracles?

To put it a little bit more technically, we have bumped into the twin questions of form criticism and the hermeneutical circle. You may protest that what I saw in the far-see was an advertisement, in which the prepos-

---

[4] I am translating by parts a German technical term, *Fern-sehen*.

8.1 Returning to Miracles

terous routinely happens. You may not *know* what form criticism is, but you have demonstrated that you are quite capable of *doing* form criticism.

In the hermeneutical circle, we understand the parts of a text on some assumption about the genre of the whole. Then we iterate back and forth from parts to whole, to show that the reading of the text is consistent and coherent. To enter the hermeneutical circle with the assumption that the Resurrection texts are reports of an event does not give a reading that is consistent and coherent. The anguished literalist cry above for at least a hearing founders on the reply, "consider the possibility of *what?*" On the literalist assumptions, what exactly are we supposed to consider the possibility of? They have no answer except that it is a sacred mystery. To that I would reply that there is indeed a sacred mystery here, but the literalist reading doesn't get it.

The hermeneutical circle is not difficult to understand. The issue of circularity was seen already in *Being and Time*,[5] and it was developed in Gadamer's *Truth and Method*. Heidegger already was sensitive to anticipate charges of logical circularity, and his counter was that there are always already assumptions in the interpretation of anything in the world. Gadamer supplied enough concrete detail to give the hermeneutical circle some usable texture. He spoke of a logically circular relationship, long known, between parts and the whole (of a text); it was in Schleiermacher, among others, but was not raised to the level of a fundamental principle as Gadamer himself claimed it to be. He says, of the interpretation of a text,

> the repeated return from the whole to the parts, and vice versa, is essential. Moreover, this circle is constantly expanding, since the concept of the whole is relative, and being integrated into larger contexts always affects the understanding of the individual part. (190)

> The harmony of all the details with the whole is the criterion of correct understanding. The failure to achieve this harmony means that understanding has failed. (291)

In other words, it is an iterative process, and it may or may not converge to a stable reading. Mathematically literate readers (not Gadamer's intended

---

[5] Heidegger, *Being and Time*, section 32, "Understanding and Intepretation"; Macquarrie and Robinson, 194; German, 152–153. Understanding self and world is circular, but this circularity is not vicious.

audience) would see parallels to their own iterative approximations.⁶ In hermeneutics (unlike mathematics) there is no metric, and convergence cannot be measured, so the analogies with mathematics are quite limited. But the same issue arises in both contexts: Does the iteration *converge* to a stable reading? Failure to converge may not indicate meaninglessness; Wayne Booth acknowledged unstable ironies, ironies that can never be resolved.⁷ Some have remarked that many parables of Jesus are unstable, resisting any simple reading.

What Gadamer did not note (it was not germane to his own inquiry?) was that a line of thought that is *hermeneutically* circular when read as a confessional *explanation* of faith becomes *viciously* circular when taken as an apologetic *proof* of faith. (The phenomenon of multiple readings of texts and events will always be with us: sometimes the ambiguity will not go away.)

As Gadamer says, the initial genre assumption about a text (or event, equally) can be broadened to its larger context in the world from which it came, ultimately reaching all the way to assumptions about the world as a whole, and to ultimate reality. That is what was happening just above when the inquiry reached the larger question about what to do with the pains of life — ultimately.

In what follows, we look at a reading of the structure of Mark on the assumption that both the whole and the parts are an invitation to faith. The other (and more traditional) reading is that they are reports of events. There are undoubtedly other possible interpretations but these two matter now. It may or may not be possible to infer events from an invitation to faith; that question is secondary to reading the texts as such an invitation.

Some have taken the Resurrection as a matter of faith, not an objective historical fact that could be used to support believers and confute unbelievers. My knowledge is limited, but I was lucky to have a teacher who saw one path to integrating all the texts into a coherent reading.⁸ How does one enter the hermeneutical circle and iterate around the circle enough to come to a coherent reading? I think Edward Hobbs made a good start in an-

---

⁶ It was Timothy Axelrod, a physicist and astronomer, who pointed this out to me.

⁷ Booth, *A Rhetoric of Irony*.

⁸ It should be emphasized that there may be more than one coherent reading of the texts. For those who crave analogies to mathematical iterative approximations, it suffices to remember that Newton's method of finding the roots of a function can be used to find multiple roots, if there are more than one.

8.1 Returning to Miracles

swering that question, at least in outline. He was quite cautious, and never published his ideas to my knowledge, because he was aware of how little we know about first-century culture, worldviews, and conceptualities. One would like to show that the ironies in the miracle and Resurrection texts were intended by their authors, but that is much harder than merely observing that the texts are full of ironies. Nevertheless, texts can mean more than their authors know or intend,[9] and the intention that we *can* see in the texts — an invitation to faith — is consistent with reading the texts as advertisements for faith. We don't even know whether the author of Mark was an individual, a community, or the sense of a tradition.[10] This will take some unpacking. It began, logically, in an observation that implicitly takes the miracle texts as a different kind of part, which entails a different kind of whole.

Edward Hobbs saw that the miracle *texts* have the same literary structure as modern TV advertisements.[11] In both, a client with a problem gets the problem solved by a product being advertised, usually with something preposterous happening along the way. This raises problems for us because the evangelists *appear* to believe the "miraculous" healings "literally," even if we don't. What is more, the product is not consistently named — unlike TV ads, which tend to be repetitious with the pertinent product name.[12]

In this section, we lay out how to enter the hermeneutical circle on the assumption that the Gospels are invitations to faith, not primarily reports of events, especially in respect to the miracles and the Resurrection. The relation of the parts to the whole of Mark needs to be spelled out. After a reading of the structure of Mark as the prototype Gospel, it will be possible

---

[9] The thesis that says the meaning of a text is equal to the intended meaning of its author is known as the "intentional fallacy."

[10] There have been speculations, for example, that the order and choice of pericopes in the Synoptic Gospels was the result of matching oral traditions to Synagogue lectionary readings. No such theory has gained general acceptance, but they do attest to the degree of our ignorance. The effective authorship is in the Church that later canonized these four Gospels — and not the many others.

[11] See also above, p. 43. Hobbs, "Gospel Miracle Story and Modern Miracle Stories." In *Gospel Studies in Honor of Sherman Elbridge Johnson*. Hobbs was not the only one to spot the parallels. Gary Dreibelbis, in an AAR/Wecsor paper, "Moving Mountains and Money: A First Union Bank Commercial," Wecsor program, March 2001. The paper was about TV ads and theology, and saw TV ads as miracle stories.

[12] That suggests to me that these texts are the intuitive sense of the Markan community rather than a deliberately intended borrowing of the literary form of a TV advertisement — one that was presumably not available to them, though its similarities for us are uncanny.

to return to the older readings of the Gospels as reports of a Resurrection "event" and see the problems in the older, more conventional readings.

In analogy with a comparison of two paradigms, we then (in the next section) can look at one through the lens of the assumptions of the other. It may be that one explains the successes and failures of the other better than the other itself can.[13] For an example that explains the development of the Resurrection traditions (other than my own speculations, above) one could take Bernard Brandon Scott's work. It ends with a turn to ironic and literary meditations on the limitations of life, instead of the quest for a coherent literal reading of the texts.[14] This is not a proof because the two paradigms do not share enough common presuppositions on the basis of which a proof could be possible. It is a call for a choice, and that, after all, is in the logic of the Gospels. It is also the theme of the present study, the accountant's question, which is also a call for a choice.

Sketch the structure of Mark:

> the title at the beginning:
> "this is the good news of Jesus Christ"
> call for *metanoia*
> the baptism
> calling the disciples
> a series of cleansings, raisings, and feedings,
> interleaved with teaching
> At the end,
> the cleansing of the Temple
> the feeding of the disciples
> the crucifixion
> — and where we are led to expect[15] a raising,
> we get only a message, "he is not here."

The opening title: "The beginning of the Good News about Jesus Christ, the son of God" (JB). The term translated as "Good News" in the Jerusalem Bible, and as "Gospel" in many other translations, is εὐαγγελίον, a new

---

[13] For a definition of the phenomenon, see MacIntyre, *Whose Justice? Which Rationality?*, 363–364.

[14] Scott, *The Trouble with Resurrection*

[15] That expectation is attested in the words of the bystanders, "He saved others, he cannot save himself."

8.1 Returning to Miracles

concept, and a new genre not quite like anything before it in Greek or Latin literature.[16] The good news is an invitation to *metanoia*, both by John the Baptist (1.5), and Jesus (1.15). Translators usually render *metanoia* as "repentance," but its literal meaning is closer to "change of mind," or in effect change of perspective. The word occurs three times in Mark, more in Matthew, more still in Luke.

For those interested in the miracles, Mark gives us a sequence of them leading up to the three at the end:

The first five:
1.21 a demoniac
1.29 Simon's mother-in-law
1.40 a leper
2.1 a paralytic, lowered through the roof by his friends
3.1 the man with a withered hand

The second five, with feedings interspersed:
5.1 the Gerasene demoniac
5.21 Jairus' daughter
5.25 the woman with a hemorrhage
6.30 (five loaves)
7.24 the Syro-phoenician woman's daughter
7.31 the deaf-mute
8.1 (seven loaves)
8.14 (the 13th loaf)

The third five:
8.22 the blind man at Bethsaida
9.14 a man with a deaf and dumb spirit
10.46 blind Bartimaeus
11.15 the cleansing of the Temple
14.22 (the feeding of the disciples)
16.1 "He is not here."[17]

The cleansing of the Temple, the Last Supper, and the Resurrection are

---

[16] The *word* is not new; in the New Testament it is Pauline (e.g., 1 Cor. 15), and it occurs in the Septuagint and Aristophanes (among other authors) before that. The word is common after the New Testament.

[17] Edward Hobbs made the list, and it was published with his permission in my *By the Waters of Naturalism*, section 7.2.

the goal and climax of a series of miracles. Each is the last of its series: cleansings, raisings, and feedings.

Even though Mark's miracle stories have the same form as TV advertisements, the product they offer is not so simple as a household product or cultural concept that one could buy or buy into easily. The product is more elusive than that; beyond calling it *metanoia*, it didn't really get a name. To put it in a modern idiom, Mark is "messing with your mind."[18] Did the evangelist know that? Are there other examples of irony in Greco-Roman literature? I don't know how to answer those questions. Others may. The question of "miracles" appears explicitly, in Mark 13.22 when he deprecates "signs and wonders." The other three evangelists do the same, as we shall see shortly. For the moment, the import of the messenger's words in the short ending of Mark is, "You're looking in the wrong place." It is a last call for *metanoia*, change of perspective.

In effect, the series of "miracles," ending in the cleansing of the Temple, the feeding of the disciples, and the "He is not here" (16.7d), is a series that ends in a whiplash. The expectations that are built up as the series moves forward are dashed in its last member. The miracles could be characterized as the work of a θεῖος ἀνήρ. We could mistake Jesus for a *theios anér*, but the ending doesn't fit that. The text catastrophically undermines that reading. Call this the Markan "whiplash" — one that the long ending and other post-resurrection appearances seek to defang.[19] The short form of the Gospel of Mark, ending with ἐφοβοῦντο γάρ, emphasizes the whiplash.

So much for a sketch of the structure of Mark's Gospel, placing its internal parts in a whole. The whole of a text is but a part in a larger whole of its circumstances, world, and environment. The horizon of context keeps expanding. Some of those larger contexts may be noted; it is impossible to find them all.[20]

This inquiry presupposes an ontology in which the constitution of the parts is determined by the whole chosen for their context. We respectfully demur from those who think it is possible to isolate parts first and construct

---

[18] The pious don't allow the Bible to mess with your mind. Those who have been ambushed by the Bible know better.

[19] The whiplash has this much in common with many jokes: you thought you were in one story, but in the punch line you find yourself in some other. The Joke was on us.

[20] What follows is one lesson drawn from reading Mark. It is not the only meaning in Mark; the Gospels have many lessons to offer.

8.1 Returning to Miracles

wholes later. That may work in physics, but it doesn't work here. The parts always already involve the whole, and the whole is a choice, a matter of basic life orientation. The ontology of physics is one in which parts *can* be isolated without reference to wholes.[21] But human life is more than its naturalistic substrate.

As an aside, notice that the relationship between parts and whole is circular or reciprocal: each determines what the other is. Though we focus here on how the larger contexts determine the reading of the parts, the parts also determine the sense of the whole. In particular, it is the Christian contention that the death of the Lord is one answer to the question, "Where does your proposed ultimate reality show itself in the world?"[22] That part ontologically determines the meaning of the whole. To pursue that would take us into the doctrine of the Work of Christ, which is well beyond the ambitions of this book.

Look at ten larger contexts for the Gospel of Mark. Some of them may overlap. Each pericope gets its meaning from its place in the sequence of all of them together, and from the teaching, the parables. As much applies to the Resurrection texts. The whole collection gets its meanings from the world that the Gospel fits into.

For a first larger context, the structure of Mark, in both parts and whole, is constructed as Exodus typology, as we have already seen in section 3.1.[23] Matthew and Luke saw this, and they filled in parts of the story that Mark left out. They followed roughly Mark's arrangement but with changes for their own characteristic theologies.

In a second larger context, on close examination, the Gospel of Mark has a very poor opinion of the disciples. Theodore J. Weeden Sr. explored this some years ago.[24] Mark's polemic against them is easy to miss, until the reader sees Luke in comparison. As an old saying goes, "Luke spares the Twelve." The disciples represent will-to-power, and they are also very slow to understand Jesus's real intentions. The issue, once again, and stated in our terms, not Mark's vocabulary, is whether we are saved *from* or *in* the pains of life.

---

[21] See *Living in Spin*, section 3.1, "Systems ontologies and distributed ontologies."

[22] "When we eat this bread and drink this cup, we proclaim your death, Lord Jesus, until you come in glory." This is the mystery of faith in the middle of the several canons of the Mass. Quoted from p. 364 of *The Book of Divine Worship*.

[23] This was argued at a little more length in my *In the Beginning, Exodus*. Again, this reading of the texts comes from Edward Hobbs. Others have argued this at more length.

[24] Weeden, "The Heresy That Necessitated Mark's Gospel."

In a third larger context, look at the miracles against the background of some of the teaching in the Gospels. This is not a trivial question, since the teaching is notoriously elusive, not always easy to pin down, and full of ironies, even when it is not being pushed in Gnostic directions. Consider only one pericope, the laborers in the vinyard (Matt. 20.1–16). It is in Matthew, not Mark, but Mark could hardly be read to disagree. Permit me one observation from Edward Hobbs. The lesson is a simple maxim: "accept the limitations of life in gratitude and joy, without invidious comparisons between your neighbor's lot and your own."[25] This would seem to be incompatible with reading the signs and wonders texts as promising a way to get out of limitations. This is developed more in sec. 3.3 and 8.8. The teaching about Limitation parallels that about Exposure and Need, to which we come momentarily. Exposure, cleansing, usually appears in the Gospels as cleansing from demons.

In a fourth larger context, the whole of the New Testament is one side of a bitter quarrel (especially in John), and we do not have the other side, the rabbinic counter-arguments, if there were any. One could call it a choice between Christ and kashrut. In slightly different words, both daughter religions born out of the ashes of Second Temple Judaism continued the covenant with a transcendent Other but in different ways. For one, the transcendent Other is present in obedience to his laws and prescribed observances.[26] For the other daughter religion, the transcendent Other is present as incarnate in a person in history. Both have deep roots in the Common Documents. Both are social constructions, and in this we follow a Chalcedonian method: in one side of a Chalcedonian description, the social sciences tell us a little of how religions are constructed; in the other, we trust that ultimate reality really is present in our socially constructed realities. That a responsible choice was made is thematic in this book. Paul, in Galatians, claims a responsible liberty of interpretation for the Church. Would that he had recognized that the same liberty was given to the Synagogue (cf. p. 221 below).

For a fifth larger context, consider late Second-Temple Jewish apocalyptic, which supplied much of the idiom of the New Testament. It was at least one of the conceptualities[27] of the New Testament world and a fair

---

[25] The phrasing is very close to Edward Hobbs's.

[26] These prescribed observances are more liturgical than legal, to put it in terms that Catholics could understand. They welcome a real presence of the transcendent Other, just as Christian liturgies do.

[27] Gnostic terms in John are another.

8.1 Returning to Miracles

amount is known about it. We saw the distinction between conceptualities and "understandings" above, in section 1.8.

The context for apocalyptic was three centuries of disaster imposed on the Jewish people in the land of Israel, first by the Hellenistic monarchies (Antiochus Epiphanes, 167 BCE), then eventually by the Romans (67–73 and 135 CE. The message of apocalyptic was a promise of restoration, with a resurrection of the just dead. For a contrast from before the apocalyptic period, look at Psalm 89, which is divided in two parts in the Breviary, on Wednesday and Thursday of Week III. On Wednesday we rehearse the promises to the monarchy and on Thursday bewail the promises broken in the downfall of the monarchy. Psalm 89 fits the Exile; the apocalyptic period came a few centuries later, under the Greeks and then the Romans. The literature of the time looks forward to a justice in which wrong is punished and the unjustly killed will be raised up and restored to life — the narrative elements which the Gospels take up and use to frame the story of Jesus. Among those who have surveyed the apocalyptic literature are Paul Hanson and George Nickelsburg.[28] Hanson focuses on apocalyptic in the biblical texts, and Nickelsburg surveys also some of the extra-biblical sources. See especially Nickelsburg's chapter 8 on apocalyptic elements in the Markan Passion narrative. My own comment would be that (apart from vaticinia ex eventu) Mark uses the language of apocalyptic but uses it to undermine its practical application. This is particularly true of chapter 13, sometimes called the "little apocalypse," in which specifics of time and manner are removed, thus rendering it unusable for actual predictions.

Biblical literalists ignore that, for practical predictions for our own time are exactly what that they want. That is, they ignore the difference between conceptuality and "understanding," and that determines what meaning can be retrieved for our own time.[29]

In a sixth perspective on the larger context of the Disasters of the First Century, the emergence of both Christianity and rabbinic Judaism is one stage in the long history of world-affirming historical religion. This is part of the continuing development of historical religion in contrast to nature religions and exilic religions, among others.[30] What happens when one views the New Testament within the context of the inheritance from the

---

[28] Hanson. *The Dawn of Apocalyptic*, and Nickelsburg, *Resurrection, Immortality and Eternal Life*.

[29] Sheehan, "Easter, Apocalypse, and the Fundamentalists" Part One. *The Fourth R*, 28-3 (2015/May–June) 3–20.

[30] The allusion is to the last three chapters of Merold Westphal, *God, Guilt, and Death*.

Second Temple and then views that inheritance in the larger context of the history of religions? The dynamic of the hermeneutical circle changes, for the New Testament becomes a part in something bigger, and the part-whole relationship changes. The NT becomes a continuation of the covenant at the Exodus, and it becomes a continuation of biblical religion, not its origin. Christianity is more than just Christology; it is world-affirming historical religion, something that is not an abstraction but is grounded in its history — all of its history, not just the Disasters of the First Century.

Much scholarship of the New Testament and early Christianity has perplexed itself because it cannot get access to the kind of "facts" that Christianity is supposedly based on in enough detail to quiet its anxieties. That kind of history was offered in historicism, which was supposed to give the objective "facts" in as much detail as one might wish. It also offers a kind of objectivation. The New Testament is about real history and real people, but it is an invitation to faith without objectivating that faith, whether in signs and wonders or any other way. You can see well enough what kind of faith is intended.

For a seventh larger context, consider man-in-the-world viewed under the aspect of "success" in living (or not). Man is face-to-face with ultimate reality; to be human is to be engaged with ultimate reality. The question of ultimate reality is a question in somewhat loose language of *success* in life. What has to happen for someone to "succeed" in life?[31] To live well? People have quite various answers, people do not all agree on the answers, people do not all even think about the question in these terms. But everybody has answers, in the sense that answers are implicit in human actions and in the narrative coherence of human lives. Most cultures have ways (typically in myths) of locating themselves in the larger and eventually ultimate realities. When we don't use "myths," our "science" nevertheless performs the function of myths.

For an eighth view, among the largest contexts is the choice of what to do about the pains of life, of which we take Exposure, Limitation, and Need as exemplary. How the Resurrection can make sense depends in large part on how the question of the pains of life is handled. It is the ultimate context in which the day-to-day pains and sufferings we see in the miracles and the teaching culminate. It is your answer to the basic question of philosophy of religion: how does your proposed basic life orientation

---

[31] Note, the question does *not* ask "what does one have to *do*" — it leaves open the possibility that some things have to be done to me or for me.

8.1 Returning to Miracles 153

deal with the pains of life?[32]

For a ninth larger context, we have said above that *metanoia* would better be translated here as change of perspective than as repentance. At this point, one ought to ask change of mind *to* what perspective? That comes out only slowly in the course of the Gospel. In some ways, it is left unspecified in order that it may not simply be dismissed by those who reject it. It is like a joke: one gets it or not, and spelling out the joke is a poor substitute for just getting it. Sometimes a conversation comes to an impasse, and explaining the joke is the best that can be done. Then the irony of the joke moves on to some other clearing in life, like a traveler refused admittance by a "No Vacancy" sign. Irony will stay with those who can welcome it. Some get it and some don't. The attempt to drive out irony is one kind of quest for power and control. No one ever really gains control, though some think they do. They may succeed in driving out irony.

Consider a tenth perspective. The miracle texts put the reader to the question. The Resurrection texts drive the question home to the heart and then twist it. We have seen the question before. Here, it takes the form, "Can you welcome blessing in the Limitations of life? And in Exposure and Need?" More generally and more abstractly, the question is, "Where does your proposed meaning of life show itself in the world?"

To embrace the blessings that come *in* the pains of life (rather than in getting *out* of those pains) requires a change of mind (*metanoia*), as the opening of the gospel of Mark candidly announces. To put it a little differently, the Resurrection texts (and miracle texts more generally) ask for a *choice*; but they don't offer to make that choice for you (by objectivation).

What gets changed is the ultimate wider horizon within which the events are to be contextualized. We have said, following Gadamer, that the meaning of the parts depends on the larger whole, and the largest whole is a person's sense of ultimate reality. But that always involves a choice: are we saved (do we find life) *in* Exposure, Limitation, and Need, or in getting *out* of them?[33] To demand "proof" is to change to a different choice. The *form* of trust that the pains of life fit into a larger whole that is good is, "We trust that the future will reward our faith as the past has." The claim that the past rewarded our forbears' faith can easily be misinterpreted as proof,

---

[32] Cf. pp. 11, 14.
[33] See sections 3.3, 8.7, and 8.8.

especially if the past is edited selectively. Sometimes we simply trust that God was there with us, acting for us, even when we cannot see how.

The structure of the texts is more complicated than a naive reading would indicate, for the texts were not all written at the same time. In the short ending of Mark, there are no Resurrection appearances, and the story has "grown in the telling" in the long ending of Mark and in Matthew, Luke, and John. The other evangelists have evidently gratified the crowd's appetite for signs and wonders, amplifying the story that Mark gave them. St. Paul's Resurrection tradition is more rudimentary: appearances, but no empty tomb. That is, the concept of being "raised" for Paul means appearances (of which he knows many); it doesn't involve a tomb at all. The Resurrection texts in the post-Markan Gospels appear today — to many readers — to offer signs and wonders on which to base faith. The Gospels tolerate signs and wonders, though they don't like them.[34] So what *is* the logic of the Resurrection in the gospels?[35] And how did those texts come to be? Probably, or at least plausibly, by the inference of the faithful, filling in what "must have" happened, or what "probably" happened. Craving for signs and wonders then took over.

Let me summarize this reading of Mark, starting with the assumption that it is an invitation to faith, not Rankean history: The miracle texts are to be read as like TV advertisements, for a product named *metanoia*. They are a series of cleansings, raisings,[36] and feedings, culminating in the last three: the cleansing of the Temple, the feeding of the disciples, and the absence of Jesus.[37] This reading is to be fitted into several larger perspectives: The Synoptic gospels are Exodus typology, because they have the

---

[34] This is a change from the signs and wonders in the plagues of the Exodus. There the text appears (credibly, I think) to believe in the miracles of the plagues, but it notes that Pharaoh's magicians also worked signs and wonders. Here, in the Gospels, we are not to base faith on signs and wonders *at all*.

[35] That is our question. Mark asks the same question, in 9.10, where after the Transfiguration, "among themselves, they [the disciples] discussed what 'rising from the dead' could mean," evidently without Jesus explaining it to them. The verb is $ἀναστῆναι$, which does not have the breadth of meaning of $ἐγείρω$, so Mark is indulging the craving for signs and wonders, but in the mouth of the disciples, whose intelligence he doesn't think much of. In any case, he flags his question and ours as the central issue of his Gospel, and it is a question that he does not answer explicitly. This is characteristic Markan understatement, a clue hidden in plain sight where no one will find it.

[36] If you translate $ἔγερσις$ as *raising* rather than as *awakening*. Liddell and Scott list awakening as a meaning of the word, but not raising.

[37] It was Edward Hobbs who saw this structure.

8.1 Returning to Miracles

same structure as the Exodus. Mark is a critique of the disciples' quest for power. The Gospels have a place in the quarrel with nascent rabbinic Judaism, and in the choice between Christ and kashrut. They have a place in the Disasters of the First Century and in the emergence of two daughter religions from the ashes of Second-Temple Judaism. A modern reader may paraphrase the challenge. The *metanoia* proffered appears in a question: do you want to find blessing *in* Exposure, Limitation, and Need, or in getting *out* of them?

This is what we get in a reading of the Gospels as invitations to faith, not primarily as historicist (Rankean) accounts of "facts," as reports of an event. The legacy of nineteenth-century historicism lives on, unrecognized, at so deep a level as to be hard to eradicate. We look at the interpretation of the texts as reports in the next section.

The conspicuous alternative to reading the miracle texts as advertisements is to read them as *reports* of events: "signs and wonders," σημεῖα καὶ τέρατα, in the language of the New Testament. The Gospels — all four of them — address the issue. They deprecate faith based on signs and wonders, though they allow it. See Matt 24.24, Mark 13.22, and John 4.48; all reproach the crowd's unwillingness to believe "except they see signs and wonders." Even Luke, who does not repeat Mark's rejection of signs and wonders, speaks of signs in terms that are not very complimentary. Luke 11.29: "The crowds got bigger and he addressed them, 'this is a wicked generation; it is asking for a sign.'" Interestingly, the Gospels also predict signs and wonders by *false* prophets.[38] They appear to mean *real* signs and wonders. Acts 5.12 says the apostles worked many signs and wonders. How are we to interpret that? Do the texts ever ask our question, about the difference between the preposterous in advertising and "real" events?[39]

What did the ancient world (and the evangelists in it) really think about the possibility of what we call miracles and they called signs and wonders? What did *they* think in answer to *our* questions? That is more than I know, and possibly more than NT scholars know. It may simply be that they did not ask, much less answer, our questions. We do not have to answer these questions for present purposes. What the NT writers thought was

---

[38] This, too, is in its lowly way Exodus typology: at the Plagues, Pharaoh's magicians worked counter-miracles aplenty. So the "miraculous" (i. e., preternatural) character of an event does not by itself make it an act of God.

[39] No. Neither do TV ads or TV news; they assume we can do form criticism.

possible, and what they thought actually happened, are questions about the *conceptuality* of that age, and there were probably disagreements among the various writers and traditions.[40] Those questions are not easy to answer, especially in an inquiry with historiographic ambitions as modest as this one's. The theology in the texts is another matter; to that, we have some access.

Paul knows no tomb; resurrection is still ill-defined.[41] He knows many appearances, but what appearances meant we do not know. The issue of the "how" of resurrection does arise (1 Cor 15.35), and he dismissed it as a category error. Mark's tomb is a literary device with the same purpose as Paul's dismissal in 1 Cor 15.35: He is not here; you're looking in the wrong place, you will find him in Galilee (i.e., in your lives). The Emmaus story makes much the same point. The tomb narratives in the other three Gospels are a case of "the story has grown in the telling." The growth may be both to gratify craving for signs and wonders and simultaneously to undermine that craving — the texts are ambiguous. The theology is available to us in the texts and in the ways we iterate around the hermeneutical circle in reading the texts in their many contexts. This is an invitation to faith, to a change of perspective (*metanoia*). It is not apologetic literature, argument, or proof. It deprecates objectivations (signs and wonders) but tolerates them. At this point, the only reading of the miracle and resurrection texts that can help is ironic, and it makes no sense to the irony-challenged.

I would not say that the message in the short ending of Mark is the *only* Resurrection theology in the Gospels, merely that it is sufficient to fend off the craving for objectivation in literalist readings of the texts.

In one summary of the theology, the perspective on life that Mark offers is one that takes all of life as good, in full view of its pains. That's not easy. It's also a choice, not something that can be proven. We come to it only slowly, in sections 8.4, 8.7, and 8.8.

---

[40] Cf. Edward Hobbs on conceptuality, in section 1.8 above.

[41] Thomas Sheehan observes that in one meaning of ἐγείρω Jesus was "awakened." "The primary and literal meaning of the verb *egeirō*, from which *egegertai* is derived, is 'to awaken someone from sleep.'" Sheehan, "The Resurrection, an Obstacle to Faith?" *The Fourth R* 8-2 (1995 March/April), 3–9, reprinted in Scott, ed., *The Resurrection of Jesus: A Sourcebook*. This reading of ἐγείρω is supported both in Bauer and in Liddell and Scott.

8.2 Literalism and the Resurrection

Turn from reading the miracle and Resurrection texts as an invitation to faith to the more common reading of them as reports of objective events. As invitations to faith, these texts are literary constructions devised in order to make a theological point. The short ending of Mark is only the first example (he is not here; you're looking in the wrong place) — and the others have grown in the telling. But they are ambiguous: they can be taken as literary irony, and they can also be taken as reports of events, signs and wonders. As irony, they offer good news, for those who can hear it. For those who cannot, but still would walk the road to it, the reading as signs and wonders is available. But even then, the texts do not give readers the kind of access to the "event" that a physical description would.

The alleged events have attracted attacks, and the attacks have attracted apologetic defenses, arguments in favor of the historicity of the miracles and the Resurrection. Such arguments (and there are many), simply *assume* (thereby evading alternatives) that the texts are reports of objective events, and are to be read as such, leaving only one further question, whether the reports are "true" or not. More than the entry into the hermeneutical circle is assumed here.

Elaborate arguments are mounted in defense of a "bodily" Resurrection, without saying what *bodily* really means. It is assumed (again, silently, to deflect attention from the question) that *bodily* means *physical*. But 'bodily' is a term from one discourse and 'physical' from another. For the many meanings of 'bodily' one could consult the TDNT article on σῶμα, σωματικός.[42] The situation is complicated by the literalists' insinuation that 'body' is used in contrast to soul or spirit, meanings known from Plato. Paul, however, uses σῶμα to mean the whole person, which does nothing to support the literalists' project.[43] If anything, the contrast to *soma* in the New Testament is sin, not soul or spirit.

For the physical, many resources could be consulted; my choice would be Landau and Lifshitz. The physical, as we know it, was unknown in the First Century; it dates from the seventeenth. There are doubtless places where the ancient concept of the bodily overlaps the modern concept of

---

[42] *Theological Dictionary of the New Testament*, vol. VIII, 1024. "Σῶμα, σωματικός, σύσσωμος," by Eduard Schweizer and Friedrich Baumgärtel. Body of Christ? Body and blood, in the Eucharist? Body as whole person?

[43] Sheehan, "Easter, Apocalypse, and the Fundamentalists," Part Two. The Fourth R, 28-4 (2015/July-August), 11.

the physical. We can *sometimes* infer physical effects from ancient texts about the bodily.[44] That does not suffice to accredit the ancient world with an understanding of the physical as modern science understands it.

If there were some physical anomaly, it would leave traces. Would all be impossible to detect? We do not know; few ask. But to treat the Resurrection as a *physical* event is to open the door to many lines of inquiry that would undermine or distract from the theology in the texts. Unsurprisingly, the literalists would protest that to ask about the physical particulars of the Resurrection is to miss the point. In this, they would be right. Typically, they claim a sacred mystery. There is a sacred mystery here, but violations of physical laws are not it. In this the literalists are partly right and partly confused. When looked at carefully, the arguments from a literal reading of the Resurrection texts are incoherent. It will take some work to unravel the threads of the problem.

One issue is worth some emphasis. The literalist approach to the Resurrection texts seeks to prove something objective about it, and thereby get the Resurrection "event" to take the responsibility for the faith of believers. This would relieve them of a great anxiety, and that is the point and purpose of literalist hermeneutics. It lets literalists defy the heckling of nonbelievers, but the responsibility of a confessional commitment should never be dodged or evaded. That, of course, is exactly what literalism is designed to do.

Literalists in effect demand validation of their defenses. They want not only the "objective" facts to take the responsibility, they also want other people to validate their "facts." It would be odd to call it faith, because the objective is not really a matter of faith. They are also in defiance of critical history, even when they attempt to argue within its canons of evidence and inference, because the resulting arguments are incoherent. The basic mistake was in accepting the planted presupposition of their adversaries, that the texts are to be read as reports of an objective event.

Typical of the literalist genre is N. T. Wright's work, but there are many other authors also. It is a peculiar genre because it constructs long and detailed and extremely learned and scholarly arguments in favor of literalist readings of the texts as reports of events. N. T. Wright says as much: "The main conclusion that emerges from these four studies of the

---

[44] The logic is not really an inference but rather a diagnostic relation. Cf. Ricoeur, *Freedom and Nature*, 13.

8.2 Literalism and the Resurrection

canonical evangelists is that each of them, in their very different ways, believed that they were writing about events that actually took place."[45] A literal reading would mean a "bodily Resurrection," but it never quite tells the reader what (in modern scientific terms) a "bodily Resurrection" might actually be. It takes for granted the meaning of "bodily resurrection," and the reader may not notice that it is never spelled out physically.

Wright is aware of the problem, and he introduces the term "transphysical" to mean "the nature of the future resurrection body." He goes on: "This new mode of embodiment is hard to describe,[46] but we can at least propose a label for it.... The word 'transphysical' ..."[47] We never do find out where the molecules went (or came from).[48]

Literalist arguments for the historicity of the Resurrection fail to discharge the obligations of such an argument. If they make a claim about where the molecules of Jesus' dead body went, they don't say. They are not candid. If they are not a claim about where the molecules went, they give no convincing reasons why we should not assume they went where they usually go (into the dirt and the water table). If the molecules went someplace out of the ordinary, where? Presumably they went *someplace*. Are there any lasting physical traces of such a violation of natural laws? If the molecules simply dematerialized (i. e., violated conservation of matter and energy), would they leave traces of such a deviation from law? In physics, there are microscopic (but undetectable) deviations in the trajectories of every other body on earth, and far from earth, too. But detectable effects, with traces somehow imprinted on near-by matter? Once such questions are raised and offered to the tender attentions of physicists, it would be impossible to contain them.

If I talked the way N. T. Wright does, I would fault myself for monophysite theology of divine action, though the issue is on the border between Christology and acts of God outside Christology. We saw the problem at the beginning, in section 1.5. It has dogged the Church ever since. The appeal to supposed violations of natural laws is ignorant of the biblical

---

[45] Wright, *The Resurrection of the Son of God*, 680.
[46] Sic; said without irony.
[47] Wright, *The Resurrection of the Son of God*, 477.
[48] The problem has been satirized. The cartoonist Sidney Harris showed two scientists before a long algebraic derivation on a blackboard. Step two says, "Then a miracle occurs." The response is "I think you should be more explicit here in step two." The cartoon is all over the Net.

treatment of such violations.[49] Violation of a natural law (contrary to Deist metaphysics and sloppy modern illiterate literalism) is not proof of an act of God. In the Exodus, Pharaoh's servants work violations just as much as Moses and Aaron do. Mark predicts signs and wonders by evil people just as much as by the faithful. St. Paul in 1 Corinthians 15.35 ff. makes it clear that the Resurrection was not a resuscitation or anything like it, and even to ask such questions is to misunderstand what it was all about.[50] To argue that "miracles" and the Resurrection "actually happened" is like arguing that ghosts are real, and belief in ghosts is the price that has to be paid in order to enjoy Hamlet. It confuses conceptuality with basic life orientation.[51]

Recall the larger contexts for the Gospel of Mark, p. 148 ff. above. A recurrent theme was the choice about the pains of life: are we saved from them, or in them? Wright argues to the effect that something must have happened, for otherwise, the faith of the disciples after Jesus' death is inexplicable.[52] Why? Must there be a way out of Limitation? Must the Resurrection texts be reports of an event showing that way out of Limitation, otherwise they don't make sense?[53] In other words, if the Resurrection, whatever it "was," had not shown a way out of Limitation, it wouldn't have done any good, and the faith that came after it wouldn't make sense. This reading is at best an instance of monophysite theology of divine action; at worst, it doesn't really believe the pains of life can be integrated into creation — a good world. I would say that the Resurrection texts make a challenge to find good and blessing *in* Limitation. They do not promise a way of getting out of it. To misread texts designed to challenge as ways to evade challenge is to miss the *metanoia*, the change of perspective that Mark does offer. That is what taking the texts as reports of an event does: the event they supposedly report promises a way to get out of the challenge of Limitation.

---

[49] Cf. p. 170.

[50] "Whatever you sow in the ground has to die before it is given new life" (15.36, JB) — in other words, the body went into the ground as it usually does after death; by what route, the texts do not tell us.

[51] As on p. 118.

[52] This is implicit in many places in Wright's book, but often presupposed in ways that are not obvious. One place where he says it is on p. 6, where he promises to show "the difficulty of accounting for those beliefs except on the hypothesis that they were true." The beliefs are about something objective, and to be "true" means being objective.

[53] Whether Wright intended that is for him to say, not me; he may speak for himself.

8.2 Literalism and the Resurrection

Presumably the NT writers did not understand their Gospel miracle stories as an analog of TV advertisements, for they had no TV, and their culture accepted a more or less literal understanding of signs and wonders. Did they intend the miracle stories literally? I think we don't know. What examples of irony are there in Greco-Roman or Hebrew literature? As literary creations, the Resurrection texts lead to the challenge of the short ending of Mark, or the Emmaus story. The texts are a challenge and invitation to faith, posing the question, "What will you do with Limitation in your lives?"

To say that the stories have grown in the telling is by now widely accepted. Reginald Fuller argued as much in *The Formation of the Resurrection Narratives* (1970), and a more recent survey can be found in Bernard Brandon Scott, *The Trouble with Resurrection: From Paul to the Fourth Gospel* (2010).[54]

The voices in the Bible, in both testaments, are a movement, not a thesis or a theory. They offer a way of life, but I don't think they can prove themselves. They can only invite faith.

So what is going on in literalist readings? The believer craves objectivation, since it gets him out of responsibility, and gets him out of anxiety — the inevitable anxiety that comes with facing human mortality. It would be better to surrender signs and wonders and admit that we read the Resurrection texts as posing a question: Do you want to find blessing in the Limitations of life, included among which is mortality? We answer in the affirmative — which is exactly the *metanoia* (change of perspective) that Mark invited in the beginning of his Gospel.

Put it another way. The Resurrection texts can be read in at least two ways: In the more obvious, we are rescued *from* Limitation and ultimately get out of it — Jesus was raised literally, and though delayed, we shall be also. In the less obvious, the texts are not to be read literally, and blessing comes *in* Limitation, not in getting out of it. The ambiguity of the texts is something we have to live in. It may be intentional.

The incoherence of literalist hermeneutics does not mean it is faithless or worthless, though it is seriously confused and does real damage. For some, it is a stage on the way of faith. Literalists are not doing what they think they are doing, and their problems have grown worse in our own time. They are examples of the domestication of transcendence and

---

[54] Fuller, *The Formation of the Resurrection Narratives*; Scott, *The Trouble with Resurrection*.

seeking to understand what cannot be understood.[55] Both are diseases of modernity.

8.3 The Gospel of Peter

The issue of objectivation arose already in the first century, though it was understood differently. The pertinent text is the Gospel of Peter. Hennecke and Schneemelcher date the Gospel of Peter to the mid-second century. (1963 edition, p. 180.) A small minority (Crossan, a few others) date it between Paul and Mark, as the first of the (surviving) written gospels.[56] That is not a disagreement that I can adjudicate, though it is fair to observe that the issue appears already in 1 Corinthians 15: What happened at "the" Resurrection? Physically, bodily? If Peter was written before Mark, then it is possible to make sense of Mark as a response to Peter. If Peter was written in the second century (the majority opinion), it merely reflects disputes then. Mark also makes sense as a response to ideas that were available and attested in the first century. But it is Peter that states the idea that Mark (and the Church) elide, the thesis that the Resurrection was a bodily, physical resuscitation. If it was not a resuscitation, then how did the texts develop? That is a phenomenon common enough: Historians, whether technical or colloquial, make inferences about what "must" have happened, and the story grows in the telling. This we have seen in regard to the Resurrection traditions generally.

What is of interest here is that the inferences have gone further than what the canonical gospels give us, and in a direction that takes us well out of their understanding of the Resurrection. The canonical gospels (and Acts and Paul) give us visions, apparitions of the risen Lord, but they do not give us the event of the rising itself. To do that would approximate a resuscitation, not the Resurrection. The canonical texts give us personal encounters with the Lord, in the way that that culture understood such encounters. Their descriptions are rarely part of our experience, and when people today have such visions, the rest of us don't know what to do with them.

There are many differences in theology between Peter and the canonical gospels. Hennecke and Schneemelcher put its origin in Syria, but they leave such inferences as conjectural at best. What matters for us is that the

---

[55] Cf. Placher, above, in sec. 6.1.
[56] Crossan, *The Cross that Spoke*, 18 and passim.

8.3 The Gospel of Peter

canonical gospels do not give us the actual event of the Resurrection, if it even was an event. They can be read as theological commentary on the significance of the crucifixion. Peter cannot. The canonical gospels, like the miracle stories before them, can be read as advertisements for *metanoia*. The Gospel of Peter, by giving us a visible way out of Limitation, makes that kind of *metanoia* impossible.

> [35] Now in the night in which the Lord's day dawned, when the soldiers, two by two in every watch, were keeping guard, there rang out a loud *voice in heaven*, [36] and they saw the *heavens opened*, and two men *come down* from there in a great brightness and draw nigh to the sepulchre. [37] That *stone* which had been laid against the entrance to the sepulchre started of itself *to roll* and gave way to the side, and the sepulchre was opened, and both the young men entered in. [10.38] When now those soldiers saw this, they awakened the centurion and the elders — for they also were there to assist at the watch. [39] And whilst they were relating what they had seen, they saw again three men come out from the sepulchre, and two of them sustaining the other, and a cross following them, [40] and the heads of the two reaching to heaven, but that of him who was led of them by the hand overpassing the heavens.[57]

The modern editors feel obliged to emphasize the contrast between the Gospel of Peter and the canonical gospels. Among the many differences is this:

> What, however, distinguishes it [Peter] from the New Testament Gospels is its massive apologetic reasoning. The testimony of belief is replaced by apparently direct proof of truth.[58]

> The difference in climate is apparent in the second place in the misunderstanding of the scriptural proofs in the Gospels. There the passion and resurrection of Jesus are presented as the eschatological fulfillment of the old covenant. This deci-

---

[57] Hennecke-Schneemelcher, *New Testament Apocrypha*, I:185–186.
[58] Hennecke-Schneemelcher, *New Testament Apocrypha*, I:181.

sive element of the presentation is not perceived by the author of our Gospel.[59]

In other words, Hennecke and Schneemelcher understand that the canonical gospels are advertisements, (I would add that they are dependent on Exodus typology); the Gospel of Peter is an attempt at objectivation.

8.4 Not as Literalist as They Think They Are

Several times above, I have said that the literalists are not as literalist as they think they are. So what is going on?

The test of conservative theology, insofar as a Pew survey was capable of understanding it, was adherence to this apparently simple proposition:

> Jesus rose from the dead
> with a real flesh-and-blood body
> leaving behind an empty tomb.[60]

The Pew study tells us something: People like "literalist" theology more than Liberal theology. Other possibilities were not even acknowledged in passing. "Literalist" theology offers comfort — both solace and strength — that is not available from Liberal theology. Liberal theology doesn't offer real transcendence any more than does literalist theology, though literalist theology appears to. Literalist theology, however badly it describes transcendence, nevertheless really is *about* transcendence, in the way that, for example, the phlogiston theory of combustion (however bad a theory it is) really is about flames — unlike poetry about hearts on fire. Whether literalist theology is in good faith is quite another question. Bad faith, in the sense of Peter Berger's *The Sacred Canopy*, can be quite empowering, endowing its partisans with fanatical strength.[61]

As we have already seen, the people who sound like literalists do not mean their literalist language in a literal way: they do not draw the logical

---

[59] Hennecke-Schneemelcher, *New Testament Apocrypha*, I:182.

[60] See Haskell, "Liberal Churches are Dying but Conservative Churches are Thriving." See Haskell, Flatt, and Burgoyne, "Theology Matters: Comparing the traits of Growing and Declining Mainline Protestant Church Attendees and Clergy." The question above was number 9 (of 10) addressed to laity and number 16 (of 17) addressed to clergy; pp. 525 and 529 of the study just cited. A related study from Pew: Cooperman, Smith, and Ritschey, "America's Changing Religious Landscape: Christians decline as share of population; unaffiliated and other faiths continue to grow."

[61] Berger, *The Sacred Canopy*, 94.

conclusions that would follow if it were literally true. In the first Christian centuries, this was recognized in practice even if not in theory in the rejection of the Gospel of Peter, which sought to draw conclusions from the canonical resurrection tradition that would be appropriate to a truly literal interpretation. This brings us to the salient question: If the literalists are not really literalists, what *does* their language mean, and how *does* it function in their lives? Literalist language is peculiar inasmuch as it forbids the conclusions that would appear to follow from its apparent meaning. I think it tries to engage real transcendence, but how?

What is going on when the literalist believer claims that Jesus was "raised" from the dead? In what looks like a resuscitation but supposedly was not, but something more mysterious? Or in its more overt forms, a real resuscitation, as in the Pew study? What is going on when the believer (and many theologians) translate ἠγέρθη not as "he was awakened," well within the meanings of ἐγείρω,[62] as Thomas Sheehan has pointed out,[63] but as "raised from the dead," meaning resuscitated in all but name?

It should be possible now to give a tentative answer to the question asking what literalist language does for those who use it. It is about transcendence, and the immanent presence of transcendence in the world. Transcendence is about unanswerable questions, and literalist language, as we have seen, doesn't quite handle it that way. It pretends to be literal language but it both commands and forbids attempts to take it literally. It *appears* to answer ultimate questions, thus providing "answers" for adversaries who demand answers. But that is incoherent, and the incoherence is often not noticed. It uses monophysite theology of divine action, claiming divine interference in the natural order, but forbidding further inquiry into what physically happened. Thus it can fend off hecklers — or at least comfort its own anxieties in the face of hecklers. The trouble is that it does this by objectivating divine action, and by hiding from itself its own choices of faith.

Allow me an aside about objectivation.[64] The problems of this chapter have attracted much comment in the twentieth century, when theologians first began to take seriously the implications of critical history for the Bible

---

[62] It is the *first* meaning in both Liddell and Scott and also in Bauer-Arndt-Gingrich. That incidentally puts the miracles of "raising" in a different light, especially in view of Mark's initial call for *metanoia*, change of perspective.

[63] Sheehan, "The Resurrection, an Obstacle to Faith?"

[64] Cf. Porter, *Unanswerable Questions*, sec. 5.2, "Objectivation."

and biblical religion. They arose in concentrated form in Rudolf Bultmann's proposal to "demythologize" the New Testament and its kerygma. Readers can find at least three senses for the term 'myth' in Bultmann's work. (1) Myth says something about the transcendent by portraying it as immanent within the world.

> Myth is here used in the sense popularized by the 'History of Religions' school. Mythology is the use of imagery to express the other worldly in terms of this world and the divine in terms of human life, the other side in terms of this side.[65]

(2) Myth is a way to make objectively visible certain truths about human existence. Roger Johnson quotes one of Bultmann's commentators and critics, H. P. Owen:

> "Demythologizing would be more accurately called deobjectifying."[66]

(3) Myth simply comes from a strange culture's worldview. Accounting for the NT worldview was a frequent issue for Bultmann. There are more meanings, but these are enough for now. The first meaning is the way into the second, which we have just bumped into: objectivation.[67] We saw the third sense early, in section 1.8, in Edward Hobbs's distinctions about the conceptualities of alien cultures and the life orientations expressed in them.

Objectivation of faith happens when people take the language of myth literally. It appears in signs and wonders and in biblical literalism, but not only there. Interestingly, TV advertisements qualify as myth on Bultmann's definition, but we don't think of them as mythological because we understand them without interpreting them literally. Another example of "myth" would be Gary Larson's *Far Side* cartoons, which give us a fine portrayal of the limitations of creaturehood.[68] What if real events in history were portrayed in the style of *The Far Side*? The mistakes of literalism

---

[65] This is Bultmann's primary meaning, and it appeared in note 2 on p. 10 of *Kerygma and Myth*. Johnson (p. 7) cites and quotes the original, *Kerygma und Mythos*, p. 22.

[66] Johnson, *The Origins of Demythologizing*, 8–9; he is quoting Owen, *Revelation and Existence*, 15.

[67] To take the first sense literally is both to move to the second sense and also to move into a monophysite theology of divine action. I don't think Rudolf Bultmann had the resources to solve his problem as he posed it, but we do what we can here.

[68] Cf. *Unanswerable Questions*, 106, which correlates Gary Larson with Reinhold Niebuhr's *Human Nature*, ch. VI, par. 1.

are akin to taking *The Far Side* literally. To do that is not just to misunderstand, it would be painfully grotesque. The situation is complicated when the imagined texts in the style of *The Far Side* are about real persons (Jesus of Nazareth), and those complications have never been well explored.

How does contemporary naive literalism work in engaging transcendence? Typically, the believer thinks that Jesus was "physically" raised, and at the same time (if well-catechized) that the raising was not a resuscitation. Problems are dismissed with "it's a sacred mystery," and no further inquiries are made. The believer gets on with the pilgrimage of the life of faith. As we have seen, this colloquial literalism will not withstand inspection; it is incoherent. We are not in the land of propositions, the Principle of Sufficient Reason, the law of noncontradiction, and the other standards of logic that properly apply in the discourse of a naturalistic science. This is how primary naiveté works. The naive are quite *sophisticated*, which is to say they have mastered the details of a language game that is quite subtle and also freighted with many ironies. Sophisticated is not the same thing as self-consciously *critical*: They do not cross into explicitly critical thinking until somebody challenges them, or charges their language game with incoherence, contradictions, make-believe, the unscientific, and so on. All those charges *presuppose* a logical and discursive context of the natural sciences, but that is not what naive literalism is doing. We may ask, once again, what this literalist language game of faith *does* for believers, its users.

> It expresses the transcendent
>   in terms of this world, of the immanent.
>
> It starts its users
>   on the way to embracing all of life as good,
>   in full view of its pains.
>
> It places their lives in history,
>   and the pertinent history changes who they are
>   and what they do with their lives.

The first is Bultmann's definition of myth or objectivation. The last two, of course, are what the Christian faith does for *all* believers. If the first is taken as objectivation without irony, it becomes deeply pathological.[69]

---

[69] It is also monophysite in its expression of divine action; how to do better than that is

The last two are probably not something that a literalist could be very comfortable with. What is more, literalist theology does *not* candidly embrace the pains of life as part of a good life, not when signs and wonders offer to get people out of the pains rather than bring blessing even in the pains of life. Is it really necessary to hide what the faithful are doing when, working through the griefs of life, they embrace the pains as part of a world that is blessed as good?

Typical laypeople think that they are required[70] to read the Resurrection texts "literally," and they know that such things do not happen now, and they know quite well how to get on with their lives in faith without "miracles" today. That this approach shields them unnecessarily from some challenges in theology is never spelled out and never remedied.

More could be said, obviously, but this is enough to get started. This appraisal presupposes the logic of the distributed ontology of human action,[71] in which people do not always know what they are doing, and there are many narratives of their actions. Trouble arises when naive naiveté, challenged to critical thinking by hostile adversaries, becomes tenacious naiveté. Tenacious naiveté is a contradiction in terms. It is also usually undertaken in bad faith, as we have seen. It is an attempt to objectivate the believer's faith, and in so doing, to evade responsibility for his faith.

This book has complained about three best-selling strands in traditional theology, all of them repudiated by the Church from time to time: They are neglect of the inheritance from Second Temple Judaism in Marcionite theology; monophysite theology of divine action; and a cluster of theological instincts that has no single name, but of which objectivation is typical. It is a way of misrepresenting the choice for faith as necessity, by objectivating it, as Peter Berger maintained in *The Sacred Canopy*. Bultmann railed against it in the last chapter of *Jesus Christ and Mythology*.[72] Berger called it bad faith, though it might be simpler just to call it irresponsibility: evasion of responsibility for the faith.

More can be said in answer to our question, "What is going on in biblical literalism?" The believer is, unstated and uncandidly, in the process of wrestling with God in dealing with Limitation. The question always

---

still an incompletely solved puzzle.

[70] By whom? Society? Tradition? Historical accidents? Anti-Christian hecklers?

[71] The distributed ontology was explored in *Living in Spin*.

[72] Bultmann, *Jesus Christ and Mythology*. See also Johnson, *The Origins of Demythologizing*, 2.

arises whether Limitation can really, ultimately, bear blessing. In biblical religion, the answer is affirmative, but there is no proof, for we cannot *see* ultimate reality. There is no answer to the taunt, "Where now, O Israel, is your God?" And so, instead of admitting his role in struggling with God, the believer has conjured up something "objective" that will answer hecklers, quiet internal doubts and anxieties, and get the believer out of responsibility for his chosen act of faith. The allegedly objective events are carefully protected from inspection and criticism, prying scientific eyes, questions about what "actually happened." This reading of the texts serves to validate the effort to get out of Limitation, rather than seek blessing *in* Limitation. It holds out hope that in the end, we are let out of Limitation. But this is only one possible narrative of what the believer is doing. As was argued in *Living in Spin*, virtually all human acts are open to multiple narratives, often in tension with one another.

There is another way to interpret the literalist reading of the Resurrection texts. It allows some comfort in the painful process of spiritual transformation (Mark's *metanoia*) whereby the believer comes to make peace with Limitation in the living of his life as a pilgrimage. The allowable limits of comfort given to those who want signs and wonders were marked in the refusal to canonize the Gospel of Peter. But can the Church still pamper those who want signs and wonders after the Exposure that comes with critical history? That has become more difficult.

The way the texts handle the problem — at least on the reading of them proposed above — is to allow the believer space to grow in the faith, without forcing the believer to grow faster than he is ready to. This appears to be the policy of the Church, not just the text. It was spelled out in Romans (among other places) where Paul counsels against forcing too rigorous application of dietary laws (or anti-laws?) on the scrupulous. He counsels forbearance toward those who *appear* to be "weak." (For what it is worth, it is not at all clear to me that they really are weak, nor that they are unsophisticated just because they are un-academic.) The advice not to push people faster than they can go is incidentally among the marks of the virtue of chastity (respect for others) in Bonnell Spencer's account of the monastic vows.[73] In the perspective of our own culture, or at least the subculture informed by the sciences, this would seem to be tolerance for scientific "heresy" — views that really are inimical to the sciences (as with creationism), and so to the faith in divine trustworthiness that under-

---

[73] Spencer, "The Vows," 7–8.

lies the sciences. In effect, when the Gospels tolerate signs and wonders, they have set a precedent for tolerating monophysite theology of divine action in the world. Was the Church right to do as it did? If it was right then, is it still right in the present? These are only questions. I do not have answers. But it does seem to me wrong to cover up now what was done then, even if it was right then, as in some ways it may have been. The situation has changed since the first century. It may no longer be possible to pamper those who want signs and wonders without driving away those of greater faith who find signs and wonders unnecessary and unbelievable. We shall see this again in the discussion of Ezekiel 34, on p. 223 below.

The believer walking on the way of the Cross moves by stages from primary naiveté through critical thinking to secondary naiveté.[74] The challenge to the Church, and to pastors, is how to care for those capable of critical thinking and in need of secondary naiveté, without traumatizing those still in primary naiveté more than is necessary. To do that would be a form of disrespect, as Bonnell Spencer argued. This was the issue in "The Santa Claus Problem."[75] Yet those who tenaciously hold onto primary naiveté in face of critical thinking obstruct faith for others for whom taking primary naiveté literally is incredible and in bad faith. They have reached critical thinking and need a way to a responsible secondary naiveté. As Lewis Mudge said, "We have no alternative today to working through criticism toward a second naiveté because the first naiveté available to us in our culture is so deeply idolatrous."

The logic of the idolatry of tenacious primary naiveté is simple enough. Modern apologetics based on "miracles" is not just incoherent, it is unbiblical. It flies in the face of what the Bible actually says. Those who defend "miracles" defend primary naiveté against a culture that has moved on in some measure to critical thinking. They protest "no fair" and blame the Enlightenment when people who argue from the no-exceptions presuppositions of modern science dismiss "miracles" as unscientific.[76] The apologetic of miracles would claim that the supernatural, in and of itself, is objective evidence of divine action in the world. That is not how the Bible handles the issue. The plague stories in the Exodus are as clear an example of a pre-scientific worldview as one could hope for. But

---

[74] The terms appear in Paul Ricoeur, *The Symbolism of Evil* 351–352. They appear in Lewis Mudge's introduction to Ricoeur's *Essays on Biblical Interpretation*, nn. 17–18, citing *The Symbolism of Evil*.

[75] Porter, *In the Beginning, Exodus*, Section 9.2.

[76] For only one example, Keener, *Miracles*.

the text goes on to say that Pharaoh's magicians worked counter-miracles aplenty.[77] Neither the plague stories nor the parting of the Sea of Reeds later on get the reader out of the choice put to Israel in the end of Joshua: "Which gods will you serve?" It remains a choice, not something objective. The same is true in the New Testament: signs and wonders by false prophets.[78] The Markan whiplash, undermining the objectivating reading of his miracle stories, works the same way. The Bible discreetly but expressly rejects the miracle apologetic so dear to the literalists. So what is going on in the literalist reading of the miracle stories?[79] Miracle here is not seriously different from magic, and the purpose of both is wish fulfillment, getting out of Limitation rather than dealing with Limitation as it is. Not all theology is this corrupt, as Merold Westphal remarks at length in the first eight chapters of *God, Guilt, and Death*, but literalist miracle theology is pure junk. Why is the Bible forbidden to speak in ironic and non-literal language that we know well? Why is the Bible restricted to a sacred language that was conjured up in the nineteenth century to shield the pious from the facts of life?

What happens if one asks the literalists, "Why do you *need* signs and wonders?" What if the texts were not meant in a literal way (as in section 8.1)? Or what if the texts reflect the strange but mistaken conceptuality of a different culture? (Liberal theology uses this as grounds to dismiss any challenge by the miracle and Resurrection texts; literalism uses it to dismiss the challenge of ironic readings.) Then the presuppositions of the literalists would begin to come out, and we would begin to see some candor, and probably some confusion as well.

Return to the basic question of philosophy of religion, "Where does your proposed ultimate reality show itself in the world?" Christians answer with the events (among others) of the life of Jesus in the first century. Those who are not Marcionite would place Jesus in the context of the prior history, shaped by the Exodus, simply because the evangelists themselves do that. They use the prior history to make sense of Jesus — not the other way around.[80] The question asks where ultimate reality shows itself in

---

[77] E.g. Exodus 7.11. Cf. p. 160.

[78] E.g. Mark 13.22, Matthew 24.24.

[79] Its theology is satirized in modern saccharine portraits of Jesus that have been photoshopped to show Jesus with a Superman shirt underneath his first-century costume. Google "Jesus as superman" and you can easily find several.

[80] See the remarks about Exodus typology in the New Testament, section 3.1 above.

the world *as it is*,[81] but the literalist readings of the Resurrection texts allege significant interference with the world as it normally is, as would be characteristic of a monophysite theology of divine action. The alleged exception is not innocent. It serves to validate a quest to get out of Limitation *ultimately*. It silently presupposes that the world as we know it is defective. Whether it is recognized or not, this takes exception to the goodness of the created world (and God) declared in Genesis 1. The rejection of the pains of life as barren is a concession to exilic religion that doesn't really belong in historical-covenantal religion.[82]

8.5 Violations of Laws of Nature

Discussions of the Resurrection today inevitably entrain questions about violations of natural laws. It is not a law of physics (though it might instantiate some) that animals (including humans), once dead, do not come back to life, but we take it as a natural law. We do not know of any exceptions in fact, though mistakes still continue to be made: the comatose are mistaken for dead until they revive. And there are obviously many exceptions in fiction, traditional myths, and legends. How should we interpret the Resurrection texts? My reading of the texts above is that they work to put the reader to the question: can Limitation really bear blessing? The answer is a choice, not something objective or empirical.

Most of the Church would like to have it both ways: In effect, they claim that the Resurrection was not a resuscitation but worked as one nonetheless. This gets them out of the responsibilities of a falsifiable claim, but it still gives them the comforts of an objective claim. It shifts the responsibility for faith from the believer to the alleged events but it does not spell out what those events might have been. It is objectivation, and objectivation is an evasion of responsibility, in bad faith.

There are whole provinces in the literature of theology and philosophy of religion where people try to find ways for the Resurrection texts to be literally true, reports of an event rather than a theological meditation on the significance of the Cross. They never fully spell out what they are

---

[81] This does not mean the Church has to accept the secular world's ontology and metaphysics; I shall take exception to them in section 9.1 below, "Naturalism, Nominalism, Materialisms."

[82] Cf. Westphal, *God, Guilt, and Death*, chapters 9–11.

doing. Are they making claims about where the molecules of Jesus' dead body went? They seem to claim that the molecules went someplace out of the ordinary. Having been uncandid and inexplicit, they cannot be held responsible for claims they did not really make, but they seem to have made such claims anyway. I experience such theology and its arguments as tedious, boring, and depressing — oppressively, suffocatingly depressing. It is yet one more attempt to get out of Limitation, and it is self-deceived and in bad faith.

What we say is that the pains of life (including Limitation) have borne blessing for us in the past, and we trust they will in the future as they have in the past, but there is no formula to calculate how that might happen.[83] That is the answer to the challenge of the Resurrection texts.

Return from the Resurrection to the healing miracles in the Gospels. There is a professional association for those who have healing touch: those who can, with a laying on of hands, sometimes induce healing. Healing Touch (a trademarked term) is a method used by nurses. The American Holistic Nurses Association has published on the therapeutic technique, and the Veterans Administration has made a film on Healing Touch. Unexplained medical healings do happen all the time, yet we would never think of starting a new religion based on them.[84] As much (more rarely) goes for healing touch:

> http://www.healingtouchcalifornia.com/
> http://www.healingtouchprogram.com/about/what-is-healing-touch

Nobody seriously thinks there are any violations of natural laws involved. Unexplained medical healings are common.[85]

We give thanks, heartfelt thanks, to God when such unexpected healings happen. But what is going on when we ascribe an event to God? Are

---

[83] This is to restate the two most basic elements of biblical faith: In the first, we embrace this world as good, in full view of its pains, which is not an easy commitment. In the second, we construe human life in this world as essentially historical, not just part of nature; and we can see where ultimate reality has shown itself *in history*.

[84] We also would never think of vivisecting such patients to resolve questions about violations of natural laws (or seek *new* natural laws).

[85] This depends on what passes for an explanation. Healings after changes in diet and exercise are certainly common, though we do not understand in biochemical detail. Some others may be perplexing and are infrequent but not rare.

we talking about physical causes or is this some other discourse of causation?[86] What is going on when we give thanks to God for an event that cannot be traced to him as "cause" in any physical sense? Is it objectivation and is subjectivity really the only other alternative? Is objectivation bad faith? Denial or evasion of responsibility? Is there only one discourse, only one logic by which we can deal with events for which we have more thanks to give than just to particular other human persons?

Belief in something like signs and wonders can be found today, but outside biblical religion, and with a theology markedly different from biblical theology. Joseph Laycock and Daniel Wise survey some of the recent literature on the paranormal.[87] What we are calling signs and wonders they call the paranormal. Modern Christians who would read the miracle texts literally, that is as reports of signs and wonders that violate natural laws, become strangely Troeltschian about reports of such phenomena outside of a Christian context. Why do they treat reports of the paranormal that they like differently from those of many cultures, well attested by anthropologists, that they don't like?[88]

I think there is a simple answer, and we saw it above, on p. 170 with the plagues in the Exodus. In the ancient world, from the Exodus to the first century and perhaps beyond, what we would call the paranormal, preternatural, or otherwise unnatural was for them a sign of some human reality. A "miracle" could disclose the work of any of the gods; which one is not determined simply by its anomalous character. *Which* existential reality was disclosed had to be known on other grounds, usually a choice, to be made by people who can tell the difference between one god and another. Today, we have forgotten all that, and biblical literalists take the miracle stories to be proof of an act of God, simply because they violate natural laws.[89] Thus the ancient perspective on the paranormal as posing a *ques-*

---

[86] There are many senses of causation, not just Aristotle's four. Other senses of *efficient* causation can be found in Collingwood, *Essay on Metaphysics*, chapters 29–34.

[87] See Laycock and Wise, "Recent Scholarly Approaches to Paranormal Belief." *Religious Studies Review* 40 no. 2 (2014/06) 69. For a wide bibliography, see the course syllabus of Nurit Stadler at Hebrew University in Jerusalem: http://pluto.huji.ac.il/˜msstad/AnthropologyOfMiracles.htm.

[88] Keener supplies many examples also. But one might well ask of his argument, does it really take a thousand pages to notice that pre-scientific cultures and subcultures have pre-scientific explanations for how things work? Keener cannot see that his argument for the supernatural and against science is circular; it has presupposed its conclusions, not proven them.

[89] This, of course, is exemplary of modern monophysite theology of divine action.

8.5 Violations of Laws of Nature

tion of faith has been replaced by a modern perspective on the paranormal as objective *proof* of faith. Violation of physical law as the work of other gods is not considered. Such violations have to be rebutted (usually on Troeltschian grounds) because they would threaten a literalist and monophysite hermeneutic of divine action if allowed to stand.

Why do we say that there are no exceptions to natural laws? And what you mean "we," theologian? Who is "we"? Probably the majority of Christian theologians still admit of exceptions to natural laws, but not all do. I am in the minority that does not.

So why do we reject the argument that "God made natural laws, so God can suspend them at will, at his pleasure"? It is not just that we agree with Aquinas when he says grace builds on nature but does not interfere with nature.[90] We do, but we disagree with Aquinas in the next breath, about nature itself. For Aquinas, the model for nature was Aristotelian biology, in which one can make generalizations, but generalizations admit of exceptions. Aquinas, so far as I am aware, knew nothing of natural *laws* in the sense of seventeenth-century physics. Conservation principles are only the first of natural laws, and physics knows a lot more than just conservation laws.[91]

Our faith in the orderliness and knowability of nature is based on our biblical faith in the goodness and reliability of God. Faith in the intelligibility of nature comes from the doctrine of creation; Michael Foster showed that in three articles in *Mind* in 1934, 1935, and 1936. But faith in the reliability of natural laws, without exception? That comes also from faith in God, of trust in his faithfulness, his troth.

A Chalcedonian theology of divine action has no disagreement with so-called scientific atheists about exceptions to natural laws. There are no exceptions. Monophysites of divine action, of course, insist on violations of natural laws, and they purvey the theology that rightly infuriates the atheists (and saddens Chalcedonians).

We may not know the laws of nature, but that doesn't matter very much. To put it a little differently, Chalcedonians and atheists agree that ultimate reality is such that nature follows natural laws without exceptions or deviations.[92] That sets aside questions about God, history, hermeneu-

---

[90] *Summa Theologica*, 1.1.8 ad 2, among other places. "Gratia non tollat naturam."

[91] Spielberg and Anderson, *Seven Ideas that Shook the Universe*.

[92] Chalcedonians and scientific atheists also disagree about something else that is very important. For what it is worth, the atheists usually think that the *monophysite* (not Chal-

tics, literature, and the meaning of life outside of the sciences. About all those things we doubtless disagree. That the world is intelligible *sub specie naturae* we agree. Why? For "atheists," I suppose it just is.[93] (So far, so good.) "Why is nature intelligible?" is an unanswerable question; the intelligibility of the world as nature simply has to be accepted. It is an assumption and it is an act of trust — trust in the troth of ultimate reality. Without it, ultimate reality has failed us. Without it, science would be impossible. For Christians, leaving unanswerable questions without comment is not quite the last thing that can be said. We approach the mystery of the intelligibility of nature on a personal basis, even though that mystery is not itself a person. In other words, in Chalcedonian theology, the issue of the troth of ultimate reality is spelled out. To follow that inquiry would take us beyond the scope of this book into the meaning of transcendence.

8.6 Acts of God

Restate the problem of acts of God. We saw it in *Living in Spin*, section 5.3.2, "Acts of Nature, Acts of God," but there the problem was only noted and then postponed. This book so far has brought us through the career of world-affirming historical religion of the Christian variety from the beginnings to the present, showing us a little of the perplexities of our own time. The themes have been generalized monophysite theology, half-Marcionite theology, and a general evasion of responsibility for confessional commitments. They have come to a focus in the interpretation of the Resurrection texts because a literal Resurrection[94] is the last fallback defense of the three theological mistakes just named. Having shown a different way of reading the Resurrection texts, how might one generalize it to the action and presence of God more generally? The answers we can propose here

---

cedonian) interpretation of the Catholic faith is the correct one — it just happens to be false. So prospects for even limited agreement that theological concerns are not admissible as explanations in the natural sciences are fairly dim.

[93] Like analytic theists faced with demands for proofs, Carl Sagan endeavored to provide them. He thought the intelligibility of the natural world was empirically demonstrable. Langdon Gilkey knew better. The exchange was discussed in my *Where, Now, O Biologists*, sec. 7.4, p. 215. In effect, Sagan was taking lessons in how to be bad from bad Christian apologetics: trying to prove what is in fact a confessional commitment. The logic of such a confessional commitment is, "we trust that the future will be good to us as the past has," but that is not an empirical proof. It also does not say *how* the future will bring blessing as the past has.

[94] I.e., a resuscitation or something like it.

8.6 Acts of God

must be preliminary and a mere sketch. That is enough for the present book. There is more to come in *Unanswerable Questions*.

Relating to God happens on a personal basis, and that grows out of human interpersonal relations, which we know first (temporally if not logically). Interpersonal relations have not preoccupied philosophers, who prefer to understand humans first as individuals and then add other people later if at all. Exceptions are infrequent. There is a place in Heidegger's *Being and Time* where it is possible to spot the mistake and begin to correct it, starting from what he does give us. We shall see that other people, or better, interpersonhood (to give a barbarous name to what we do not understand), is part of the ontological constitution of everything. Heidegger mostly overlooked this, though not everywhere. It was discussed in *Living in Spin*, section 3.4.1, "Heidegger's Dasein and Other People." Human being is different from the being of things in the world: it is the sort of being that has a stake in its own being. This was a very perceptive insight but it leaves out its most interesting part. Any particular human being is not the only one who has a stake in its being. Other people do also, even before it was born and after it is gone. This Heidegger left out in his definition on p. 12 of *Being and Time*. In Kierkegaard's language, a human self is "a relationship that relates itself to itself" — but it is constituted as such by an Other. To jump directly to a transcendent Other is to move a little too fast; we are constituted as human proximately by ordinary other humans, and in the logic of coming to understand oneself, God (the transcendent Other) comes later in time if earlier in logic. It is that logic we are interested in here, in aid of understanding the action and presence of God (to the extent that they even can be understood). In effect, to be a self, to relate to oneself, to have a stake in one's own being, can be done only by and through simultaneously relating to other people. A human can be a person only by relating to other persons. Personhood is always interpersonal.

What Heidegger does give us in Section 26 of *Being and Time* is the presence of other people in the constitution of ordinary things (tools) in the world. In a tool we meet other people for whom also the tool is useful. As much could be said of mere inanimate nature, from sunsets to rocks big or small. They are all part of a place where humans can dwell, part of the world as "home." Third parties are also present in our knowledge of other people, but that is not in Heidegger's account.

Other people are present as critics and judges, as collaborators in the social construction of reality, and as existential support in joy and sorrow.

These are but examples; they can be developed in many ways. Focus for the moment on other people as critics. They can validate my ideas of myself and of things in the world, and they can correct me. They challenge, simply by being present. What if they are wrong, as they often are? All of them save a few, as in the early stages of a scientific paradigm dispute? With what logic does one criticize *them*? They are not infallible, and they may not even mean well. Yet to make sense of anything in the world, things or selves, is implicitly to be in conversation with them.

The traditional solution to this problem, at least in the Greek-based philosophy of the Western tradition, is Platonist. It posits "correct" answers to all questions, in ideal forms. The Aristotelian version is (in my opinion) better but it is still Platonist at heart. The approach proposed here is different. There are no other persons to whom we could appeal *ultimately*, real or ideal, particular or generalized, in this world or any other. We seek an interpersonal troth after all persons have done what they can. We seek beyond them. This was explained by D. Z. Phillips in regard to why-questions.[95] Some think that all why-questions have answers; some know they still ask after reasons and answers have done all they can. The situation with persons parallels that with questions about the structure of the world (that's what why-questions ask about). This is a claim that is not defended or even expanded here, and even in *Unanswerable Questions* it will remain very incompletely explored. But for those in biblical religion I think it makes sense. This is not an argument for biblical religion, but only an explanation of it. Inasmuch as it is a confessional commitment, not something that could be proven correct, there are many ways to get out of biblical religion for those who want out.

Look more at what we have so far. We relate to other persons in our relating to everything. Beyond other persons we still relate in a personal way, after intramundane other persons have done all they can. But there is no other beyond all persons, and so we are up against something that is more like the void of H. Richard Niebuhr's "Faith in Gods and in God."[96] When Moses asks for a name at the Burning Bush, all he gets is "I shall be with you as who I am shall I be with you."[97] The answer speaks to

---

[95] Phillips, *The Problem of Evil*, 133–134. It is quoted in my own *Basic Concepts of Biblical Religion*, 82.

[96] In Niebuhr, *Radical Monotheism*, 122. It is worth some note that Niebuhr did not capitalize "void," as I did out of instinct for many years. But Niebuhr was right, and I was wrong.

[97] Murray, *The Problem of God*, 10. See also p. 29 above.

8.6 Acts of God

our relating-to-others without giving us an other. It also speaks directly to our fundamental anxiety, enabling us to live in it without allaying it. Such is the transcendent Other of biblical religion. Is this a category error? Probably. Is this a deliberate category error? Possibly. Is such an error wrong? That depends on your basic life orientation — or your philosophy and theology. Remember Stephen Mulhall's observation that for Anglophone analytic philosophy, a contradiction is a sign of a logical dead end, but for Continental philosophy, it may offer real insight into human existence.[98] What goes for contradictions goes also for category errors. Biblical religion is not for the irony-challenged.

At this point, we can take the definition of action from *Living in Spin* and instantiate it with respect to God. "Action happens when a contingency affects someone's interests and is narratable."[99] The actor is implicit in the narrative.[100] When the contingency is simply something intramundane, I don't think asking for connections to other intramundane phenomena (ordinary why-questions) can ever get to God. To ask how things in the world fit together is always to ask how they fit together *for humans*, or as a home for humans. In other words, to ask about things in the world may not mention humans, but they are always implicitly present because what such questions ask about is a home for humans. The meaning of "why" changes if ultimate reality is sought. To ask about a contingency that affects our interests and turn the questioning to ultimate reality produces a narrative in which the implicit actor is beyond all intramundane persons. To ask where and how ultimate reality shows itself in the world is to ask about acts of God. An act of God is more than just a clearing in which it is possible to see ultimate reality as it shows itself. It shows the presence of ultimate reality as personal and as in some sense in a personal relationship with humans.[101] It is this interpersonation beyond all intramundane persons that enables us to live in the world.

Biblical religion may not be for the irony-challenged but it is usually packaged for them.[102] The irony has been tamed, defanged, domesti-

---

[98] Mulhall *Philosophical Myths of the Fall*, 12.

[99] Porter, *Living in Spin*, 5 and passim, especially in chapter 5. Note in passing that an act depends on its possible narratives (of which there are many), and so it arises ontologically in narrative.

[100] Sometimes an actor hovers above a narrative. Implication is not always obvious.

[101] "I shall be with you as who I am," etc., Exodus 3.14.

[102] On a more positive note, the pilgrimage of faith usually means growing into the irony of biblical religion.

cated, hidden, objectivated — or just eliminated. In monophysite theology, the irony of transcendence is drawn into the world on the world's terms; with even half-Marcionite theology, the roots of Christian transcendence in the prior history of world-affirming historical religion are obscured; with evasion of responsibility, anxiety-conducive confessional commitments are hidden in so-called "proofs" of the validity of Christianity. The present book does not seek a phenomenological understanding of our not-understanding of transcendence.[103] Something less is sufficient: if we know a little of what we are doing in speaking of God, it is possible to trace through Christian history the problematic engagements that have preoccupied this book: monophysite acts of God, half-Marcionite theology, evasion of responsibility, sacred canopies, and just trying to get out of the pains of life ultimately, leaving the pains unredeemable.

8.7 Confessing the Resurrection

At the end of section 8.1, I mentioned Thomas Sheehan for calling attention to the many meanings of ἐγείρω (to raise, etc.), some of them as un-physical as common usage in English. It may help to pursue the possibilities that Sheehan opened up. Sheehan is working in a much larger tradition that has reconstructed the history and growth of the Resurrection texts (at least in a provisional way) without resorting to violations of laws of nature, the modern supernatural, literalism, objectivation, evasion of responsibility, the transphysical, and so on. Bernard Brandon Scott provides a summary of the results of work on the Resurrection texts.[104] In its final section, "Reclaiming Resurrection," designed to recover the Resurrection from literalists, Scott traces his exploration through many examples, some in literature, some in real life, of people whose actions were shaped by the Resurrection, but he doesn't actually *state* the Resurrection itself. It is a strategy that has much to commend it: it speaks only of what we *can* see and keeps silence before what we cannot see. So it is with some considerable trepidation that I attempt in this section to spell out a little more, with as much respect as I can for what we do not and cannot know. Some things we have said already, in the question whether we are saved *from* or *in* the pains of life. That question may be repeated in the form, "What

---

[103] *Unanswerable Questions* will have a little more but not a definitive solution to the problem.
[104] Scott, *The Trouble with Resurrection*.

does it mean to say that we are saved *in* the pains of life?" And how does that apply to Jesus? What follows are fragments of an answer to another persistent question here,

> Where does your proposed ultimate reality show itself in life, the world, history, or human experience?

We follow Sheehan in his observations about the meanings of ἐγείρω but we start in English, for the English verb *to raise* has as much ambiguity and wealth of meaning as the Greek does. It is not as if some Greek text between the Passion and St. Paul has already said this. We are speaking on our own, or I am, on my own responsibility. That is legitimate, for eventually we have to answer for ourselves. Even if we say that events in the past have ontologically transformed our lives, they cannot take for us the responsibility for our choices. It does not matter that we do not know the history of the tradition from the days after the crucifixion to its first expressions in New Testament documents. There can be many answers to the question above but the one here best advances the present inquiry:

> Ultimate reality has raised up Jesus in his this-worldly ending as a clearing in which it is possible to see what really living really is.

It is a preliminary statement, and it says nothing that would turn the Resurrection into something *objective*, something that would take the responsibility for the faith off the shoulders of believers.

"Ultimate reality:" we do not name God in personal terms yet, acknowledging that God rests in mystery before we come personally to what is not a person among other persons.

"Ultimate reality:" this cautious term also reminds readers that people do not agree on what ultimate reality is, and so the statement above is a confessional commitment, not something objective. Those who want to will dismiss it as "subjective," i. e., irresponsible, without any claims on other people. On the contrary, it makes a strong existential claim on them, which is why they have to dismiss it.

"Raised up as a clearing": This is an answer to our question about where ultimate reality (u-r, for short) shows itself. A clearing is not objective. Literalist readings of the Resurrection texts pretend to be. Nevertheless, it is an *ontological* claim, even if it is not *objective*. It is about who we are and what made us who we are. If we disagree about ontology (and people do[105]), that is a separate issue.

"The *ending* of Jesus": the wording is cautious and it includes more than just the Passion (and even that story is complex). We are saved in the pains of life but that does not mean we like the pains for their own sake. Jesus didn't like pain any more than we do; that is clear from his prayers in Gethsemane. He wanted out, and so do we, but that doesn't always happen. To re-understand the problem of pain, notice the institution of the Eucharist. What the Eucharist gives us as a remedy for the pains of life is the presence of ultimate reality on a personal basis. That gives us something more, the constructive presence of ordinary other people. This is an ontological phenomenon that we will develop in *Unanswerable Questions*. There we shall introduce a neologism, "interpersonation": we interpersonate in everything we do, even as individuals. That is, we relate to other people, actual and possible, whether we acknowledge it or not. Other people are part of the ontological constitution of our actions and, indeed, of our selves. While it is true that some Christians reenact the Passion from time to time, it is not the primary focus of the clearing in Jesus' ending. That focus is in the Eucharist, which reenacts the interpersonation between the Lord and his friends. As Gregory Dix has said, "Men have found no better thing than this to do" for all the occasions where we want to place our lives in their largest context.[106]

The text above is, in a sense, a claim because it does make a claim even on those who disagree: In the same sense I would make a claim on other people even if I believed that the earth is flat. Not a credible or plausible claim, and a claim easily fended off, but a claim nonetheless. The Resurrection is not an objective claim, it is not a demonstrable or provable claim, it is an existential claim, as all human commitments about ultimate reality are. A little bit of such claims was developed in *Living in Spin*, but not much, and probably not enough.

The extent and power of the claim can be seen in the responses to it. Those who choose differently cannot bring themselves to meet head-on the claim that u-r has raised Jesus up in his suffering as a clearing. They respond to it as if it were (in other meanings of $\dot{\epsilon}\gamma\epsilon i\rho\omega$) an objective claim about a resuscitation; and so interpreted, the objective claim can be dismissed easily. When challenged by objectivist hecklers, some believers

---

[105] See section 9.1.

[106] Dix, *The Shape of the Liturgy*, 743–745.

8.7 Confessing the Resurrection

accepted the planted assumption and bought into objectivation and resuscitation themselves. This was not innocent, for objectivation has many comforts, as we have already seen. Human suffering makes a claim on other people, and it is that claim that we are trying to understand.

The paraphrase above does not, so far as I am aware, appear in so many words in the New Testament, and not obviously in the early texts. Something like it does appear in Peter's speech in Acts 3.13 (a late text), where he says, "it is the God of Abraham, Isaac, and Jacob, the God of our ancestors, who has glorified his servant Jesus ..." (Jerusalem Bible; the RSV is similar). Peter doesn't even use the verb ἐγείρω, to raise. The text has ἐδόξασεν, to *glorify*, whose effective meaning is closer to the above answer to the basic question of ultimate reality than to any literalist reading of texts about raisings. Acts was written late in the first century and does not by itself get us to earlier tradition. So once again we are proceding on our own responsibility, not on the basis of any text from before Paul, for there are none.

In the confessional statement above, "What really living really is," a Greek phrase with a somewhat different meaning is ζωή αἰώνιος, frequent in John. Literally, it means eternal life (endless in time), but in effect it also means authentic living, really living. It is about the answer to questions about ultimate reality. To tell what ultimate reality is is to tell what really living really is.

Others before me have said that ultimate reality comes not to get us out of an evil world but to bless us in a good world: "God enters into the world to save his people, not by freeing them from the world, but by being with them in it."[107] What to do about the pains? Edward Hobbs put it that "suffering for others (both *because of* others and *for the sake of*) others is what God does; and so *Suffering for others is part of the calling of those who would share in God's life* (ζωή αἰώνιος)."[108]

What if you don't care for *this* suffering as the clearing in which u-r blesses us in this world of pain? There are plenty of others. Elie Wiesel, watching the Nazis hang three prisoners in a concentration camp, answered the question, "Where is God?" by replying, "Where is He? Here He is — He is hanging here on this gallows ..."[109] One can find it in the Bavli, Menahoth 29b.[110] The text alludes briefly to rabbi Akiba's suffering and

---

[107] Westphal, *God, Guilt, and Death*, 222.
[108] Unpublished instructional materials, 1970s. Some italics removed.
[109] Wiesel, *Night*, 76.
[110] Soncino edition, Seder Kodashim 1, 190.

death in the siege of Jerusalem in the Bar Kochba revolt, circa 135 CE. But any suffering will do. What I think one may not do is transfer the clearing to all the others and hide the fact that the Jesus's suffering became the pivotal change in the history of biblical religion. It was in the Passion that Christian believers worked out the place of suffering in ultimate reality. The passion became the presence of ultimate reality to us in our own sufferings. The other clearings are what St. Bernard called "the third comings of Christ."[111]

Are the texts ambiguous? Yes. Are they intentionally ambiguous? Maybe. Could the New Testament writers have intended ambiguity, especially without spelling it out or labeling it *as* ambiguity? Maybe. We live in ambiguity, and respecting it gives people room to grow in their own faith and on their own pilgrimage into conversion of life. By leaving ambiguity open, the Gospels defend themselves against being turned into another theory of everything. In doing so, they remain a challenge. A respectful challenge. Is the truth of the matter ambiguous? Certainly. But that is another story, for another book.

8.8 Exposure, Limitation, and Need

The choice of a basic life orientation is always circular in its logic because some of it has always already been presupposed in talking about the world at all. If what follows is just an explanation, the circularity is hermeneutical. If the explanation is taken as a proof, the circularity becomes vicious.[112] The hermeneutical circle is in some ways analogous to a mathematical iterative approximation.[113] In both, the progress to some sort of convergent solution is signaled by a discrepancy, showing how the reading still fails to converge. In basic life orientation I would conjecture that that role is played by the pains of life: they signal the failure to come to ultimate happiness, in which all pains are comforted, all hearts are open, all desires known, and no secrets are hid. We have met those pains under the terms Exposure, Limitation, and Need.

Many times we have said that the challenge posed by the Gospels is a

---

[111] St. Bernard, Sermo 5, In adventu domini, 1–3, Opera Omnia, editio Cisterc. 4 (1966), 188–190. It is translated in the Breviary for Wednesday of week 1 of Advent. He says that the third comings of Christ are between the other two — in everyday life, now.

[112] See section 5.6, "Hermeneutical Circularity" in *Basic Concepts of Biblical Religion*.

[113] Not in all ways: there is no metric, and it is not objective as mathematics is.

choice whether we are saved in getting *out* of the pains of life, Limitation conspicuously, or saved *in* them. Limitation comes with Exposure and Need. These we saw in sec. 3.3, in our first reading of the New Testament.

A fair answer to the basic question of the philosophy of religion, "What is your proposed ultimate reality?" has to deal with the pains of life. The Gospels do that through many narratives, and I would like instead to propose a summary in a more philosophical vein, despite all the risks that entails. It was promised early, on p. 15 above, and most of my own writing has been based on it. I learned it from Edward Hobbs.[114] All of human life falls into three broad categories and the pains of life follow the pattern. The roots are cultural, in the Indo-European tripartite worldview. The story is well told elsewhere and need not be repeated here, though some credit may be given. It was Georges Dumézil who discovered the pattern in Indo-European mythology and C. Scott Littleton who canvassed his work to bring it to the English-speaking world.[115] That tripartite perspective on life has not attracted much attention or criticism from philosophers, and contrasts from outside the Indo-European language family have not been sought. So the present study has given hostages to future research and controversy. Nevertheless, thinking in these terms is what we have, for the time being. This analysis is itself an example of cultural relativity conditioning religion.

To proceed, there are three aspects of life: order, action, and sustenance. Disappointment in them comes respectively as Exposure, Limitation, and Need. To affirm human life in this world as good in full view of its pains is to embrace each of Exposure, Limitation, and Need as blessing-bearing. The Gospels show Jesus's actions as cleansing, raising, and feeding those in need — in effect, meeting Exposure, Limitation, and Need.

The series Exposure, Limitation, and Need has an application in the life of theological education. Every non-literalist seminarian quickly learns that the principal challenges to theology come not from science but from critical history, historical and cultural relativity, and religious pluralism. Some of these don't require a seminary education: many have seen the challenges from pluralism, and many of them have given up on unique

---

[114] See especially his remarks quoted in Porter and Hobbs, "The Trinity and the Indo-European Tripartite Worldview."

[115] Littleton, *The New Comparative Mythology: An Anthropological Assessment of the Theories of Georges Dumézil*.

claims of biblical religion, because they don't know any cogent unique claims of biblical religion. In critical history, the truth about our history comes out. In cultural relativity, we see our roots in human choices made in the history of religions. In religious pluralism, we encounter others in their humanness and demands on us.[116]

We trust that the truth will bring blessing — but that is not always easy. Just ask your students, "Does the truth do you any good when the truth hurts?" They will answer in the affirmative, but unless they are *very* pious, they will hesitate before answering, because they know how much the truth can hurt. We trust that Limitation bears blessing also, but in it we are destroyed in the end, sometimes at cost of horrendous injustice and suffering. Embracing Limitation can only be done by faith and appeal to examples in history. It is not something that can be proven. Need is similar: we would all like to think of ourselves as benevolent (this we learned from biblical religion), but we also put limits to how much we will give.

We don't embrace the pains themselves, but we trust that good comes *in* Exposure, Limitation, and Need, rather than in spite of them. Trusting them to bring some sort of good is the only thing that makes it possible to live without platonist certainty. It is what enables us to leave unanswerable questions unanswered, instead of pretending we have answers. It enables us to give up the Platonist quest for control and learn to live with the precariousness of creaturehood. It is what makes it possible to bear being wrong and found out as wrong. It is what makes it possible to bring grieving over Limitation to its final stage (as in Kübler-Ross), one of hope. Need is what opens us to other people, and with them, a constructive and hopeful response to the pains of life. H. Richard Niebuhr said "the causes for which we live all die."[117] Why? There is no reason or cause, but the phenomenon is real nonetheless: he spoke of it as a void from which all things come and to which all things return.[118] Why is this a kind of hope, rather than despair? It would be an error to mistake it for nihilism and despair, but those still devoted to one or another "cause" readily do that. Such "causes" are defenses against the limitations of creaturehood and accepting creaturehood means accepting not being in control.[119]

Embracing Exposure, Limitation, and Need is what makes biblical

---

[116] See Porter, "History, Relativity, and Pluralism."
[117] Niebuhr, *Radical Monotheism*, 122.
[118] I don't think he meant to invoke Neoplatonism wholesale in these remarks.
[119] Niebuhr, *The Nature and Destiny of Man*, vol. I, chapter 6, first paragraph.

faith possible in the (post)-modern world. It is what makes the pains of life bearable in faith, hope, and trust; especially change in history, meaning critical history, historical and cultural relativity, and religious pluralism.

This is what comes with rereading the Resurrection texts as an invitation to *metanoia* rather than as a promise of getting out of the pains of life. My purpose in this brief J-walk through the technical problem of reading the Resurrection texts is to reassert the basic faith that God provides blessings even in the pains of life, without putting conditions on God in that faith. This is one instance of the central contention of this book, that the Church has lost some of its chief commitments, but also that the Church has ample resources from within its tradition to correct its mistakes.

Chapter 9

Problems in the Culture

We concluded our historical survey with chapter 7. In the initial applications in chapter 8, we focused on monophysite theology, with less attention given to the kinds and degrees of Marcionite theology. Monophysite theology of divine action plays into a general evasion of responsibility in objectivation. It is time to look at some of the problems in the world. The Church has not done a particularly good job of clarifying its disagreements with the world, and it may help to do a little of that work here.

9.1 Naturalism, Nominalism, Materialism

Naturalism is a way of approaching problems so as to bracket history, narrative, choice, responsibility, ambiguity, art, beauty, morality, and probably more. What is left is what we know (scientifically) as *nature*. In this perspective, things be and move according to rules and both the motions and the rules are unambiguous. In some sciences, the motions and changes are quantifiable, thus inviting mathematics into their discourses.

This bracketing is all to the good, in order to ask and answer questions in physics and other modern sciences. It is not so good if the banished questions are not just banished but abolished, never to be returned to in any other discipline. That would not just bracket the humanities but eliminate them. In my own lifetime, the fate of the humanities has been grim. They are misunderstood or forgotten, and what they have to offer is more and more just lost.

History, by contrast, is about human actions, and there are many ways to conceive of human actions. The traditional way, going back at least to Aristotle, borrows the language and logic of naturalism: An action is a caused motion, in an entity whose motions come from causes within itself. I argued against that conception of action, taken from Aristotle's *Physics* and *On the Soul*, at length in *Living in Spin*. The way to do that is to notice that choices have been made already in the discussion of any human act: They answer the question, "Yes, but *which* motions? And *which* causes?" In other words, an act presupposes a narrative, and the relation of motions and narrative is circular.[1] There are many motions, and which ones matter is not a question of physics or any other natural science. Mattering is not a naturalistic concept. It is human-relative in contrast to physics (among other natural sciences). In physics, human involvements have been abstracted from, to the extent that that is possible. As a general definition, an act can be said to happen when some contingency affects someone's interests and is narratable. Motions come later, if at all.

Some consequences: Acts (human and otherwise) are ambiguous, open to multiple narratives, possibly narratives that are simultaneously true but mutually inconsistent, or at least in great tension. (This can occur when different narratives answer "why did such-and-such happen?")

Contrast the ontology of the world of physics: That world is subdividable into *systems*[2] that have unambiguous *states*, states that are a mathematical function of *time* (i.e., they, or their material substrates, have *trajectories*). In physics, it is usually clear what is in the system and what is not.[3] Approaching the world through the lens of a systems-states-trajectories ontology is built into physics from the ground up. It doesn't matter how you subdivide the world into systems and subsystems; the laws of physics work the same way in all cases.[4] This begins in the differential calculus, where derivatives and integrals are defined as limits that can be approached from any direction.[5]

---

[1] See Porter, *Living in Spin*, section 4.5, looking at Paul Ricoeur on narrative. An act presupposes a narrative of it, but narratives presuppose the act that they narrate.

[2] These distinctions between the ontology of systems that have states that are a function of time and things that are not systems at all appeared earlier in *Living in Spin*, chapter 3.

[3] I am well aware that in quantum mechanics, some of these distinctions are blurred, but those phenomena are not yet well understood, and in any case, they are not part of the problems of this book (ambiguity and choice in the history of biblical religion).

[4] I don't think quantum mechanics is an exception, but showing that would take us far from the present inquiry.

[5] One might think of Stokes' and Gauss's theorems as examples where that invariance appears in the large. Earlier, the first two of Newton's laws of motion tell you that for the most part, you will be dealing with second-order differential equations. The third law

By contrast to science and engineering, the humanities have shown people up as being not in control, not even in control of their own narratives. The cultural instinct to defend oneself against the depredations of hermeneutics is to retreat to naturalism, which offers some measure of control.

This is slightly ironic. People know how to interpret the world, often with great skill, subtlety, and sophistication. But in a naturalistic culture, they would like to deny that they are interpreting the world — at least in high-stakes situations. In nature and the natural sciences, explanations ideally produce phenomena that are determinate. When phenomena are indeterminate, there is still order in their indeterminacy. (Think quantum and statistical mechanics.) The order of nature is invoked to explain human actions: it is nature that acts in me, so I don't have to take responsibility for my actions, or hold others responsible for theirs. But nature doesn't have enough order to explain history or human actions. Those require narrative, not creative statistics.[6] Admitting their own role in interpreting the world *exposes* people as *responsible*, and also sometimes as not being in *control*. This is part of the root anxiety that comes with moving from a world of nature into a world of history. In a historical world, you never entirely know what you are doing, many things are not under your control, and you are nevertheless responsible.[7]

The second feature of secular assumptions about the world after naturalism would be nominalism. There are many accounts of nominalism and its alternatives (platonisms, various realisms). Fortunately, what we need here is less than a comprehensive history of that issue. Nominalism is a way to restrict language and eliminate (or downgrade) modes of expression that cannot be controlled, kinds of expression that raise anxieties. That kind of distrust of language is characteristic of nominalism. We certainly live in a period when language has become problematic. Doris T. Myers remarked as much, and she got it from Wilbur Marshall Urban, in *Language and Reality*.

As philosopher Wilbur M. Urban has pointed out, each turn-

---

underwrites the division of the world into systems and subsystems that is required for differential equations to work properly.

[6] The entertaining counter-position is, of course, Isaac Asimov, in the *Foundation* series. Some philosophers in the twentieth century tried to explain history with laws like those of physics, but they didn't get anywhere.

[7] This was in *Living in Spin*, in a little detail.

ing point in Occidental history has been marked by intense concern about the nature of language. Every time such a period occurs, there are what he calls high and low evaluations of language. The high evaluation involves a belief in the reality of universals and connects the word closely with the thing it designates. It identifies reason with the Word, the Logos, and is therefore closely connected with the Greek-Christian tradition. The low evaluation of language involves some form of nominalism and detaches the word from the thing. It is the characteristic underlying assumption of all periods of empiricism, and Urban calls it the "beginning of skepticism."[8]

The features of distrust that we need appear in the attempt to limit language to propositions, in which terms are allowed only to *refer* (as names do), and refer to things in the world that can be comprehended in such referential acts. That means that the challenges of irony (even the comic strips), fiction, any kind of language other than propositions literally interpreted can all be dismissed and thereby evaded. Most of the power of narrative may also be evaded. Chapter 8 was enough to show that literalist instincts, whether nominalist or platonist, domesticate or just undermine much of the Gospel challenge. Nominalism is the other side of platonisms, in this case, disappointed platonisms. This was argued in *Living in Spin* in section 8.4. Platonisms and nominalisms come in cycles, starting with a platonism, disappointment, nominalism in reaction, and a return to platonism out of reaction to the failings of nominalisms. Platonisms and nominalisms disagree about the structures of reference and of what is referred to but they share a desire for control. Platonisms think control can be had, nominalisms still hope for control but have been burned, and they are more cautious. Nihilisms despair of control. Critical thinking about language, its capacities and limits, its subtleties and responsibilities, is much harder. To banish its subtlety and irony is to evade all challenge of (non-domesticated) transcendence.

Nominalism has a simple strategy to restrict the power and scope of language. A sentence is required to *refer* to a state of affairs in the world, and nouns within the sentence are required to refer to things in the world, without irony, without nuance, without expressive character. And that, of course, renders irony unreal, which was the goal and purpose of nominalism. Wittgenstein's *Tractatus* was one example of that program but there

---

[8] See Myers, *C. S. Lewis in Context*, 1. She cites Urban, *Language and Reality*, 21–24.

were others as well. It was quite popular in the first half of the twentieth century.

One idea that travels with nominalism is the instinct to start with parts and leave wholes for later. It even works in some circumstances, if it is not allowed to crowd out other paths of inquiry. John Ellis remarked an instinct to start from small things and build up solutions to larger things from the prior understanding of their component parts. His focus was on its occurrence in theories of language but it is much broader than that.[9] The alternative is to solve the big problems at the outset. The mistake is

> the assumption that descriptive words like square or cat are simpler and easier to understand than evaluative words like good and that the former are therefore more basic and thus a better model to take for understanding how language works (15–16).

He continues a little later:

> The more general form of this second misstep embodies an important misconception about scientific thought and procedure: the assumption ... that science begins by taking the clear cases and then generalizes from them to formulate the principles that are used to deal with the difficult cases. The movement of thought is assumed to be from simple to complex (16).

After nominalism consider materialism. There are many materialisms. Sometimes a materialism can even be good, as when biblical religion affirms the goodness of this material world instead of deprecating it before some other immaterial reality.[10] For Marxists, materialism means the denial of idealism (i.e., transcendence), a dispute we may pass over. Materialism may be a synonym for greed, gluttony, and lust.

What is denied in the materialism pertinent for us is the *problem* of formal causes, thinking that material causes are enough by themselves. Formal causes answer the question "*What* is that?" Not what preceded it or followed it, or what it is made of, but why it is whatever it is. How

---

[9] Ellis, *Language, Thought, and Logic*, 15–16. We shall see John Ellis again, in *Unanswerable Questions*.

[10] This among other meanings of materialism is noted in *Spin*, sec. 3.3.2, 63, n. 34.

does it be whatever it is? Why are its parts parts of one whole? Some, on the other side, would separate formal and material causes, and give formal causes an existence independent of their material instantiation. More than one kind of error is possible here.

The answers to questions about formal causes are not always Aristotelian-Thomistic substantial forms. That tradition assumes (whether tacitly or explicitly I do not know) that the form of a thing is inherent in the bearer. Some forms are not: The "form" of a chair is equipment for sitting (by humans), which is clearly human-relative. The form of a key depends on locks someplace else.

In *Spin* it was shown that what some things are (acts in particular) can be changed after the fact.

I would conjecture that what people are also changes in time and what an individual is in the present involves things in the future that are not yet known. Many things are not systems that have states that are a function of time, even if their material substrates are. (Hence my scolding those who think that material causes alone are sufficient.)

There is something intuitively natural in this sort of materialism. It relies on familiarity with the things whose formal causes are dismissed; we know what such-and-such is because we know how to use it. We don't need no stinkin' formal causes (*Spin*, p. 64). (This is intuitive because we don't do Aristotelian philosophy, and we also don't know the limitations of Aristotelian concepts of form.) What is natural to this dismissal of formal causes arises from our familiarity with things in the world and that is part of being-in-the-world, as Heidegger called it. In effect, we can get away with dismissing *philosophy* of formal causes, in general or in particular, because our *familiarity* with things already does the work of formal causes.

9.2 Individualisms

The last feature of this group of errors is a pathological kind of individualism. People usually think questions about individuals and society belong in political philosophy, how to structure a society. That is beyond the scope of this book and its sequel, though it will be prudent to say a little about it in a moment. My complaint is that by starting with individuals and coming to interpersonal relations later if at all, the instincts of Western philosophy have made it difficult to understand some parts of the Bible and, indeed, of world-affirming historical religion itself. Though the focus here is on the consequences of pathological individualism for philosophical theology, others have dealt with the consequences for politics and social structure. Patrick Deneen may serve as an example, for he has distinguished clearly between the pathologies of modern "liberal" political philosophy and the parts of "liberalism" that are medieval or scholastic, i.e., premodern.

> Many of what are considered liberalism's signal features — particularly political arrangements such as constitutionalism, the rule of law, rights and privileges of citizens, separation of powers, the free exchange of goods and services in markets, and federalism — are to be found in medieval thought. Inviolable human dignity, constitutional limits upon central power, and equality under law are part of a preliberal legacy.[11]

Deneen continues with the pivotal assumptions that carried the modern world beyond the scholastics:

> The strictly political arrangements of modern constitutionalism do not per se constitute a liberal regime. Rather, liberalism is constituted by a pair of deeper anthropological assumptions that give liberal institutions a particular orientation and cast: 1) anthropological individualism and the voluntarist conception of choice, and 2) human separation from and opposition to nature. These two revolutions in the understanding of human nature and society constitute "liberalism" inasmuch as they introduce a radically new definition of "liberty."

The distinction is useful for us for it illuminates a change not just in philosophical anthropology but inevitably in how the world and transcendence are viewed by man re-understood in a "liberal" anthropology. Relations to the natural world we can bracket for now. The roots of modern democracy (for those that have it) lie in a centuries-old understanding of creation.[12]

Unrestricted choice in regard to society and human nature is new. Many times in other books I have said that you can declare any kind of covenant with reality you want, but be very, very careful, for reality's interpretation of your covenant may not be entirely what you had in mind.

---

[11] Deneen, "Unsustainable Liberalism."

[12] There is more in O'Connor and Oakley, *Creation: The Impact of an Idea*.

9.2 Individualisms

In other words, you really do not have the kind of arbitrary choice that you think you do. This is true in particular in regard to human and social reality. Sociology of knowledge brackets truth claims (other than its own), but that does not mean there is no truth and it does not mean all social constructions are equal; some are better than others.

To concentrate on only one of Deneen's claims, the difference in the understanding of individuals lies in whether individuals exist before interpersonal involvements (and acquire sociality later) or whether individuals are social from the beginning (or before). The issue appears already in the Bible and has run through philosophy since.[13] Alexander Blair traced it through the history of the Common Era, across many philosophers.[14] It is his contention that the Common Documents presuppose a corporate view of human existence but the New Testament is ambiguous. To be sure, Christians have often read the New Testament through a lens that takes humans first as individuals, but Blair's claim against the New Testament strikes me as somewhat odd if one listens to the Corinthian correspondence, where Paul focuses on the "body of Christ" and membership in it of all believers. Paul's background is not known in much detail — he self-identifies as a Pharisee but his knowledge of Aramaic or Hebrew we don't know. To be a member of the Body of Christ is to play a role different from any other member (1 Cor. 12), so humans are not generically interchangeable for Paul. What is not developed is the primordial involvement of people in other people, whether Christian or not. To be a Christian, and indeed human, can only happen by being "a part of other people" — but that is modern American slang that rarely gets much reflection or thought. Paul's remarks get some attention from theologians but little or none from philosophers. When one notices how different Paul is from most philosophy today, the lack of attention to interpersonhood becomes surprising.

This lack is what makes biblical religion difficult to understand in today's culture, for which humans are individuals and human fulfillment happens on an individual basis. *Unanswerable Questions* has more to say about this and it goes well beyond the agenda of the present book, which limits itself to criticizing a few popular but problematic ideas in theology that the Church long ago took exception to. Nevertheless, in forecast and foretaste, to be human well is to handle well one's involvements in other

---

[13] Notable modern explicit examples of "liberal" individualism can be found in Hobbes and Locke, but it is not an occasional position. It dominates our culture.

[14] Blair, *Christian Ambivalence Toward Its Old Testament*.

persons, ultimately including beyond all other persons the void we call God.[15]

In our own culture it is inevitable that a call to recover sensitivity to interpersonal relations will be interpreted by the hasty as a call for socialism, a political program, and a few words are appropriate. In passing and lest my remarks against philosophical individualism be mistaken for the premises of socialism, I despise socialisms. Socialisms turn out to be based on assumptions of individualism shared with "liberalism," though Deneen's argument at this point is beyond what we can examine. The most ambitious socialisms have given us wholesale lies, wholesale murder, and wholesale economic dysfunction.[16] Less aggressive versions offer the same vices retail in Western democracies.

One recurrent feature of socialisms is a pretended attempt to practice the virtue of love without the virtue of hope. Hope is the virtue correlated with transcendence. Transcendence is specifically excluded in the program of Marxism: in "dialectical *materialism*," the materialism is a rejection of "idealism" — which means more than just Hegel. It means transcendence in any form, and it can take many forms. The attempt to practice love without hope quickly produces atrocities, as the history of Communism amply attests.[17]

One could call the constellation of NAturalism, NOminalism, Materialisms, and INDividualisms a *nanomind* ontology. It is the hallmark of our time: fabulous material wealth and scientific progress coupled with ontological poverty and metaphysical squalor.

9.3 Confusions About Religion

In the European West, it used to be clear what "religion" meant. Together with irreligion, there were only three or four: Christianity, Judaism, Islam, and atheism. Asian religions were known but beyond the cultural horizon. Those times are long gone. Today what counts as a "religion" is unclear, and what religion does is also up for grabs. It matters because the Church, in order to get on with its own life, needs to have some idea of what it is

---

[15] Cf. Niebuhr, "Faith in Gods and in God," in *Radical Monotheism*, 122.

[16] I would say economic irrationality but that too easily can be twisted into a brief for "economic rationality," what Deneen calls "liberalism."

[17] Stéphane Courtois et al., *The Black Book of Communism: Crimes, Terror, Repression*.

9.3 Confusions About Religion

doing. It used to make sense to say that someone's god was money (or sex, power, or fame). The language was colloquial and metaphorical, and no one took it literally. Today it needs to be taken seriously and explored in depth. The confusions are manifold, the category 'religion' no longer functions as it used to, and the activities it undergirded are now hidden or themselves confused.

Some religions or religious movements present themselves as "scientific"; some simply seek the meaning of human life in the sciences; and some movements present themselves as religions in order to gain political or legal advantages that come with religion. And there are some movements that are functionally religious but present themselves as purely secular in order to gain other legal advantages. Examples may help.

Biblical creationism presents itself as science, though it is pseudoscience in fact. That story is well-told elsewhere.[18]

Environmentalist movements (of which global warming alarmism is only the latest) have predicted imminent disaster and tried to impose their preferred remedies on everybody by law. They have claimed to be based in science, but the science has not vindicated any of them. Often it has attracted charges of fraud, corruption, and sloppy scientific reasoning.

In the 1960s, many expected computers to model human consciousness in full. As things developed, this became an attempt to build a philosophical anthropology on the legacy of René Descartes. Artificial Intelligence and more recently transhumanism were the outcome. The results have been disappointing. Many useful tools have been built, some nifty, some nasty, but artificial intelligence, meaning computational personhood, is still nowhere in sight. Yet the longing for it persists among AI researchers, and a little familiarity with the people and the literature conveys a sense that for them, it is the meaning of life. In other words it exercises some of the functions of a religion.

Memetics is the idea that the differential survival of ideas can be explained much as the differential survival of genes is in evolutionary biology. That involves ignoring the *reasons* for *choice* of some ideas over others. It is a way of shaping narratives without acknowledging that one is even telling narratives. It is a not-spelled-out policy of not spelling out what is going on in the development of ideas and culture.[19] The necessary presuppositions (or at least one of them) are that "ideas" (or "memes" in

---

[18] For one history, see Numbers, *The Creationists*. There are other accounts as well.

[19] See Fingarette, *Self Deception*. especially chapter 3.

the jargon of memetics) are both well-defined and discrete in the way that genes are. But ideas and other cultural artifacts are not digitally discrete as genes are. There is at most an analogy between the differential survival of ideas and that of genes.

In yet another kind of confusion about what a religion is, totalitarian ideologies sometimes try to pass themselves off as religion, in order to gain the protections of freedom of religion. The so-called "Religion of Peace" would be one example: the Religion of Peace has a serious violence problem. Sometimes a movement that is effectively religious claims to be science, in order to gain the prestige belonging to the sciences.[20] All of these examples illustrate confusion about the categories of human existence having to do with basic life orientation. We no longer know what a basic life orientation is, or how it can legitimately be supported in community. We no longer know when people are doing what they say they are doing in a claimed basic life orientation.

We no longer know what sort of claims can legitimately be made on one's neighbors and what sort of refusal of claims ought to be protected under the freedom of religion. Should governments regulate or impose a common basic life orientation? To what extent should a society make claims on its members? Any society is engaged in cooperation for common ends so that all may benefit. But to what extent can it regulate the understanding of those common ends? When is force justified, when is forbearance the better course?[21]

Sociology of religion has documented some of this confusion about religion, but sociology has rarely offered much detail or precision about the distribution of theological ideas. Still the available results are instructive. Christian Smith and coworkers, for one example, have backed up colloquial intuition about the distribution of religious opinion, from commitment to tradition to selective observance to degrees of indifference or ignorance to articulated opposition to tradition.[22] Apart from anecdotes, there isn't much about the kinds and degrees of traditional Christian commitment. For example, there is no sociological research about the issues of interest to the present study: Marcionite theology, monophysite theology of divine action, Christian triumphalism, sacred canopies, and the like.

---

[20] As in Marxism, creationism, many environmentalisms. One could go on.

[21] Some of these issues appear again in section 10.6, "Religious Autoimmune Disease."

[22] Smith and Snell, *Souls in Transition*. See also Smith and Denton, *Soul Searching*.

One result can be inferred from both sociological research and common experience: more and more Americans are doing without much *formal* theology. Informalism is widespread.

9.4 Seeking Meaning in the Sciences

Memetics is only one example of turning to the sciences for the meaning of human life. Many trust the sciences to provide reliable truth where the humanities (including biblical religion) have failed them and so they understandably hope to find meaning in the sciences. Nothing else is reliable. Some could point out that science changes with time and history.[23] They would respond that science is still the best we have and a lot better than the make-believe of religion or the caprice and whimsy of the arts. Some of that make-believe we have seen above in the literalist readings of Resurrection texts, and more in the miracle stories.

The fact that human meaning does not appear as a category of explanation in any natural science does not slow down those searching for it in the sciences. The logical technique of finding meaning in nature Merold Westphal called "mimesis";[24] it is a form of analogy, but analogies are human-relative social constructions. They are not implicit in nature; not the nature known to the natural sciences. This analogy is typical of mimetic religions, in which human and social meaning practices[25] integrate human life into nature. Westphal remarks,

> The term "mimetic" suggests itself because semi-worldly religion seeks to integrate human existence into the natural cosmos by means of ritualized imitative participation in which religious rites not only come to have central importance in life but the very difference between ritual and ordinary life is not allowed to emerge clearly if at all.[26]

Westphal is speaking of ancient nature-focused religions, where the religious meaning is clear to modern scholars, but his remarks apply to memetics just as well. The understanding of nature has changed (it has

---

[23] Paradigm shifts are the most visible example but sometimes the changes are discontinuous, as in cosmology. Cf. Pacholczyk, *The Catastrophic Universe*.

[24] Westphal, *God, Guilt, and Death*, chapter 10.

[25] Proponents of memetics (or any other form of scientism) would not acknowledge meaning practices as worship, so a more general term is needed.

[26] Westphal, *God, Guilt, and Death*, 196, on mimetic religion.

been taken from evolutionary biology) and any recognizable features of "religion" have been removed.

The natural sciences have great prestige and people trust scientists enough so that they are willing to trust them outside the sciences as well. That is why creationists seek to justify themselves in scientific terms, religion masquerading as science. Hence the attempt to find the meaning of human life in the sciences. The quest offers prestige, power, and culturally plausible claims of knowledge.

One thing that is usually overlooked is that science gets one of its central presuppositions from biblical religion, namely, the trust that the world is reliably intelligible *sub specie naturae*.[27] In practical terms, this means that there are no violations of natural laws (i.e., no Humean "miracles"). But the connection to biblical religion has been lost or rendered incoherent.

Consider beauty. Some scientists (Richard Dawkins and Carl Sagan are typical) boast about the beauty revealed in the sciences but dare not say that it is *real*, for to give it ontological status would (for them) raise the possibility of transcendence, and that would be anathema, unbearable. Beauty is real enough but not in the way matter is real, and they can think of no other way of being real.[28] They cannot conceive that there could be more than one mode of being — that of material being. How to say that beauty is real but not material is impossible in a nanomind ontology. Heidegger in *Being and Time* well and truly nailed that problem — demonstrating that people, tools, and rocks have very different ways of being what they are. And that was only the beginning, but it was successfully confined to philosophy departments where it could not threaten the culturally dominant naturalism, nominalism, materialism and individualism.

9.5 Loss of the Humanities

It is a commonplace observation that the humanities in higher education have been vandalized by several generations of nihilists, and most lately by proponents of identity politics in place of the inherited morality. That morality is obnoxious, and in any case the politically correct are more interested in their own power. There are dissidents trying to save classical

---

[27] Michael Foster demonstrated this in *Mind* in the 1930s. Others have questioned details, but the essential thesis has survived, largely forgotten. Cf. section 6.2.

[28] Hence my indictment for monophysite theology: in this case, monophysite of the intramundane, fending off both real transcendence and what would cause too much anxiety.

9.5 Loss of the Humanities

and Christian education, but they are a minority. Yet in the early twentieth century the humanities stood on the threshold of a rich land, new and unexplored; phenomenology and hermeneutics are part of it. Those disciplines survive, like classical education, in refuges from the mainstream. How it will turn out we do not know. What is ephemeral and what is a long-term trend is unclear.

Philosophy in the twentieth century was faced with many assaults. In Bruce Wilshire's[29] words,

> Imagine a schizophrenic. Suddenly feeling overextended in his ambitions, and unable to sustain his ground, he retrenches radically: he will attempt to hold something, however distorted and denuded — a very small, highly fortified area.

The result was logical positivism, which Wilshire characterized in the words "... positivism, whose function was to create the illusion of being a science."[30] What goes for positivism goes as well for scientism.

The early twentieth-century breakthroughs in the sciences were accompanied in the humanities, but only the sciences survived. The humanities were on the edge of a world beyond the nanomind ontology and they turned back. Nanomind has taken over cultural imagination. In parallel, and spread out over more years, were the fruits of Neo-Orthodox theology. That, too, was abandoned after the 1960s. Both the secular world and the Church bumped into a rich metaphysical world, and turned back.

There is a haunting parallel in the Exodus, when Moses sent scouts to reconnoiter the promised land from the South: Numbers 13.17 ff. The scouts find it rich but are intimidated by the resident Amalekites. Moses is disgusted and orders the Israelites to desist and turn away. The text (in two traditions, J and P) condemns them. Numbers 14.20–25 (J): none save Joshua and Caleb shall enter the promised land. And 14.26–38 (P), an even more dismal forecast, forty more years in the wilderness (v. 34). Though some attack against Moses' orders (14.39–45, J), they are defeated.

How long will we have to wander in the wilderness?

The loss of the humanities has been noticed, there is some pushback, and there may be more. Will it be able to escape from Cartesian nanomind ontology? Will it find a way to transcendence without crude platonisms or supernatural dualisms?   Wait and see. Will it recover from today's fashionable nihilism? Wait and see.

---

[29] Cf. p. 112 above. Wilshire's description applies to biblical literalists also.

[30] Wilshire, "Fifty Years of Academic Philosophy in the United States," 414 and 418.

A central part of the humanities is transcendence. We saw transcendence domesticated above, in section 6.1. Language that was meant to explain transcendence construed it in such a way that in the end it was abolished. We are back to the plight of the Church in the ancient world. What Sokolowski said about ancient secular understanding of gods in the world[31] goes today for any kind of transcendence: The secular world can only conceive of transcendence as phenomena within this world or invisible extensions of it. When we answer the question, "Where does your proposed ultimate reality show itself in the world?" as we do, we are intelligible to the secular world only on the interpretation that we are talking about phenomena within some extended world.[32] The possibility that there could be a reality that is not simply a worldly phenomenon but nevertheless shows itself *in* worldly phenomena requires a subtlety that the secular world refuses when it can even understand it. Mostly, it is unthinkable. In the end, one root issue is familiar. Transcendence was driven out by a quest for control and Cartesian scientistic naturalism serves that quest well. It bears notice that when the culture needs to deal with transcendence without admitting what it is doing, it is quite capable of doing so. Just read the comic strips.

9.6 A Technology of Disrespect

This book is mostly about theological quarrels that easily qualify as dusty, slow, and dry. They are a history of theological errors, most long ago repudiated by the Church but still peddled to an eager market for such ideas. Most readers will be much more interested in sex, and in the sexual changes in our own time. Highschool teachers observe that their male students have sex on the brain for eight out of every fifteen seconds and so you have seven seconds to get your message through. The sexual chaos of our time can be related to the other problems in theology: both are instances of will to power, revolt against creaturehood. Our selected theological adversaries (half-Marcionite theology, monophysite theology of divine action, and evasion of confessional responsibility) are all instances of will to power. But sex is where the rubber hits the road and leaves skid marks.

---

[31] Sokolowski, *The God of Faith and Reason*, 36.

[32] They think we are peddling some sort of dualism: a dual world with natural causes in the dual world and effects in this world, overriding normal natural causes.

9.6 A Technology of Disrespect

There are reasons for this section. Most would not miss it if it were left out, and Liberals would prefer that. In fact, Liberals would love to use the arguments in the rest of the book to beat conservatives[33] over the head, effectively making the rest of the book, in our social context, an argument for Liberal theology and the sexual practices it has plagued us with. To forestall that, this section is a way to poison the book for Liberals.

Given widespread cultural assumptions today, rejection of monophysite theology of divine action is easy to mistake for Liberal theology. Anything Chalcedonian undercuts the monophysite theology that is widely used to backup traditional morality, so it must be Liberal. Or so people easily think. Monophysite theology objectivates — but it can be used to objectivate any theology, conservative, liberal, revisionist, or traditional, as experience around seminaries can easily confirm. There are other, and better, if harder ways to enforce responsibility.

So if you claim to like the arguments in the rest of the book, show me some evidence of serious pro-life commitment, and also rejection of the technology of disrespect (i.e., agreement with at least the conclusions of *Humanae Vitae*.) Without that, we don't agree on the most basic core of biblical religion. Biblical religion is pro-life when life hurts: that is its whole point. To carve out exceptions when the pain of life is an unwanted pregnancy or even when it is the duty of respect for another person's sexuality is to cut the heart out of biblical religion. And to try to get around the intrinsic sexual nature of human bodies is an instance of trying to get out of creaturehood. Both undercut the affirmation of human life in this world as good, in full view of its Limitations. This book does not spend much time repeating arguments laid out in earlier books, affirming human life and pointing out how this life orientation shows itself in history. But the so-called "sexual revolution" works to undermine the central biblical affirmation of human life in the face of Limitation.

So — as a grotesque sort of comic relief, let's talk briefly about sex. That would mean the technology of disrespect: the technology that was designed to give males all the choices about sex, to allow males to get and get away with any kind of sex they want and then skip town when it comes time to take responsibility for their sexual activity. (We live in an equal-opportunity society, so we see not just male but also male-pattern irresponsibility.) Some acts merit censure, but the censures are disjointed

---

[33] I would say traditionalists, but not all conservatives are traditionalists.

fragments of an older morality that has been lost, without any principles that could give it unity or coherence.[34]

Some will of course reply that contraceptives are precisely the means of respect — so that they can get their desired sex without making the significant other of the moment pregnant. To say that is to reassert by presupposition precisely what the technology of disrespect is all about: predatory males getting away with whatever sex they want, usually at the expense of women (and lately, younger males). And so you will undoubtedly proclaim that contraceptives are the technology of respect, thereby begging the question at issue and uncandidly reasserting by silent presupposition the purpose of the technology of disrespect: to give males any kind of sex they want.

The technology of disrespect has transformed both our theological and moral anthropology and also the meaning of human sexuality. We have become sexual predators, whether we want to be or not, because that's what sex has become: a pastime for the available, on a supposedly consensual basis. The sexually strong get what they want, those less effective in sexual competition are crowded out, and people are driven to other ways of fulfillment. Most of the damage is done by ordinary predatory heterosexual males, but that is banal. The culture reviles the vile — other kinds of sexual abuse, especially sex involving children — in order to deflect attention from the banal. The vile is really, really, really, really, really, really vile.[35] Got that? About the banal, there is nothing to see here; move along, folks.

Gay marriage is a clearing in which we can see something essential about marriage, something that is denied as often as it is affirmed. The result is incoherent. The marriage liturgy asks the witnessing congregation to support the union that is beginning, and so marriage used to have a corporate dimension.[36] The support of society and other people used to be very important. Sociology and law can also attest as much. But the new sexual morality operates by the rubric that consenting adults should be allowed to do anything that "does not harm anyone else." This passes

---

[34] This was the opening thesis of MacIntyre's *After Virtue*.

[35] For an extended if brief description of the pertinent facts and their consequences, see Weigel, *The Irony of Modern Catholic History*, 277–291. He lays out the obvious consequences if the sexual abuse crisis is not thoroughly remedied. Whether that will happen is an open question.

[36] I don't know how old the explicit support of the congregation is in the liturgy. It may have been simply implicit, taken for granted, and then spelled out recently when it became clear that it cannot be taken for granted. Or it may be ancient.

9.6 A Technology of Disrespect

in silence over the possibility of harm to the sexual partners and very effectively hides the possibility of indirect harm to others. It utterly subverts the corporate dimension of marriage. What people do in private can do great harm to others near and far, for it transforms the participants, and they meet and deal with other people far away. And if private behavior becomes known, it works to legitimate that behavior.

The result is radical individualism, the denial of a place for others' support for a marriage. Why was the community's support needed and asked? Because it's not easy to get married, and it's not easy to stay married. That's the practical reason but there is more. All human actions get their being from a community of interpreters, among whom an act may be criticized and given definition and meaning.

In the so-called sexual revolution, the meaning of sex and everything related to it, marriage especially, has been transformed utterly. What it means to be a sexual being is changed; this is at the heart of a theological anthropology. Demands by the sexually revolting are demands to legitimate their anthropology, and opposition to those demands is a movement for an older and quite different anthropology. What can be said in a book like this (a digression, after all) is quite limited. Let me simply cite some of the work in criticism of the sexual revolution. Begin with Mary Eberstadt. In a series of articles in *First Things*, she reviewed other people's work showing that the sexual revolution is dysfunctional.[37] Eberstadt speaks of the vindication in four trends after contraceptives became widely available and accepted:

> a general lowering of moral standards throughout society;
> a rise in infidelity;
> a lessening of respect for women by men; and
> the coercive use of reproductive technologies
>   by governments.[38]

These are not side effects, they are the main point. In other words, what the US Supreme Court inflicted upon us all in Griswold v. Connecticut is exactly a technology of disrespect. It touches everybody, whether they use it or not. The studies Eberstadt relies upon often *support* the sexual revolution, and *still* show it to be dysfunctional.

For a more technical perspective turn to Janet Smith, *Humanae Vitae: A generation later* and *Why Humanae Vitae Was Right*. In the first, Smith

---

[37] See the Eberstadt titles in the bibliography.
[38] Eberstadt, "The Vindication of Humanae Vitae," part II.

provides a history of the debate that led to the encyclical and its publication in 1968 as well as the aftermath. This is the place to look for a scholarly history of the technical controversy in depth. For the history before the modern period she assesses John Noonan's work as reliable, despite the fact that Noonan himself in the end supported relaxing the prohibition of contraceptives.[39]

For a general perspective on the sexual revolution, consider Ephraim Radner's remarks. They were written specifically about gay marriage, but I think far worse damage is done by ordinary predatory heterosexual males, for whom, after all, the technology of disrespect and the sexual revolution were launched. He points out, by analogy with the revival of slavery (previously banned in Christian Europe) that progress is not inevitable, and battles won in the past can be lost again in the present, at great cost in human suffering.[40] The problem is not gay marriage, though that is a sad symptom of it. The problem is the redefinition of human sexuality as essentially predatory, a redefinition accomplished by the technology of disrespect. The result has been a radical shift in moral and theological anthropology.

We who do not participate in the sexual revolution watch in helpless bewilderment. It has wrecked many lives and hurt many more, yet we hope you can succeed in your quest for happiness despite all expectations to the contrary. Typically, you are friends or family, and we love you — but we have to weep for you. Prohibition of the technology of disrespect may not work. Simple prohibition has never worked very well against other kinds of dysfunctional behavior. Returning to the past is supposedly impossible. You, the revolting generation, will have to solve this moral problem. You have declared independence from the authority of tradition, and you have gotten your wish.

What is the connection to the rest of this book? The new sexual anthropology is about power, disrespect, and evasion of responsibility — which also animate most of the dysfunctional theology that we inherit today. The so-called sexual revolution is but one manifestation of the new elements of "liberalism," namely the idea that human nature is malleable and open to arbitrary refashioning at the whimsy of individuals. We saw this with our brief quotations from Patrick Deneen above, p. 194, on the "voluntarist conception of choice." Is this a coincidence? No.

---

[39] John T. Noonan, *Contraception*.
[40] Radner, "Same-sex marriage."

9.6 A Technology of Disrespect

One consequence of the sexual revolution is simple. Birth rates have fallen below replacement level over much of the world, especially among the bearers of biblical religion and the Western tradition, with the notable exception of the State of Israel. This is an index of despair. It is a sign of unwillingness to pass on the gift of life to another generation.

We were told in the 1970s that overpopulation was our future, and we would all starve from a Malthusian crisis. Quite the opposite is upon us. That ought to tell how imbecilic the predictions were, especially those from proponents of the sexual revolution.

It apparently is not obvious that a quest for power and control could be a form of despair, but Kierkegaard said it long ago, in *The Sickness Unto Death*. What is surprising is how thoroughly he has been vindicated.

Chapter 10

Problems Not Faced in the Church

We have followed engagements with life and history in the Church that could have been handled better. It is possible to collect some of them together here. Usually there are overlooked resources from the tradition that could help.

These are not all the problems in the Church, just a few of interest to one highly opinionated philosophical theologian. I knew about most of them in a primitive sort of way before I became Catholic, and the problems are usually worse among Protestants, even though it may fairly be said that Protestants keep us honest. Sometimes we do better, as when the Church remembers to be pro-life and to demur from the technology of disrespect. And among the Church's commitments, she has often remembered to help the poor and disadvantaged. It's not all bad news.

But here, in prospect, let me list some problems peculiar to the Church.

Nobody, neither real people nor philosophers, has a very good idea of what it takes to give a human life coherence or a basic orientation or purpose. Some people do better, but in practice, not in theory.

The Church all too often forgets its own central commitments: affirmation of life in this world as good in full view of its pains — a costly and difficult commitment. She has always treasured her history but what it means to live in history has changed subtly in recent years. Revelatory events in history transform what and who we are today, and that is not quite the traditional way of understanding history. Lastly, we are confused about transcendence — unable to escape from monophysite theology of divine action and presence.

The possibility of change in covenants in history was seen long ago, and turned away from (cf. Aphrahat, below).

The perennial temptation to Marcionite theology — beginning de novo with Jesus — is still with us.

These initial errors are reflected in the history of love between Christians and Jews.

The critics of Christianity find it to be unbelievable, offensive, and in bad faith. When the criticisms are examined, they are largely directed against the errors in focus in this book: Marcionite theology, monophysite theology, evasion of responsibility for confessional commitments, and garbled transcendence. (That does not mean that the so-called "New Atheists" would convert if these errors were corrected; with all due respect to them, I think they have deeper reasons for not being Christian.)

Lastly, it will be possible once again to summarize our history as part of the history of religions, from the beginnings to the present, with a few brief comments on Christian answers.

10.1 Basic Life Orientation

It is a category error to think that religion is confined to the (modern) supernatural. A better definition would be a communal approach to *basic life orientation*, perhaps with some mode of recognition and intention. (We first saw this in section 1.4.) For individuals, basic life orientation means narrative coherence of a life, and hence needs ideas that go beyond the naturalism, nominalism, materialisms, and individualisms of our time (cf. sec. 9.1. Another definition of basic life orientation would simply be ultimate reality as chosen by a community and its members. The Church does not have much sense of its identity as part of world-affirming historical religion, in contrast to world-affirming nature religion, exilic religion, the varieties of informalism, and a few other options. It is worth note that a *declared* basic life orientation is not necessarily one's *real* basic life orientation. Inattention to this problem has rendered the Church incapable of making sense *of* contemporary culture and incapable of making sense *to* contemporary culture. Much of the secular culture gets along just fine without "organized" religion, rendering communication between the Church and the secular world somewhat difficult.

Along with the questions of ultimate reality and basic life orientation goes the question of how they show themselves in life as we know it. We saw it first in section 1.6. It does not attract much attention colloquially or in philosophy of religion today, though it is often handled informally. Failure to deal candidly and explicitly with these issues makes the Church all the more unintelligible to the culture.

In effect, we live in a culture that is ahead of the church and professional philosophers, but nevertheless a culture that functions without theory, without spelling out what its various subcultures are doing to make sense of life and the world. At the same time, we live with disagreements and diversity on a scale broader than anything in European history. The wars of religion in the sixteenth and seventeenth centuries were between parties whose religions were much closer to agreement with each other than what we see in the spectrum of formal and informal life orientations in Western culture today. One difference is that five centuries ago, the disagreements were violent; today they are comparatively peaceful, amounting almost to indifference. Another is that there is no general agreement on what a "religion" is, and many think they can live perfectly well without "religion," though they would never think their lives have no coherence or orientation.

Freedom of religion was invented in the seventeenth century in order to bring peace instead of strife among religions that were very close to one another. But in a culture where "religion" and shared basic life orientation have become different categories, how long can freedom of religion endure? It used to mean freedom of ecclesiastical polity in a society with a common biblical life orientation. There is no longer a common basic life orientation, and there are attempts to secure parts of various orientations in law, on the way to establishing one of them comprehensively in law. We are starting to see people ask the question, "What is a religion?"[1] In what sense can a society presuppose common assumptions about life and the world? How much agreement can be assumed, and more to the point, how much agreement and common commitment can be *enforced* in order to enable a society to cooperate in coherent projects?

---

[1] The question has already arisen in the courts, in the Flying Spaghetti Monster case if not earlier. The headline was, "Federal Judge Rules That Worshiping a Flying Spaghetti Monster Is Not a Real Religion." See Reisman online.

10.2 The Heart of Historical Religion

If the culture is confused about religion, the Church is confused about its own religion. We no longer have an easy shared understanding of what we are doing with our lives. Yet we still think the Creeds answer such questions and so we *appear* to ourselves to understand what we are doing with our lives.

Between the scholastic and modern periods, the solid premodern theology evaporated unnoticed, and what was left was a theology that conceived of divine action only as interference with the natural world. And when modern monophysite theology of divine action and presence became incredible, there was nothing left. Without monophysite theology, there was no way to make sense of biblical religion.

Basic commitments of biblical religion were lost or rendered unintelligible: that the world is good, in full view of its pains; that this ultimate reality shows itself in biblical history; and that transcendence can support such a commitment. We are saved in the pains of life, not in getting out of them, and in our pains we offer ourselves up to God. The pertinent history is not just the occasions when this way of life was disclosed to us, and so dispensable or non-essential, as in the *occasions* when one learned basic algebra, which fade into irrelevance while the algebra remains. By contrast, biblical history is ontologically effective: its events transform our lives and actions today.[2] They constitute our lives as faithful, which is a lot more than just being the occasions when our forebears received the "deposit of faith," as if it could be captured and passed on in propositional form. That ontological constitution of human actions was explored in *Living in Spin*.

By stages the covenant community has transformed its faith from an encounter with a God who is holy into a way to control and evade that encounter while appearing to embrace it. We can no longer live with H. Richard Niebuhr's insight in *Radical Monotheism*, that "the causes for which we live all die" (p. 122). The Church listens to the world, and the world takes such words to entail nihilism and despair, not hope.

If Niebuhr spoke of human life and disappointment at its largest scale, we have turned away from small-scale disappointments, common Exposure, Limitation, and Need. We are loth to accept history, relativity, and

---

[2] This is an instance of formal causation that is ruled out by the materialism in a nanomind ontology. The formal effects of events far away on events here and now was explored in the distributed ontology (*Living in Spin*).

pluralism as instances of Exposure, Limitation, and Need. Some seminarians hear about this but when they become pastors they don't pass it on to their laity.

What monophysite theology of divine action and of divine providence gave people was a hope to get out of Limitation *ultimately*. When monophysite theology of divine action lost its credibility, people simply continued (outside of the Church) seeking to get out of disappointment ultimately, because that was a more candid way of doing what they were already doing inside the Church: trying to evade Exposure, Limitation, and Need.

There are some patterns in these failures. We have (as all human beings do) tried to evade the pains of life, leaving them as barren. We have tried to domesticate our relationship to history and get control over it. And we have bungled transcendence on the way to evading our responsibility for our own religion. These will take some unpacking, though at this point they are mostly review, since we have seen them already.

Begin with the pains of life, Exposure, Limitation, and Need. By now they should be old friends. In the life of the Church and its theology, these pains show themselves as critical history, historical and cultural relativity, and religious pluralism. Section 6.6 introduced biblical criticism and with it critical history. It was announced in section 1.3, and critical history appeared again in section 8.8 above.[3] Critical history has dismantled monophysite theology and exposed many errors in our own confessional history. In showing that things did not happen as our inherited stories claim, critical history has usually also showed some of how things really happened, and so made the roots of faith stronger, not weaker. It makes the past intelligible, so that we remember more, and can fit it all together in a coherent narrative. "History also works as exposure, for revelation resurrects the forgotten and buried and embarrassing past. The sins, betrayals, denials, follies, what we had denied and suppressed, all come back in the light of the revelatory moment. Unburyng the past is confession of sin."[4] We shall see examples momentarily in reviewing the relations between Christians and Jews.

Historical and cultural relativity are an instance of a general principle:

---

[3] For my own treatment of the issue, see Porter, "History, Relativity, and Pluralism."

[4] The quotation is from Porter, "History, Relativity, and Pluralism." It is a paraphrase of H. Richard Niebuhr, *The Meaning of Revelation* chapter III, "Reasons of the Heart," section II, "Interpretation through Revelation," 113 (1st edition) and 60 (3rd edition).

10.2 The Heart of Historical Religion

Human religions are human social constructions, even biblical religion in all its forms. We would like to get out of responsibility for our own hand in the construction of our own religion. The usual way to do that is to recite the story of divine action in our history and then ban the history of religions and the sociology of knowledge as they apply to our own religion. That is to eliminate one side of a Chalcedonian description of the phenomenon and intrude the other in its place — a paradigmatic example of monophysite theology. The alternative is to pray,

> Lord, we are unworthy that you should enter
> into our human and socially constructed realities,
> but only say the word,
> and we shall be made whole.

The instinctive objection seeks truth independent of social constructions, but consider that social construction applies even in mathematics. There are two kinds of numbers, counting numbers and measuring numbers. Mathematics since the seventeenth century has fitted both into one and the same real number line but they have different origins. The real number system that we have was fashioned in the nineteenth century[5] in order to underwrite Newton's calculus and classical physics. What would the measuring numbers look like if they were created with quantum measurement in mind? I have no idea, since I am just a scruffy engineer and not a real mathematician, but this much can be said: We trust that reality enters into our socially constructed reality, and we are not really in control.

Religious pluralism[6] is the last of the trio history, relativity, and pluralism, but it was the first to be seen and cause people anxiety. Religious disagreement is a fact of life. Anxiety arises when it is noticed what the disagreements are about, when their logic is seen: the *starting* point for making sense of the world. Starting points cannot be reasoned to, only from; so all explanation of them is circular.[7] Once again, we are not in control. What is more, we are in the face of other people who see the world differently, and so it is not possible to get them to validate our social constructions. What results is anxiety. Those others, whoever they are, nevertheless make a real claim on us, whoever we are. The claim arises

---

[5] The litany of the saints begins with Cauchy and Weierstrass.

[6] Plurality, really, not plural*ism*. It's not an "ism," a social project.

[7] If we are dealing with a mere explanation, the circularity is hermeneutical. If the explanation is treated as a proof, the circularity is vicious. This was explored in a little more detail in *Basic Concepts of Biblical Religion*, section 5.6, "Hermeneutical Circularity."

because we share a world, and share in its interpretation, even if we disagree. We have stakes in each other and in each other's interpretations of the world, so the phenomenon of religious pluralism embodies religious Need, especially when we disagree. Sometimes it is possible to come to some kind of agreement, but not always. Some disagreements should be nurtured and treasured, as we shall see with respect to Christianity and rabbinic Judaism in section 10.4.

We still have a long way to go and old habits die hard. Thomas Joseph White remarked on mid-twentieth-century French Neo-scholasticism that it moved from exclusive triumphalism to an inclusive triumphalism,[8] without really owning the logic of a confessional stance, without really giving up triumphalism. In other words, everybody else is supposed to give up and become Catholic.

10.3 Evading History

One sometimes hears from conservative Catholics that the teaching of the Church is unchanging.[9] This is faithful in a strange sort of way, but it is not even aware of John Henry Newman. I would have said the Church's faithfulness is in the sense of "semper fidelis," not the platonist absoluteness of things that (mathematically) do not change in time. Absoluteness unrelative to history is Platonism, not biblical religion. The eternal faithfulness of the Church (and of God) need to be explained in terms other than Platonist absoluteness unrelative to history. This is not a new idea, not even new with John Henry Newman. It appears in Aphrahat, a fourth-century bishop in Syria.

> Law and covenant have been entirely changed. God changed the first pact with Adam, and gave a new one to Noah. He gave another to Abraham, and changed this to give a new one to Moses. When the covenant with Moses was no longer observed, he gave another pact in this last age, a pact never again to be changed.
>
> He established a new law for Adam, that he could not eat of the tree of life. He gave to Noah the sign of the rainbow in

---

[8] White, "Catholicism in an Age of Discontent."

[9] One comment from a devout, holy, and very pro-life Catholic was, "We attend and support a parish that we know teaches children the Faith according to the Church's official, unchangeable and perennial teaching."

the clouds. He then gave Abraham, chosen for his faith, the mark and seal of circumcision for his descendants. Moses was given the Passover lamb, the propitiation for the people.

All these covenants were different from each other.[10]

Aphrahat was aware of what he was doing, and had some conception of what it means for a covenant people to live in pilgrimage through history, with covenants that change as appropriate to changing circumstances in history:

> We know, dearly beloved, that God established different laws in different generations which were in force as long as it pleased him. Afterward they were made obsolete. In the words of the apostle: *In former times the kingdom of God existed in each generation under different signs.*
>
> Moreover, our God is truthful and his commandments are most trustworthy. Every covenant was proved firm and trustworthy in its own time, and those who have been circumcised in heart are brought to life and receive a second circumcision beside the true Jordan, the waters of baptism that bring forgiveness of sins.

Aphrahat incidentally was well aware of reading the Gospels as Exodus typology. He continues:

> Jesus, son of Nun, renewed the people's circumcision with a knife of stone when he had crossed the Jordan with the Israelites. Jesus, our Saviour, renews the circumcision of the heart for the nations who have believed in him and are washed by baptism: circumcision by *the sword of his word, sharper than any two-edged sword.*
>
> Jesus, son of Nun, led the people across the Jordan into the promised land. Jesus, our Saviour, has promised the land of the living to all who have crossed the true Jordan, and have believed and are circumcised in heart.

---

[10] This and the following texts are from the Breviary for the Office of Readings, Wednesday in the First Week of Lent: "From a Demonstration by Aphraates, bishop; Dem. 11, De Circumcisione, 11–12: PS 1, 498–503."

Yet as so often happened in the history of the faith, Aphrahat did the right thing but did not go far enough. He admits development in the history before Jesus but turned Jesus and the (then) New Covenant into the final solution to the problem of history and historical anxiety. He could be defended on the rationale that he went as far as was needed in his time, and since more than that was not needed, he should not be faulted. That almost works, but not quite. In the perspective of the history of religions, he was certainly right about his past, but there was and is no reason why development should stop with the Disasters of the First Century and the Jesus movement. It is too easy to turn Aphrahat's position into a rejection of development in the life of the faith. That is why I have called it "the final solution" to the problem of anxiety in history.

With Aphrahat and many others like him, we bump again into the ambiguity of history and events in history. Is the New Testament, are the events of Jesus and their aftermath, to be regarded as a continuation of a pilgrimage through history fraught with change, or are they to be regarded as the *end* of change in history? Do they continue the covenant people's pilgrimage, or are they a final solution to the anxieties of history? Aphrahat is clearly right about change in the sequence of covenants before the New Testament. He also thinks Jesus is the final revelation. The New Testament itself does not raise this question. It cannot, for it was not written for twentieth-century postmodern readers with a developed history of religions and hermeneutic of history. We can, however, ask whether the New Testament understood its place in history in the same way the Common Documents do.

Reinhold Niebuhr, in the opening pages of *Human Destiny*, explains what a "christ" is. A christ, with a lower-case c, is an event in history that enables the covenant community to carry on its covenant in history. It doesn't reveal what can only be known at the eschaton but rather just enough to carry on in the present. How long the "present" will last is never known. So on Niebuhr's reasoning, it would be improper to set limits on God, to say that He is not allowed any more revelation between Jesus and the final end, the eschatological consummation of human history. You can tell God there is something He is not allowed to do, but I wouldn't. Yet those who think Jesus is the final solution to the problems of anxiety in history do just that.

In effect, Aphrahat never really escapes from Marcionite theology, even though he is never really a Marcionite. That may sound like a paradox, but it isn't really. To really escape from Marcionite theology would require more than what Aphrahat gives us, an acknowledgment of the open history beyond our present. Is that implied in what he does give us? Is it ruled out by what he gives us? The texts themselves are open. We need to be allowed to re-understand the history in the Common Documents in terms of our own secular cosmology, starting with the evolution of life and language. (Since the first chapters of Genesis start with two mutually incompatible and inconsistent cosmologies, what I ask is not something unbiblical.) What will come in the future we do not know. Aphrahat turned Jesus into a way to get out of the anxieties of history, and I think that is a mistake. In *Cosmos and History*, Mircea Eliade saw as much for biblical religion in general, though he didn't deal specifically with Christology.

10.4 Christians and Jews

Rabbinic Judaism has been a clearing in which it is possible to see the Church's failed engagement with its own responsible liberty of interpretation. This is its longest-running failed engagement. It focuses at least two of the central concerns of this book: Evasion of confessional responsibility and half-Marcionite theology. The history of relations between Christianity and rabbinic Judaism has been recounted by many people. I surveyed some of them in chapter 8 of *Elementary Monotheism*. Norman Beck has scoured the New Testament for its kinds and degrees of anti-Jewish theology.[11] The New Testament that we have is one side of a bitter quarrel between the Jesus movement and the Judaism of the rabbis. We do not have the other side of the quarrel. Both were responses to the loss of the Second Temple in the first Jewish Revolt, of 67–73 CE. Liberal Theology was never particularly fond of rabbinic Judaism so it is not really a remedy for the problem. We need a new perspective.

To make sense of the parting of the ways that began in the First Century it is necessary to back up some and begin with some of Merold Westphal's characterizations of biblical religion. In effect, he says that the covenant community is traveling through history in company with a transcendent Other. My words, not his; but look at what he does say:

> "I will be there (for you) as I choose to be there" (a rendering of Exodus 3.14, with citations in note 82 to p. 238.).

---

[11] Beck, *Mature Christianity in the 21st Century*.

> "This promise of a personal accompanying leadership adds to the law a second, more personal dimension of divine guidance through history," (Westphal's own summary, p. 238)

Westphal speaks of several covenants, those with Moses, Abraham, and David, and he characterizes them as an obligation covenant (Moses, the law) and promise covenants (Abraham and David, the people and the monarchy). One could add the covenants that Aphrahat reviews as well as the new covenants forged in the New Testament and the Mishnah, in the first centuries of the Common Era, by the rabbis and the Jesus movement. Indeed, one could well say that you can make any kind of covenant you like with ultimate reality. That is true, but it would be wise to be very, very careful, for it is ultimate reality, not you, that will interpret and implement your covenant. Its interpretation may not be your interpretation.[12] Many places in the Bible, the human authors lament as much. See Psalm 89 for one extended example in regard to the covenant with the Monarchy.

One more resource and we can draw some conclusions. Human being, human personhood is commonly taken to be an individual thing, with other people added on later if at all. I think this is a mistake and have said so elsewhere.[13] Human being is the sort of being that matters to itself — a breakthrough insight — but it also matters to other people. The consequence is that other people are always already involved in the being, the ontology, of a human being. People know this, whether or not they *know* they know this. Relating to other persons is always already part of being a person, and when we relate to the world, in that relating to the world we also relate to other persons with whom we share the world.

It is now possible to observe that the covenants by the rabbis and the first Christians exemplify two different ways to relate to the transcendent Other. When a person acts as another person wishes, desires, instructs, commands and so on, the first person is relating to the second.[14] The second person is present in the ontological constitution of the first person's actions. This is true in particular when the other person is the transcendent Other. Typical in the Bible is Psalm 119, the love-song for the Law. The Law is a human social construction, but we trust that ultimate reality enters

---

[12] See *Basic Concepts of Biblical Religion*, section 3.3, "Covenant," especially its ending; or *By the Waters of Naturalism*, section 6.5, "$\pi = 4$."

[13] See for example *Living in Spin*, section 3.4.1, "Heidegger's Dasein and Other People," and 3.4.2, "Kierkegaard's Self-Relating Self."

[14] It should be obvious that this is true of disobeying as much as of obeying another person's wishes.

10.4 Christians and Jews

into our social constructions, and the wording of the giving of the Law in the Common Documents reflects that faith.

When a person relates to particular other persons, he also relates in a personal way beyond all intramundane persons, simply because in relating to anything in the world, other-personhood is always present in the background.[15] That is the way into a long story in theology, the idea that in Jesus of Nazareth God could be present to the covenant community, with echoes of the Davidic covenant. In its careful statement, some four centuries later, that meant two φύσεις[16] in one πρόσωπον.[17] Suffice it to say for present purposes (I have not written a Christology) that the Christian and rabbinic ways of continuing the covenant inherited from the Exodus, the Monarchy, the Exile, and Second Temple Judaism were different and incompatible. In effect, in a process that took several centuries, Christianity and rabbinic Judaism became two daughter religions born out of the ashes of Second Temple Judaism. The parting of the ways began early but continued slowly until the fourth century. Daniel Boyarin tells the story.[18] The separation was not really final until the Theodosian Code (438 CE).

In a short digression, it is possible to observe that, contrary to Paul and the Reformers, observance of Jewish Law is not a form of works righteousness. Works righteousness is a theory alleging that observance of the Law makes one righteous before God in a way that gives the believer a claim against God, and in any case gives the believer control over his relationship to God. Paul seems to think he was up against such a theology, and inasmuch as it gratifies a believer's craving for control over the relationship to God, the allegations are plausible. We have seen such craving in Christian theology in the domestication of transcendence above (section 6.1). Works righteousness is not my experience of observant Judaism.

It could be said of the Law (halakah) as of any other world-affirming historically religious socially constructed reality, that we are dependent on ultimate reality to enter into our human socially constructed realities. It is not only *we* who need grace, as in Paul, but the Law *itself*, among our socially constructed realities, that needs grace.

The Law functions in the way that liturgy functions, not in the way that

---

[15] More of this in *Unanswerable Questions*.

[16] None too helpfully translated as *natures*.

[17] Usually mistranslated as *person*. None of my teachers were happy with that translation, and other translations are found first in Liddell and Scott and (at much greater length) also in Bauer-Arndt-Gingrich and Lampe.

[18] Boyarin, *Border Lines: The Partition of Judaeo-Christianity*.

paying taxes or the rent functions. Liturgy defines someone's intended basic life orientation. How that works is not susceptible to the sort of inquiry of analytic philosophy of religion, or of the Reformers, or of any who would try to calculate. It does not give humans (or philosophers) *control*. It does not provide what the tax man would call a "safe harbor" — do this, do such-and-such, and you are guaranteed to be right with God. Safe harbors are not given to us; we are always dependent on grace, even in our knowing God and our naming God.

Perhaps an example might help. It is a story I have told many times. Over the years I rented out rooms to students, one of whom was a more or less observant conservadox Jew. I would go around the house at the end of the day, to turn off lights, lock doors, make sure everything was in order, etc. One Friday, I found the oven on and turned it off. A week later, the same, and somehow I had the sense to leave it. How that happened is forgotten. Apparently, as it was explained to me, it is within kashrut to turn the oven *up* on Shabbat but not to turn it *on*. Details of why don't matter, and are not a matter of calculation but of tradition. This is liturgical, not legalistic.

When I knew what was happening,[19] the result was quite striking. It was not something I could participate in, or get control of, though it was clearly possible to interfere. It was as if we had the Reserved Sacrament under my own roof, with all that that implies for a Catholic. It was not an idol — how could a warm empty box be an idol? It was utterly holy — and utterly gracious, quite beyond control or calculation. For my tenant, it was a way of relating to God and shaping his life, though it was also rather routine and unremarkable in a kosher kitchen. For me it was the presence — real presence — of God in another way.

That real presence can be found in many ways, in all things,[20] even though people of a nanomind metaphysics and ontology will always succeed in protecting themselves from it.

Return to a principle invoked often in this inquiry: a Chalcedonian method in theology, together with candor in the face of sociology of knowledge. The principle is simple. Ultimate reality *shows* itself in human realities, but not by *interfering* with the world. Halakah and kashrut are a social construction, and the Incarnation is a social construction. Both are

---

[19] Note that this understanding of the being of human acts has a distributed ontology, as explained in *Living in Spin*.

[20] Some argument to that effect can be found in Steiner, *Real Presences*, which we shall meet again in *Unanswerable Questions*.

dependent on grace and should be understood in the spirit of the caution above: it is ultimate reality (not you) that will interpret your covenant in the end. Monophysite theology of divine action, of course, denies that these ideas are a human social construction and intrudes divine action *in place of* human action in the making of them.

At this point, we can harvest another result. Rabbinic Judaism is Exposure for Christianity. Its mere continuing existence attests that Christianity is a choice and a social construction, an exercise of a responsible liberty of interpretation. One need not wait for the Oven of Achnai in the Bavli, for this is well attested in the New Testament. All the passages that claim for the Church a discretionary authority in the conduct of its affairs (especially the Epistle to the Galatians) in effect claim that responsible liberty of interpretation. Would that the NT authors had allowed to the nascent Synagogue the same "liberty wherewith Christ hath made you free" as they claimed for themselves.

The story of the consequences of not fully recognizing the responsible liberty of interpretation given to the community in its discretionary authority in conduct of the covenant is a long one. There is a text full of sad irony in Mark 13.13, in the Little Apocalypse, "You will be hated by all men on account of my name" (Jerusalem Bible). Rabbinic Judaism has lived this prophecy far better than the Church has. A few Christians were faithful enough witnesses to get themselves martyred in the first centuries, but most of the dying since then has been done by Jews, though recently a few more Christians have been given the crown of martyrdom (not one they wanted, not one we want for them). What grace has been given to the Synagogue that has made it so effective and so obnoxious a witness for world-affirming historical religion?

Eucharistic liturgies for the Easter vigil used to contain a sequence of versicles called the Reproaches, of which the gist is "I brought you out of Egypt, etc.; why did you prepare a cross for your Savior? . . . ."[21] These too obviously invite an anti-Jewish interpretation, so they were omitted from the Proposed Book and the final text of the 1979 American Book of Common Prayer.

Better, today, would be,

> I brought your forefathers out of Egypt,

---

[21] One source can be found in the revision of the American *Book of Common Prayer* in the 1970s. See the Episcopal Church, "The Blue Book": *The Draft Proposed Book of Common Prayer*, 281.

out of nature into history;

And you *knew* that I gave you freedom,
> a responsible liberty of interpretation,
for you claimed that in your New Testament.

But you covered up your responsibility
> in a sacred canopy,
and when the rabbis Exposed you
> as the authors of a socially constructed reality,
> you took it out on your rabbinic brothers
> in a homicidal rage and fury uncommon in all of history.

Why, O my Christian people, why?

10.5 Unbelievable, Offensive, and in Bad Faith

The Church still has problems making sense of the sciences. Its attempts to live with the natural sciences are both somewhat clumsy and also less than candid.

For many people today, claims for "miracles" are simply incredible, implausible, a kind of make-believe. What is more, they offend against the claims of the natural sciences, and these people trust the sciences to provide a kind of reliable meaning when the humanities (and theology) no longer do. And these people know in an instinctive way that claims of "miracles" are in bad faith; they also objectivate what is not objective. They are a way of getting out of the challenges of Exposure, Limitation, and Need, and they are a way of getting out of responsibility for basic choices in life. The fact that some who still believe in "miracles" are attempting to embrace the pains of life faithfully doesn't cut much ice. If things were ever clarified, the "faith" of the faithful would elicit the question, "if that's what they are doing, why don't they say so?"

It is not as if science is a counter-magisterium over against the Church.[22] The natural sciences came from the Church, and it was from

---

[22] I say this in respectful disagreement with one of the most generous and gallant thinkers on the issue: Stephen Jay Gould, in *Rocks of Ages*. Phrased with more precision, Gould's notion of "non-overlapping magisteria" could be restated in terms of the differences in logic between the kinds of questioning in theology and the sciences.

biblical faith that they were able to trust that ultimate reality is trustworthy in a world viewed *sub specie naturae*. The sciences are built on faith in the orderliness of the natural world, and they got that faith from biblical religion. So those who side with the sciences are not against world-affirming historical religion in its understanding of nature, though they are right against the Church's mishandling of the sciences.[23]

The Church doesn't do much for people who find "miracles" unconvincing. She tolerates them, in order to pamper those who still want signs and wonders. The people who find signs and wonders unbelievable, offensive, and in bad faith could lead the Church forward — if they were given some street signs in life, if they were given some idea of where we are in the ongoing history of religions.

In a typical biography, someone was raised as a Christian and learned enough awe before the world so that as an adult he turned to the sciences as a clearing where the world could be seen with awe. The Church, as teacher, doesn't do much for these people. Unable to make much sense of history, at least they can respect the mystery of the world under the aspect of nature — in scientific disciplines that, ironically, are quite faithful to history in the conduct of their own research.[24]

Ezekiel 34 famously chastises the shepherds who fail to feed the flock, pampering the big sheep who crowd out the little sheep. They leave only muddy water for the smaller sheep to drink. That is like the Church today. Typical Catholic seminary education produces men who make good parish priests, but it does not give them enough history of religions or basic philosophy of religion to be of much use to their laity where their laity rub shoulders with seculars for whom biblical religion just doesn't make much sense. Seminaries produce men who are good pastors, preachers, and even shrewd confessors. But the typical MDiv curriculum doesn't give them the larger narrative of which they are a part: the history of religions and the place of biblical (world-affirming historical) religion in it. Despite much improvement in recent years, it still pampers literalists and the remnants of literalism, without showing the basic structure of world-affirming historical religion in the context of the other religious options or the natural and

---

[23] Sometimes the Catholic Church has interfered with the natural sciences, sometimes she has protected them from interference. Galileo is the most famous example of the first; the Church's participation as a plaintiff on behalf of evolutionary biology in the 1981 lawsuit about teaching creationism in the public schools in Arkansas is an example of the second. The first is remembered, the second is forgotten.

[24] Porter, "The Barbour-Smith-Gilkey Paradox."

social sciences. The answers to the basic question of philosophy of religion, "Where does your proposed ultimate reality show itself in the world," are fudged, obfuscated, and corrupted. Acts of God remain monophysite, *interfering* with the world as we know it rather than appearing *in* the world as we know it.

Clergy live a sheltered life; they do not confront in quite the same way as their lay parishioners do the seculars for whom biblical religion in a world of science is bunk, just bunk. Or worse, bad faith.

10.6 Religious Autoimmune Disease

The prophets in the Common Documents were a somewhat unusual phenomenon in the history of religions. Usually, a religion is just supposed to legitimate the Establishment. The prophets tried to delegitimate the Israelite monarchy.[25] Self-criticism is built into biblical religion. It occurs in the prophets, in the New Testament, in the Scholastics, in disputes about causation in acts of God, and in modern biblical criticism.[26] Whatever one may say about constructive Liberal theology, its nineteenth-century biblical criticism was heroic. It was willing to risk all in order to turn on itself the tools of criticism. For some, what resulted was a biblical faith that was strengthened, not weakened. For others, the challenge has not been met even today. Christian self-criticism has in the late twentieth century mutated into something more than that, something that strikes me as pathological. It is a religious form of autoimmune disease.

Autoimmune diseases occur in biology when an immune system can no longer reliably recognize the difference between self and other, what is healthy self and in need of protection, what is sick and needs healing, what is other and to be removed. In a similar way, self-criticism in biblical religion today has trouble distinguishing between what is authentic to biblical religion (of either variety) and what is a superstition, or syncretism, or compromise with another basic kind of religion. Not recognizing what is authentic to biblical religion (world-affirming historical religion if you like) we saw in chapter 9. Many no longer understand what religion is

---

[25] So also did the Deuteronomistic historian, but that story is complex. The Deuteronomists were often associated with the prophets.

[26] Indeed, one could take the New Testament itself as an instance of religious self-criticism, though that reading ought to carry some caution with it inasmuch as the disputes between the Jesus movement and nascent rabbinic Judaism were a lot richer and more complicated than a simple case of corruption and reform. We have seen this above.

10.6 Religious Autoimmune Disease

and does. We do not even ask what gives a human life a point and purpose, what gives a human life narrative coherence in a world where simple assent to *propositions* doesn't provide that coherence. Among the things most often forgotten are the central place of affirming life in this world as good, in full view of its pains. I have said this so many times that it may be a little tedious by now but it is not widely appreciated.

The possibility of confusion in religion is inherent in its structure. Religion is supposed to add coherence to a basic life orientation, to provide some mode of recognition and intention to the direction of a life (a life in community, be it noted). In other words, it is supposed to tell the difference between which acts fit into a chosen basic life orientation and which don't. Difficulty arises from the ambiguity of language and narrative. It is easy to talk one line and live another. Colloquial proverbs acknowledge as much, as in "Ever'body talkin' 'bout heaven ain't goin' to heaven."[27] H. Richard Niebuhr dwelt on the problem in *Radical monotheism* when he came to religion (chapter 4). Acts can be narrated many ways,[28] and we don't always know how to "tell it like it is" — how to spell out well[29] the parts of an engagement with life.

When the language of a life orientation has to draw on resources beyond mere propositions, the problems can become acute. Consider an example that we have seen already, the determination of what an act is by the larger context into which it is fitted, though that larger context is taken for granted as obvious rather than itself being spelled out. We all would like to be excused from the pains of life (Jesus certainly did), and we try to get out of them when we can. Deal with them as one likes, the *acts* of dealing with them are constituted by the larger contexts in which they are construed. This opens up the possibility of tacitly *changing* the larger taken-for-granted context.

When the conceptuality of a culture changes, its commitments have to be reformulated and re-understood. That is not always straightforward. Louis Dupré and many others have commented in this vein on the transitions from the medieval to the modern world. Differences between the biblical worldviews and our own have raised similar questions. All of these problems have attracted self-criticism, as they should.

Self-criticism has drifted into simple apostasy, in several ways. Know-

---

[27] With apologies to Fregean predicate calculus.

[28] Porter, *Living in Spin*, chapters 4–5

[29] Fingarette, *Self Deception*, chapter 3.

ing that we have problems in our history (that, after all, is the major thesis of this book) has led many critics to attack what is genuine along with what is problematic because they can no longer tell the difference. Self-attack also provides a moral status and security that biblical religion never does. For biblical religion, we are all in trouble. Among the confusions is a loss of transcendence, one that has led to loss of commitment. Loss of commitment together with the sexual revolution has led many out of Christianity. The result has been something post-Christian altogether. Why the drift into apostasy, or drift away from the center of biblical religion? It happened because of the same inability to recognize the root character of biblical religion, the inability that led to an autoimmune disease.

There are other, and related, issues that may be noticed here. The purpose of an immune system is to defend a body against adversaries and that, too, arises for an organized religion. Can (and should) biblical religion defend itself against critics? Apologetics can have two meanings: the answering of questions and clearing up of misunderstandings, and attempts to prove the validity of Christianity. Evangelism can easily be confused with the second.

Should the Church enforce its commitments on believers? What is to be done about apostates, those who leave? The problem arises in a somewhat complicated form, already in the Bible. In Merold Westphal's reading, commitment to biblical religion is irrevocable. It is a promise, and it can be broken, but it cannot be "un-promised."[30]

Some concluding questions and observations: Religious freedom for all except those who would suppress religious freedom? This presupposes that we know what is a religion; but we don't. When Western civilization has become offensive, what to do? What is it about Western civilization, religiously speaking, that is worth defending? When Gloria Greenfield and others made a movie in defense of the West,[31] they didn't say much about religion; indeed, not much about the heart of Western civilization. I would lay the fault at the door of the churches, who have not done much to explain themselves.

---

[30] See e.g. Westphal, *God, Guilt, and Death*, 234 and thereabouts.
[31] Greenfield, "The Fight of Our Lives."

10.7 The History We Live In

The present section continues a story that began in section 1.4, in the Prolog, "Some History of Religions," and sections 2.5 and 3.1. We shall return to it again as a story unfinished in section 11.3. The present section will summarize some of the material gained during the course of the argument thus far.

Revisit the place of biblical religion in the perspective of the history of religions. Some of this we have seen already. There is more, both before and after the account in section 1.4. In the beginning, obviously, was astrophysics, but astrophysics, if it is done in a way that is truly naturalistic, is but the prologue for evolution and what comes after evolution, namely history. Evolution is still utterly naturalistic, a point that is not as clear as it might be, for many Darwinians would like evolutionary biology to do for them what the biblical creation stories did for biblical believers before Darwin. They would like it to provide a philosophical anthropology for human life in the world. The anthropology projected upon evolutionary biology is surprisingly reminiscent of predestination[32] themes that do not belong in any natural science. But take naturalistic evolution as given. It has bequeathed to us features of life that matter theologically, if one can diagnose and set aside the homebrew theologies of supposedly naturalistic biologists.

If there is animal life, there is animal behavior, motion. The principal difference between animals and plants is that animals exhibit motion that is initiated from within themselves. (That much is Aristotelian enough, to give credit to The Philosopher.) What follows is that if an animal can move in many directions, something has to decide or determine which one it actually moves in. And some kinds of motions are conducive to reproductive success (and so appear in differential survival), and other kinds of motions are counter-productive. At a minimum, the animal needs to breed with conspecifics, avoid predators, and find prey. And it needs to be aware of more basic behavior that is harmful or fatal: it needs pain. Fantasies or longings for animal life without pain are incoherent.

At some point, language evolved.[33] Language gives man a world, a

---

[32] With Calvinist overtones: fitness presides over evolution in the way that predestination did for English Calvinists of Darwin's day. The alternative, corresponding to Pelagius in theology, would be Lamarck in biology. I tried to sort out some of the logic in *Where, Now, O Biologists*.

[33] The Wiki article "Origin of Language" (late 2017) is uncharacteristically cautious.

world that extends far beyond the immediate present: into the past and the future, into things far away, into things possible but not actual; what might have happened, what could happen. Language makes the difference between mere animal behavior (which is naturalistic) and true action, which is a matter of narrative. With language comes ambiguity, and narratives are ambiguous: they could be told in more ways than just one. And the same language that creates ambiguity enables us sometimes to resolve that ambiguity.

Note here in passing something that comes with language but becomes clear only later in the history of religions. The ambiguity that comes with language applies to human actions as they are narrated and evaluated. Problems arise because what is in one person's interest all too often conflicts with another's. This is one ontological origin of unsatisfactory or disappointing human actions. The Greek words behind "disappointing" ($\dot{\alpha}\mu\alpha\rho\tau\acute{\iota}\alpha$ and its relatives) were turned into a technical term for sin. Sin presupposes an understanding of human life that is open to the ambiguities of narrative (and with them, responsibility). Nevertheless, we have here bumped into one of the origins of sin, even though in nature religions it is not very obvious.

Back to the history of religions. With language, we are on the way to culture. Human memories are short and focus on archetypes when details cannot be saved. But with writing and iron, more is possible: history. Iron enables travel and with it broader horizons. Writing enables memory in ways that are not available to an oral culture.

At this point we have enough to speak of an organized life orientation, or as Peter Berger called it, a socially constructed reality — extending to the whole cosmos. It becomes possible to use language to make a home for man in the universe. It is possible to ask what makes a human life a coherent whole, what gives a human life meaning. It is possible to ask about meaning in life in ways that simply are not thinkable for non-linguistic animals, and it is possible to answer in culture, or better, *as* a culture.

When history is not seen (as it always was not in the earliest cultures), human life gets fitted into nature, as on p. 9 in section 1.4 above. This way of life was not peculiar to the ancient Near East, it is the shape of aboriginal basic life orientation everywhere. In this book, focused on the problems of biblical religion, we specialize to the history of the West, leaving other

---

Some estimates place the origin at 50,000 to 100,000 years ago, but as the article says, there is scant direct evidence. Nevertheless, the question has attracted growing interest.

10.7 The History We Live In

cultures for other writers.

Call it world-affirming nature religion if you like, because it was basically affirming of human life in this world. The problem is that naturalistic categories cannot explain all of what humans encounter. In nature, the world is in some sense regular, and it is predictable even in its irregularities.[34] Things happen in ways that are, shall we say, "characteristic" — and exceptions would be "out of character." All true, in a naturalistic perspective, but there are events enough that do not fit such a schema. They usually involve pain, ambiguity, contingency, the unexpected, and everything that cannot be subsumed under natural regularities. There are examples enough of ambiguity in Greek tragedies, to take only one sort of event that transcends nature. Consider Sophocles' Theban plays. People caught in the ambiguities of conflicting moral obligations and of narratives that they themselves do not entirely understand are thereby thrown into tragedy. Alasdair MacIntyre followed the growth in ethical conceptualities from Homer to the philosophers in *Whose Justice? Which Rationality?*[35]

The situation in the eastern Mediterranean, specifically Egypt, was more interesting. What happened was the evolution or emergence of historical religion from an Egyptian culture that was basically focused on nature.[36] It could have happened anywhere, and it would have happened, sooner or later, someplace, simply because history was becoming both visible and painful. It was bound to happen because the life-affirming instinct in nature religions cannot handle the sorts of painful events that are characteristic of history. Historical events are opaque to a nature religion, surds, unintelligible, refractory to subsumption under naturalistic categories. They don't make sense, they don't fit, and they hurt.

We have seen the emergence of historical-covenantal religion from a background matrix of nature religions, growing out of the now-lost-to-us events of the Exodus, an exodus from nature into history. What might not be noticed is the new dimension of transcendence that came with the Exodus. When Moses asks God's Name, the answer is not entirely reas-

---

[34] This parallels what modern physics does when it finds probability distributions for stochastic processes. The spirit is the same.

[35] MacIntyre, *Whose Justice?*, Chapters II–IX, tracing the growth of the problematic of ethics from Homer to Aristotle and Augustine.

[36] To say that "God acted in these events" is true, but it is also to alternate into another kind of discourse. It is to move from the intramundane side of a Chalcedonian account to the transcendent side, to a confession of faith in something transcendent. For the moment, stick to a history of religions perspective.

suring, as we have seen with John Courtney Murray's paraphrase (p. 28 above): "I shall be with you as who I am shall I be with you." In other words, Israel will be traveling through history in company with a transcendent Other. Transcendence is something that biblical religion grew into, slowly. Finding good in the pains of life is also something it grew into slowly. It is present in the earliest texts, but its depth was explored only slowly (that is why biblical religion is irreducibly historical). The texts in the Common Documents attest a thousand-year transition (from David and Solomon to the Common Era) from nature religion to world-affirming historical religion. Traces of nature religion persist almost until the Common Era. Tribal violence against neighbors, the deities of nature, idol worship, the wife of God, animal sacrifice, human sacrifice, temple architecture, witchcraft, and shamanistic divination are some of the features leftover from nature religion.

The currents that removed these elements from biblical religion also gave it a sense of difference from its neighbors.[37] That apartness was not just another instance of tribalism. The inheritance from Second Temple Judaism was peculiar but not tribal: its peculiarity lay in its shedding of most of the hallmarks of tribalism, and what resulted was an openness that grew into universalism. Biblical religion acquired that universal dimension in many authors, from the Yahwist (Gen. 12), to the Priestly editor and Deutero-Isaiah (40–55), to the Gospels (e.g. Matt. 28). The tension between peculiarity and universality is inherent in biblical religion; it is very much with us today.

The confessional stance of biblical religion was clear enough. In covenant, God called Israel out from among the nations, and the demands of covenant did not apply to other nations.[38] The problem of dissenters does not arise *as a theological problem.* For universalism, it does: The religion claims in some sense to be universal, but it clearly is not universal in the empirical sense of receiving assent from all peoples and all cultures. Sociologists call the mismatch "cognitive dissonance."

Tribal violence is common enough in nature religions, and was also in early biblical religion, but another kind of violence that has occurred all too often in the Common Era was rare before it. The characteristic way

---

[37] Its explanations in the terms of its own time were noticeably different from our explanations in our time. Their time was pre-scientific and often mythological; ours is a time of the history and phenomenology of religions. In between, of course, was a vast philosophical tradition.

[38] See Westphal, *God, Guilt, and Death*, chapter 11, esp. 234.

of wrongly protecting itself from anxiety in a sacred canopy is to exterminate dissenters. By contrast, tribal violence is just social darwinism: surviving and so being "fitter" by eliminating the competition. Eliminating dissenters is something different, even if among atrocities it doesn't look very different.[39] It is a mishandling of religious anxiety and a form of bad faith characteristic of a sacred canopy (see sec. 1.9 above). It comes with a cluster of problems that all arose together. The tensions implicit between universalism and the peculiarity of monotheism are the first, and difficulties with a responsible liberty of interpretation would make a good second.

The problem became acute in the choice between Christ and halakah, and it was radicalized at the same time, for the heirs of Second Temple Judaism had to acknowledge that they had a responsible liberty of interpretation.[40] People usually don't mind the liberty part, especially if it doesn't cause too much anxiety. But that doesn't answer the question, "what do we have to do to exercise that liberty *responsibly*? The choice between Christ and halakah could be posed at a deeper level: are we to conduct our relationship with the transcendent Other by doing what it wants us to do (keeping the Law, cf. Ps. 119), or in a more directly personal relationship, through what they called $\pi\iota\sigma\tau\iota\varsigma$ focused on a person in history?[41] Both courses raise questions in phenomenology that lie beyond this book.

The responsible liberty of interpretation seen in the First Century led in the fourth and fifth (with a little government interference) to a parting of the ways between rabbinic Judaism and Christianity. The problems of confessional responsibility, a liberty of interpretation, and the vices of a sacred canopy have been endemic in biblical religion ever since the fourth century and the establishment of Christianity. We have not solved them

---

[39] I think the atrocities of liquidating heretics and infidels are indefensible in a way that goes beyond the atrocities of tribal violence. Tribal violence can defend itself as "natural" to a naturalistic worldview. Historical-covenantal religion is supposed to know better, and on its own standards, eliminating others is indefensible. As bad as tribal violence is, extermination of unbelievers is worse. That leaves unanswered the question of what to do when the others are trying to kill you or force you to apostatize.

[40] The issue first appeared in clarity in section 4.4 above (the Oven of Achnai), but it was in the background in section 1.9, on sociology.

[41] We take that word for granted, but its meaning is not at all obvious. Calling it "faith" hides its meaning as much as discloses it. Psalm 119 says nothing about particulars of statute, and a lot about the joys of relating to God through the Law. The relationship between "faith" and human actions was incomplete then (see the Epistle of James) and still is, in two recurrent questions that I don't know how to answer very well: (1) what is a basic life orientation? and (2) what gives a human life narrative coherence?

well even today.

The establishment of Christianity worked after a fashion until the end of the medieval period, and since then, we have been in a modern or recent period. Making sense of the recent past is always risky because we do not have the perspective one gets from a long view. At the same time, the recent past is always the bearer of today's problems. So in a brutally simplified sketch, tailored to fit the questions of a philosophical theologian, here is what apparently has happened.

The doctrine of creation (that this world is good, trusted in full view of its pains), gave rise in the transition from the thirteenth to the seventeenth centuries to the faith that the world under the aspect of nature is both intelligible and reliable. The literature is vast and sometimes contentious, but the work of Michael Foster can be cited as a landmark in the beginning of recognition of the contributions of Christian faith to modern scientific thought. Several things came with the change. The earlier easy access between man, God, and the world was gone; for that, see Louis Dupré, *Passage to Modernity*. More concretely, modern physics necessarily assumes that its laws (whatever they are) apply universally, always and everywhere, without exceptions. The resulting problems with acts of God have been with us for the whole book. What goes for acts of God goes also for the presence of God. We shall see more of the presence of God and its importance in *Unanswerable Questions*, but for now I would like simply to collect the parts of the present book.

The attempt to naturalize theology in the seventeenth century didn't work very well, though it did undermine pre-scientific naive and tacit biblical literalism. In the aftermath, in the nineteenth century, came critical or scientific history, a renewed and tenacious biblical literalism, and Liberal theology. Those were, in their way, yet another attempt to recover scientific certainty. Eventually, when even that didn't work, scholars turned to hermeneutics and phenomenology, and along the way, they have recovered many parts of Christianity that were shadowed or forgotten. The crisis of the seventeenth century, monophysite theology of divine action, is still with us. Marcionite theology is still with us. The problem of objectivation of ideas that are a matter of faith is still with us. At the same time, the culture has drifted away from its former biblical religion (mostly Christian, sometimes Jewish). What counts as ontology and epistemology in culture today is not very hospitable to biblical religion. The distributed ontology of human action (as in *Living in Spin*) is mostly unthinkable in any explicit sense today, even though everybody understands it in an instinctive and un-theoretical sense. Our culture has a not-spelled-out policy of not spelling out what it has done with its worldview. Some of these issues will appear in *Unanswerable Questions*, but even there my answers do not entirely satisfy me. There is quite enough work to do just to make sense of the answers we have achieved so far.

10.8 Some Christian Answers

We have merely told a little about the place of Christianity in the history of world-affirming historical (biblical) religion, without saying much about what Christianity is (or became in the First Century and after). Backtrack and repeat some of the questions asked early in the book, and then consider some specifically Christian answers to them. Not all theologians will agree; these are my answers, and as with the rest of the book, disagreements are not hard to find.

The principal questions are:

> What is your proposed ultimate reality?

and

> Where does your proposed ultimate reality
> show itself in the world?
> What is it about life that leads you to propose
> such-and-such as the ultimate reality?[42]

A short (and incomplete) answer for biblical religion of the Christian variety is "in Jesus." A little more detail would be helpful. More context we have already seen; Christianity begins not with Jesus but with the Exodus, an exodus from nature into history. History continues with the inheritance from the Monarchy, the Exile, and Second Temple Judaism. We share this inheritance with rabbinic Judaism.

Many times we have seen the central commitment of Christianity to affirm human life in this world as good in full view of its pains. Merold Westphal puts it this way: "God enters into the world to save his people, not by freeing them from the world, but by being with them in it."[43] How? As Edward Hobbs has it, "suffering for others (both because of others and

---

[42] We have seen this question before, at pp. 3, 11, 14, 152, 171, 181, inter alia.

[43] Westphal, *God, Guilt, and Death*, 222.

for the sake of others) is what God does."[44] All humans suffer for others (in both senses) simply because in our own shared stakes in life and in our lives what is in one person's interest virtually always conflicts with what is in some other's interest. Yet to be a human person is to have stakes in other people's lives as well as one's own.[45] That can be done well or badly, but in *this* proposed ultimate reality, it means to love the neighbor as one whose life is shared with one's own (cf. Leviticus 19.18).

Where does this show itself in history? In the suffering of Jesus. The Passion ontologically transforms every other human life and action. "If this is really how and where ultimate reality shows itself in the world, then the events of the Last Supper and the Passion reconstitute believers as people who have been suffered for, by ultimate reality itself manifest in the world."[46]

In this book, we have usually passed over questions of how to explain transcendence, with the exception of section 6.1, on the domestication of transcendence. More cautious thoughts about transcendence are reserved for the sequel, *Unanswerable Questions*. The problem of transcendence is bigger than the ones that have preoccupied us here (Marcionite and monophysite theology, and evasion of confessional responsibility). Transcendence will grow out of the interpersonal structure of personhood: being in the world among other persons.

---

[44] Hobbs, "The Theology of the Evangelists, Shared Dimensions."
[45] Porter, *Living in Spin*, sections 3.4.1 and 3.4.2.
[46] Porter, *Living in Spin*, section 7.2.1, 228.

Chapter 11

Conclusions

11.1 Collecting Themes

Recall first the beginning basic parts of biblical religion: (1) affirmation of life in this world as good, in full view of its pains, and (2) viewing human life as essentially historical, not just part of nature. Both are commonly forgotten or evaded. To affirm life in history means doing so at a personal level, which is to say traveling through history with a transcendent Other. To seek blessing even in the pains of life and not just in getting out of them utterly transforms events in immediate view. In other words, what an event, an action, or a disappointment *is* depends on the ultimate context in which we construe it. This much was argued in many places, principally in *Living in Spin*.

To see human actions and human lives in the present as part of history is quite different from construing them as just part of nature. In nature, what acts in human lives is nature itself. There can be fate but not responsibility. History is open and ambiguous, for history is the result of narrative, and narratives can be told in many ways. Only in narrative is it possible to take *responsibility*. And so an act in the present is constituted by past acts and events that are part of its present narrative. Again, this was in *Spin*.

That said, the Church has a long history of failed engagements in theology:

>Substituting proofs for covenant,
>>evading its own responsible liberty of interpretation;
>
>Monophysite theology outside Christology,

using miracles as signs and wonders;
using claimed divine exceptions to natural laws
as a way to try to get out of Limitation ultimately;
using claimed "miracles"
as a way to evade responsibility in objectivation;
Half-Marcionite theology
and poisoned relations with Judaism
as a way to get out of responsibility in history;
Sacred canopies and bad faith,
growing out of anxiety and its cover-ups.

More radically, the Church all too often forgets the challenge to *metanoia* in the beginning of Mark, a change of mind in which we come to seek blessing even in the pains of life rather than in getting out of them, even though we are usually happy to get out of them if we can. (Nihilists don't think there are any blessings there at all.) The blessings in the small events of life get their ontological constitution *as* blessings from the limitations of our creaturehood, whether the pains thereof are only latent or actually patent. But I don't think one can speak of the limitations of creaturehood without presupposing some sort of transcendence, some way of dealing with unanswerable questions.

One theme needs both emphasis and more exploration. That would be the relationship of biblical religion of the Christian variety to living in history. Clearly the biblical tradition was successful in engaging living in history. The Short Historical Creed in Deuteronomy 26 (and indeed, all of the Deuteronomistic History) as well as the entire New Testament do that. They are intensely historical. What they do not do is engage the *philosophy* of history, theory of how history works, as the modern and postmodern worlds have done. Hittite suzerainty treaties don't go that far. We are still working to get it right. We have difficulty seeing that we are traveling through history in company with a transcendent Other, in a covenant that humans have written (a social construction) but which gets interpreted by the transcendent Other. Both the Church and the Synagogue have rightly claimed a discretionary authority for the covenant community in the conduct of the covenant. Neither could solve the problem of a dissident community exercising that discretionary authority differently. That is the longest-running failed engagement in the life of the Church. The New Testament, like the Mishnah, is a way of continuing the covenant that started in and grew from the Exodus. But is Christianity willing to live with the openness of history and to live with the anxiety that comes with being open to that openness? The purpose of a sacred canopy was precisely to block out that openness and precariousness. For a sacred canopy, Jesus is indeed the final solution to the problem of history. Acknowledging that Christianity is a human social construction is a good step toward undermining sacred canopies and taking the responsibility that is appropriate to covenant. To say that is to speak in a this-worldly perspective, which is only one side of a Chalcedonian method in theology. The other side is the confession of divine action in history. Inherent in its logic is that it is not allowed to contradict the this-worldly discourse of the history of religions.[1] The two discourses are misunderstood if they appear to contradict one another. If their relationship is not understood, then transcendence itself is misunderstood. But misunderstanding transcendence would hardly be new in the history of theology. Indeed, it is more common than not. It is amazing that the Bible, in the terms of its own times, really does engage transcendence.

11.2 Our Problems, in Retrospect

Consider the problems of theology. It used to be thought that the principal challenge for theology in the modern world was modern science. We have seen that that is not so; science is a challenge only to generalized monophysite theology. Chalcedonian theology can only welcome modern science. After that mistake is cleared up, what stands out next? The challenges to theology in the nineteenth and twentieth centuries were critical history, historical and cultural relativity, and religious pluralism. We have not met those challenges well even today.

The reason, I think, lies with the besetting problems of the Church: a responsible liberty of interpretation, generalizing Chalcedon, broken relations with rabbinic Judaism, and sacred canopies. These are older than the modern world and its monophysite instincts. In every case, the Church sort of did the right thing — but in the argument of this book, pulled back or just did not follow through.[2] Yet it could be phrased in a different way:

---

[1] This does not mean that description of this-worldly phenomena is infallible or above criticism. Accounts of things in this world are often wrong. What it means is that phenomena in this world are to be criticized on their own terms, without intrusion or interference from transcendence, even though they presuppose transcendence.

[2] Obviously, this book does not argue that the Church *always* did the right thing; see

Each of these crises was the beginning of something bigger than what people saw at the time.[3] Each is still fertile, open to development. That, after all, is true at the most basic level — the level at which we consent to accept blessings *in* the disappointments of life, rather than just in getting *out* of the disappointments of life. That lesson only began with the Patriarchs. It was developed in the Exodus and the Monarchy, with successively more painful disappointments that were taken into the Faith.

If we now find ourselves living in *Screwtape*, Letter VIII, we are still wayfarers on a pilgrimage through history. The end is not in sight. That Letter gives us a man who cannot see God, is tempted to despair, but obeys anyway. To ask whether perhaps we are living in Letter VIII is to notice that we have problems in knowing God, in naming God, and problems with truth.[4] This book does not answer those questions. They can be engaged, but that will have to wait for *Unanswerable Questions*.

11.3 Our Present Plight

This section continues a history that has unfolded in the course of the book: sections 1.4, History of Religions; 2.5, The Shape of the Exodus; 3.1, The Exodus in the Gospels; 10.7, The History We Live In; and 11.3, Our Present Plight (this section).

Within that larger history, it was possible to read the Pentateuch and Former Prophets as a five-act tragedy.[5] Is our situation like that? That cannot be said except in hindsight. If someday it turns out we are (or in the future were) in such a drama, we are now at most in the second or third act; we can barely see what our problems are but not how to solve them. Whether the result will be tragedy or comedy or *Heilsgeschichte* we don't know. It's too soon to tell.

Some things can be hazarded. As William Gibson said of Shakespearean tragedies, they begin when some "happening" (p. 33 above) dis-

---

the sections on atrocities. Often the atrocities came about because the Church mishandled the crises named above.

[3] One could invoke John Henry Newman, for later developments of doctrine all began with small things in earlier doctrine. Genuine development is to be welcomed.

[4] Thomas Aquinas, in the *Summa*, part 1, questions 12 and 13; Murray, *The Problem of God*, 17–19, in his third and fourth questions. About truth, there are a few conjectures in my own *Living in Spin*, section 8.3, "Revisiting the Question of Truth," and *Basic Concepts of Biblical Religion*, section 5.5, "Truth as Troth."

[5] Cf. above, p. 32.

turbs the equilibrium of an earlier state of society. Several are obvious: Modern science exposed the monophysite theology of divine action as incoherent, and the questions it led to became critical history, historical and cultural relativity, and religious pluralism. They in turn opened the way to sociology of knowledge and the recovery of a confessional responsibility in the conduct of a covenant. That has exposed the responsible liberty of interpretation of the covenant community and its sometimes shabby exercise of that liberty. Beneath all these lies the mystery of transcendence.

Most likely, theology will ignore these problems for as long as it can. It will change as little as possible and as slowly as possible. It is a temperamentally conservative discipline, and in the perspective of the sociology of knowledge, the task assigned to theology is to establish the Establishment,[6] justify social constructions, and retard change as long as possible. The job assigned to theology is to prevent anxiety, not to provoke anxiety. That's for prophets — or on a good day, seminary education. Pastoral theology has to allay the anxieties of the laity, and it often does so in bad faith (as with sacred canopies). On the contrary, the task of seminary education is to get seminarians to relish the anxiety of theology, to enjoy its thrills, and come back for more, without sacred canopies. That doesn't always happen.

Neo-Orthodox theology was occasionally called a theology of crisis, or some such words. It was (and the theology in this book is) for a time of troubles. When the Deutschmark became a hard currency, in 1948, the end of hard times was within sight, and Neo-Orthodox theology lost interest.[7] We live today in a time that is complacent and affluent, so challenges such as Neo-Orthodoxy get patronized, co-opted, and then ignored.

The risk to Catholic theology is that some other discipline will present competition that gives more effective voice to a world-affirming historically religious life orientation, more effective guidance to affirming human life in this world as good, in history, and in full view of its pains. One task of theology is to provide street signs in life, to tell you where you are.[8] It is as if today the street signs in traditional theology are in Latin or Greek; that is, you have to learn a special technical philosophy to understand them.

---

[6] This is as true of the theology of the so-called Sexual Revolution as it is of most other theologies. That theology is thoroughly at the service of establishing its proposed Establishment.

[7] Berger, *The Sacred Canopy*, 164.

[8] I owe this definition to Edward Hobbs.

If somebody were to provide world-affirming historically religious street signs in ordinary English, then Catholic theology would become obsolete.

More painfully, since anti-Semitism is all too alive and well, it should be noted that if rabbinic Judaism were to disappear, the Catholic Church would be morally bankrupt. The Church needs the Synagogue to be strong, healthy, and different; without it, the Church would degenerate into just another paganism. Rabbinic Judaism is not some other religion, it is a *different* and *necessary* part of the *same* biblical religion.[9]

The present state of Catholic theology is in some ways like Hamlet's plight. Alasdair MacIntyre characterized Hamlet's problem as not knowing what story he is part of.[10] Consequently he does not know what to do. Theology today is in a similar confusion. It has forgotten basic concepts such as the difference between religions of nature, the religion of history, religions of escape, and several other kinds of religion. It no longer understands its own commitment to finding good *in* the pains of life instead of escaping *from* them.[11] And it has forgotten the history of (and responsibility for) its own *choices*. It is ripe for some young Fortinbras to come in and provide a better account of how a world-affirming historical life orientation really works. Fortinbras need not be a person, it could just as well appear in the drift of culture. Culture could manage quite well to affirm human life in history without the conceptual paraphernalia of biblical religion. A culture could add recognition and intention to that, and it would make Christianity obsolete.

We do not as a community have much consensus on what we are doing as an organized religion, an organized life orientation, a covenant community. MacIntyre's horror fantasy in the first chapter of *After Virtue* is very apropos, one in which conceptual fragments of science survive, but how they are to be integrated together has been lost. Some of them continue but without much understanding of how they originally worked or what they mean. In regard to the natural sciences, MacIntyre's horror scenario was unbelievable and (today) impossible, which is why he chose it. His intended target was contemporary ethics, which is as confused as the "science" of his fantasy. But the fantasy applies also to theology, both

---

[9] One could find similar thoughts in Romans 11.

[10] MacIntyre, "Epistemological Crises, Dramatic Narrative," *Monist* 60 no. 4 (1977/10) 453–472, esp. 453–454. Also in my own *Living in Spin*, 107–109 and 140–144.

[11] This does not mean that the pains are good because they are painful; we would all like to get out of pain, as much as possible. But when it is not possible, then what?

11.3 Our Present Plight

academic and colloquial, as much as to ethics.

One reason I think we are in at most the second act of a drama is that there is as yet no consensus about the problems of theology. It is the work of the early acts to define the problem, show what it would take to solve it, and show why that is not trivial or easy.[12] The transition from the second or third act to the path to an ending can come suddenly. There is no drama until the problem is identified, which requires that it have been solved, i.e., there is no drama until after it is over. Before that we don't know what's happening. As it is, we know we have problems, but there is no agreement about what they are. If one were to seek an analogy other than drama (Hamlet), it might be sufficient to note that there were many Judaisms in the first century, and only two survived. That is a little more hopeful; after all, in Hamlet, all the major characters die in the end.

A lesson can be learned from Hamlet, and it is not entirely comforting. Inasmuch as human actions get their being from their larger contexts and we do not know the larger context, then it follows that we do not know what we are doing. We do know enough to know that we have botched things rather badly. To act and not know what one is doing is accounted a form of suffering. But how, then, can we know enough to function honorably and effectively? Give us this day our daily truth? Sufficient unto the day is the truth thereof?

Consider one aspect of our problems. There are more than just two temperaments in theology but two stand out: Liberal theology (the children of Schleiermacher) and the many kinds of biblical literalism. Liberal theology chooses to ignore most philosophical questions and so cannot answer philosophically informed challenges. There are both historical and temperamental reasons for this. The reactionary literalisms are not as literalist as they think they are. Nevertheless, they do attempt to objectivate the basis for their faith, and they court irresponsibility and all the vices of a sacred canopy. Hence a question: Are these the only choices we have? Many have posed this question but it is worth attending to it again. Some of us would like the confidence and determination of the "conservatives" but without a sacred canopy or bad faith. And we would like the critical candor of the Liberals without their abdication of questions of philosophy

---

[12] Compare MacIntyre, in *Whose Justice? Which Rationality?*, 362, where he says that problems in an old paradigm often are not visible until a new one comes along.

and transcendence. We would also like to escape from the errors of the Enlightenment shared by *both* Liberals and Fundamentalists.

The dilemma becomes a little more tractable if it is rephrased: If we are to do theology (and with it, life) in a way that is philosophically responsible, are we limited to the heirs of Plato, Aristotle, Augustine, and Descartes? Or are there other resources? What would the tradition of moderate realism that passes through Aquinas look like today? More hermeneutics and phenomenology? Philosophical exploration of the interpersonal relations that are so prominent in the New Testament (e.g., Corinthians) and the liturgy, but which philosophers are conspicuously uninterested in?

What do hermeneutics and existential phenomenology offer, especially as a way into sure and certain hope, but without the bad faith of reducing theology to propositions and thereby appearing to know things we cannot know? Aquinas is quite careful to admit things we cannot know, but he is easily subverted, as we have seen in the domestication of transcendence. How can we avoid that?

To put it more concretely, if we are to engage real transcendence, with the seriousness of commitment that it engenders, do we have to deny our own hand in our own social construction of transcendence (and so incur charges of bad faith and a sacred canopy)? Is the only other choice that of Liberal theology, which undermines transcendence, and with it all serious commitment? How can we have both real transcendence and critical candor in theology?[13]

This, I suppose, is also to ask what we have forgotten. For the biblical world (we think) dealt with real transcendence well enough in the terms of its own time. One definition of superstition is that it happens when people forget how some categories work but carry on their associated categorial language game as before. The concepts are not understood but we use them anyway. What was once real transcendence has become something like a cargo cult.

How might something better be recovered? I think the problem of choice sets up the problems of transcendence. The phenomenon of choice brings us up against a reality that we cannot objectivate — a place where we cannot get out of responsibility for our choices. So how do we

---

[13] This was the issue in the discussion of Paul Ricoeur's notion of the several kinds of naiveté, p. 170 above.

know that ultimate reality enters into our "children's games,"[14] our socially constructed realities? That cannot be known, only trusted. This book has focused on a few poorly handled engagements in the life of the Church: denial of responsibility, monophysite theology of divine action, half-Marcionite theology, and kindred mistakes. Behind them lie puzzles (and a few mysteries) about language, its ambiguities, and the unanswerable questions that inevitably arise for language-capable life. They are all rooted in anxiety, because that is how we are constituted: we are not in control, we would like some explanation of our not being in control, but what we really want is to get into control. That's not possible. What is the responsible way to talk about such things?

So much for the challenges we face today. Critical history, over the last few centuries, has given us a new perspective on the place of Catholic Christianity in the history of religions and the world we now live in. One can hope that the Church's leaders can bring the laity from primary naiveté through critical thinking to secondary naiveté — as was observed above on p. 170. This book and its sequel have not answered all the questions they have raised, but they have I think shown that the challenges we face can be met.

11.4 Questions

In the historical perspective of section 10.7 we can see a little of how we got to where we are today. In this book we have not dealt with transcendence. Nevertheless, at this point, some questions are appropriate, both for readers in general and for pastors.

What will you do with your life? Construe it in terms of nature alone, or history first? (Science has a history, so trying to start with science before history doesn't work — if you believe in history at all.)

Do you want to participate in responsibility? When you have to choose between pizza and beer or pasta and wine, what or who is it that chooses? Your brain cells, or just *you*? This is the choice between nature and history.

What will you do with the pains of life? Are the pains just to be escaped from, or can any positive construction be put on them? How will you come to terms with the pains of life? Into what larger context do you put them in order to make sense of them? As a friend related his prayers

---

[14] Porter, *Unwelcome Good News*, section 6.1.

after a losing a son in a vehicle accident, "Lord, you have to show me that you are in this someplace, otherwise I'm not sure I'm gonna make it." Whether howling or reduced to silence, that is how we ask John Courtney Murray's opening questions in *The Problem of God*.

What will you do with unanswerable questions? Pretend they are answerable? Forbid them? Silence them? Ignore them? Evade them? Construct a world in which they are unthinkable? Or, for biblical religion, meet them on a personal level, even though ultimate reality is not a personal being that might or might not exist?

Many questions are unanswerable but not thereby meaningless, so why do unanswerable questions arise in human living? *That* question is not at all unanswerable.[15] People disagree about it and its answers, so is it admissible for discussion?

What is the ultimate answer to these questions, for you? Where and how does your proposed ultimate reality show itself within the world as we know it? In history? In nature? In getting out of the pains of life in this world?

If you choose to define your life in terms of history, which history? Where in history does your proposed ultimate reality show itself? Which history shows what life is really all about? This was H. Richard Niebuhr's definition of revelation: the history that explains itself and explains the rest of history.[16] But that is both a choice, for which one is responsible, and also experienced as compelling: The pivotal history challenges us, it shapes my life, it ontologically constitutes who and what I am and we are. It is not *just* a choice, and that synthesis of choice and ontological challenge reflects its Chalcedonian constitution.

To pastors, I don't think you have the slightest idea of the peril you are in. Remember Hamlet: he did not know the narrative of which he was a part and so did not know what to do. If you were asked for the larger story you live in, most of you couldn't do any better than to embroider on the creeds; too many still peddle a conventional supernatural. While the

---

[15] The short answer is that language's reach exceeds its grasp. Do you want to trust language or not? And do so critically or uncritically?

[16] See Niebuhr, *The Meaning of Revelation*, variously in three editions, 93, 68, and 50. Niebuhr called revelatory history *internal* history, history told from the point of view of members of the community. Cf. 3rd Edition, 37. In contrast, external history brackets community membership and tells the story from the point of view of an external observer. Niebuhr saw clearly that the choice of which history explains the rest of history *is* a choice and not something objective.

creeds are true (and necessary) as far as they go, they don't answer some rather important questions we face today. In the perspective of the history of religions (how world-affirming historical religion arose) or of the philosophy of religions (differences between the various kinds of religion), the creeds don't help much. How did language-capable life arise in evolution? Can you explain the ontological changes that came with language acquisition? How did *zōon logikon*, language-capable life, become the sort of being whose being is ontologically constituted as, shall we say, not just personal, but "person-ready," ready for relating to other persons?[17] (That is more than what is in this book, but it can serve as a foretaste of work still to be done.)

To step outside of the traditional problematic, how can a human life have a basic orientation? What would that mean? How can a human life have (or be given) narrative coherence? These are questions that the secular culture struggles with — but inarticulately, without realizing what it is doing. If the Church is to do better than the secular culture, it needs to understand and spell out answers to some of these questions. That's not part of an ordinary pastor's job as presently understood but it needs to be done nonetheless. The time will come when not doing it will cost the Church far more than it already has.

Not all the news is bad. In my own limited experience and observation, most Catholic pastors know enough to leave nonsense about "proofs" to philosophers. They (you) know that as a practical matter, being Catholic is a choice, not the result of a logical derivation. Being Catholic in the right way is a matter of some disagreement and you have a little say in guiding people. But in some ways you are just helpless spectators, watching the lives of your parishioners, with a bizarre variety of theologies that you can't do much to inform or lead. A little differently, how do you plan to manage the menu in a theological short-order house, theological fast food of great variety, which is what your market wants?

Will you be sharing with us the laity what you learned in seminary about the origins of the Bible? JEDP and all that? They teach this stuff to undergraduates, but can it be taught in a parish? There are plenty of books about it, even from Catholic authors. *That* cat is out of the bag. I learned about it when I was in seventh grade. Explaining it is not difficult, even to beginning highschool students.

---

[17] That is to state the condition of a newborn: the newborn is always already related to other persons, even though it is still learning that.

Will you be sharing with us what you learned about form criticism? That the Bible contains many literary genres, often in a hodge-podge, woven together by the last editors? What's at stake is rather important: The Bible is the result of many voices, of a complex community in history. If you were to admit the many voices in the Bible, it would become something you could be really proud of. But you (and your laity) cling to tattered shreds of a biblical literalism that was designed to alleviate anxiety, at cost of sheltering them from historical reality. This is true even among Catholics, who know that the Church is mistress over biblical interpretation, yet interpret literally anyway. In the past, Protestants have often left out interpretation; for them, the Answers are In the Bible and you can trust it to solve all your problems. It interprets itself, but the results are still literalist.

The Bible is a collection like no other: it is easy to think of imitations of the Bible that were composed by one author[18] at the start of several obvious new religious movements, but the Bible is not like that. It is not a single argument or story given coherence by one author from beginning to end. It grew out of many centuries of a people struggling with God. If the bible is unique, so also is biblical religion. It is the life of a people traveling through history in covenant with a transcendent Other. That Other brings challenge at least as much as solace. Despite the common language of divine action, the community is not simply following instructions, as though that would get it out of responsibility. It is not as if its choices have been made for it. For we have also the testimony of the history of religions, in which all religions are human creations, human ways of dealing with ultimate reality. That does not mean that all ways are equivalent, nor are they interchangeable salve veritatem. In different religions, people do quite different things with their lives. Can you explain that to your laity?

The covenant community has an active and discretionary role in the conduct of the covenant with this transcendent reality, and that entails a certain anxiety that comes inevitably with responsibility. The Common Documents called it the "Fear of the Lord." Our "seeing" God, or maybe better, hearing God in history is an active seeing and hearing. What we hear in God's self-revelation is not a deposit of information, it is a challenge of a personal kind: we are *known*, we have no control over our being known, and so in that sense, we have no control over our own being. Part of what is revealed to us is our own not being in control.

---

[18] My favorite is Laird, *The Boomer Bible*, but it was not intended to start a new religion.

11.4 Questions 247

What goes for form criticism goes also for redaction criticism. Will you tell your laity that the Synoptic Gospels are a parody of the Exodus? Will you tell your laity that the miracles in Mark build up from small to great for a reason? They didn't "just happen" that way in historical fact; the editors are trying to tell you something. I know you know this stuff, or should. They do still teach source, form, and redaction criticism in seminaries, surely? The Neo-Orthodox were a generation or two in the past. I know Catholic biblical teachers who carry on that tradition; but did *yours*? Has biblical criticism gone out of fashion? In order to protect the sensitive feelings of seminarians, and even more, to protect the feelings of their laity? On the other hand, it may be Catholic biblical scholarship that is the strongest (not the weakest) part of seminary education. Systematics and philosophy are more than a little bit disorderly today, but the Bible has a way of getting its message through despite many readers' hermeneutics that I would not be comfortable with.

I know you can't do this in sermons, but there are more teaching opportunities than just sermons. What's your pleasure?

Will you be acknowledging that the watershed in the history of religions was at the Exodus, not in the Disasters of the First Century? As radical as the changes in the First Century were, the Exodus was more radical still. It was a move from nature into history; the First Century was merely about how best to carry on historical religion after a crisis. We disagreed, and in that disagreement, uncovered the responsible liberty of interpretation that is given in biblical religion, the discretionary authority that is given to the covenant community in the conduct of the covenant. Can you acknowledge that?

Will you be providing us with street signs to tell us where we are in life? In the vernacular, not in some philosophical language of days gone by? Above, I likened the plight of theology today to one who does not know the story he is a part of and so is vulnerable to another taking over his role and his mission (Fortinbras, p. 240 above). Pope Benedict XVI wondered whether Christianity (especially in Europe) may become a minority in a culture predominantly oriented to other ends. This makes it sound as if the responsibility belongs to apostate European culture, and that may not be entirely wrong. But in older days, the Church could provide people with street-signs in life; she doesn't do that very well now, and so the fault for secularism cannot entirely be laid at the door of apostates.

The literature of the so-called "New Atheists" was for me boring and unconvincing, though not because they are always wrong. Indeed, they criticize real faults in Catholic theology, but Catholic theology is so diverse that other theologians are innocent of the faults they criticize. The version of Catholic theology they criticize has serious problems: it thinks of God as one being among others, and as a being that interferes with natural laws, for two examples. Catholic apologists are somewhat ginger around monophysite theology of divine action, because though the New Atheists attack it, the reviewers are perplexed about whether to defend it or not. The apologists have (in their own mind) succeeded in defending the Faith against its attackers, but the New Atheists have an easy reply, one that is never heard: "If the theology we atheists attack is wrong, how come you theologians still tolerate it? How come you still coddle monophysite theology of divine action? Humean miracles, etc.?" The net result of the reviews of the New Atheists is an indictment of the Church more than of the New Atheists.[19] The conclusion I would infer is that the prominent voices in the Church have not explained the Christian faith well enough to attract those who would embrace it if they understood it; nor do they make clear what others are passing up when they leave it. None of the parties in these conversations know the history of religions well enough to situate biblical religion (in both its varieties) in a world-affirming historical basic life orientation in contrast to religions of nature or exile.

The story of Hamlet and Fortinbras is not the only possible simile from which we could learn. From within the Bible we see God make a covenant with the House of David and then rip most of it away when Rehoboam inherits the throne. He was proud, arrogant, cruel, greedy, sophomoric, and foolish. The people were oppressed, and then they departed. You are not like Rehoboam. You are pious and conservative, conserving even Scholastic philosophy, with all its solicitude for signs and wonders then and now. Today, the Church provides signs and wonders for people who want them, but very little for those who recognize signs and wonders as just make-believe. Those people were confused, and then they departed — usually quietly and politely, but they still departed. They just lost interest in a Church that offers them nothing in the world they actually live in.

About the various kinds of basic life orientation, starting with nature religions and then historical religion, can you teach your parishioners to

---

[19] I am not saying that the New Atheists would convert if they understood the Catholic faith correctly. They have other reasons for getting out of biblical religion: too much pain, history is bunk, or transcendence doesn't make any sense to them. That is their right, though like everybody else, they have to live with their choices.

recognize, understand, and reject nature religion even when it is not labeled as such? Gently and clearly but without scolding? Instead, many in seminaries (not all Catholic) want to co-opt nature religion, to sell "God" in the name of environmentalism.[20]

In the Common Documents, the prophets foretold disaster, and in that they were believed. Disaster was quite plausible. What Judah and Israel could not hear was the idea that disaster was the way to salvation. But for you, disaster is not inevitable; not yet. You could lose your shepherding of Western Culture,[21] but it doesn't have to be that way. You have resources from within the tradition to make sense of our changed circumstances, to make sense of our place in the history of religions, to make sense of the evolution of man from naturalistic beginnings to existential phenomenology, to make sense of (and even correct) the mistakes of the tradition. You can, but will you? If you abandon your role of explaining the world to people, someone else will take up that role. World-affirming historical religion, affirming life in this world in full view of its pains, with the necessary transcendence to support that affirmation, can point to the historical events wherein that chosen ultimate reality has shown itself. But if the magisteria of the churches can no longer explain it to them, people will reinvent it if necessary. It is too obvious, too inviting — for those who can accept its offer of grace. A world-affirming historical basic life orientation will continue, if necessary, without you. You are dispensible.

Will you be commenting on the difference between chastity, modesty, faithfulness — and the technology of disrespect, with the sexual chaos it has brought upon us? (Cf. p. 203 above.) Dare you remind people that the whole purpose of the technology of disrespect was to allow males to get and get away with any sex they want and then skip town when the time comes to take responsibility for their sexual actions? Can you recognize the corruption and corrosion that the technology of disrespect inflicts on *all* human relationships? The damage is done by the availability of the technology of disrespect even more than by its actual use. The availability redefines everyone as a sexual predator and redefines the point of marriage as sex rather than the ordering of human lives to passing on the gift of life.

---

[20] Global warming alarmism is only the latest version. Memories are short; there have been many others.

[21] Many say you already have.

Will you be coddling monophysite theology of divine action ("miracles," signs and wonders), or will you recall theology to a Chalcedonian way of thinking?

Will you let the faithful get away with evading responsibility for their faith by objectivating it in signs and wonders? Sometimes the laity can see through that. Some of them are ahead of you.

Will you still be half-Marcionite, or will you welcome the challenge that rabbinic Judaism brings by its mere existence? Friends in their disagreement, for your sake, as in Romans 11.28? Can you retrieve the roots of Christianity and world-affirming historical religion in the history of Israel?

The atrocities? The difference between the transformation of nature religion into historical religion before the First Century, and the attempt to silence critics after it?

Are you serious about Exposure, Limitation, and Need? And critical history, historical and cultural relativity, and religious pluralism? Applying Exposure, Limitation, and Need in history, relativity, and pluralism? Sacred canopies? Or confessional candor?

In general, for both the faithful and the clergy, what will you do with your lives? What about the pains, and what about living in history? Given where we are now in the history of religions, where are you going from here? How will you handle unanswerable questions?

As things stand, like Hamlet, you don't know the larger narratives you are living in. All you have is fragments of the Catholic faith, with poor ways to integrate them.

Bibliography

Amir, Alexander. *Infinitesimals: How a Dangerous Mathematical Theory Shaped the Modern World.* New York: Scientific American and Farrar-Straus-Giroux, 2014.

Anselm of Canterbury. *Saint Anselm: Basic Writings.* S. N. Deane, ed. 2nd ed. LaSalle, IL: Open Court, 1979

Bambach, Charles R. *Heidegger, Dilthey, and the Crisis of Historicism.* Cornell University Press, 1995.

Barron, Robert. *The Priority of Christ; Toward a Postliberal Catholicism.* Grand Rapids: Baker Academic, 2007.

Barth, Karl. *Der Römerbrief.* 1918; 2nd edition, 1922. English translation as *The Epistle to the Romans,* by Edwyn C. Hoskyns (London: Oxford University Press), from the sixth German edition. 1933, 1977.

Bacon, Francis. *The New Organon or True Directions Concerning the Interpretation of Nature.* (1620) Online at http:// www.constitution.org/ bacon/nov_org.txt. "This rendition is based on the standard translation of James Spedding, Robert Leslie Ellis, and Douglas Denon Heath in The Works (Vol. VIII), published in Boston by Taggard and Thompson in 1863."

Beck, Norman, *Mature Christianity in the 21st Century; the Recognition and Repudiation of the Anti-Jewish Polemic of the New Testament.* New York: Crossroad, 1994.

Bencivenga, Ermanno, *Logic and Other Nonsense: The Case of Anselm and his God*. Princeton University Press, 1993.

Berger, Peter L. *Adventures of an Accidental Sociologist*. Amherst, New York: Prometheus Books, 2011.

Berger, Peter L. *The Sacred Canopy: Elements of a Sociological Theory of Religion*. New York: Doubleday, 1967.

Berger, Peter L., and Thomas Luckmann. *The Social Construction of Reality; A Treatise in the Sociology of Knowledge*. New York: Doubleday, 1966.

Berger, Peter L., and Anton C. Zijderveld. *In Praise of Doubt: How to Have Convictions Without Becoming a Fanatic* New York: HarperCollins, 2009.

Blair, Alexander. *Christian Ambivalence Toward Its Old Testament: Interactive Creativity versus Static Obedience*. Eugene, OR: Wipf and Stock, 2010.

Booth, Wayne. *A Rhetoric of Irony*. Chicago: University of Chicago Press, 1974.

Bowler, Peter J. *Evolution: The History of an Idea*. Berkeley and Los Angeles: University of California Press, 1984.

Boyarin, Daniel, *Border Lines: the Partition of Judaeo-Christianity*. Philadelphia: University of Pennsylvania Press, 2004.

Brague, Rémi. *Eccentric Culture: a Theory of Western Civilization*. Trans. Samuel Lester. South Bend, Ind.: St. Augustine's Press, 2002.

Brueggemann, Walter and Hans Walter Wolff. *The Vitality of Old Testament Traditions*. Atlanta: John Knox Press, 1975.

Bultmann, Rudolf. *Jesus Christ and Mythology*. New York: Scribners, 1958.

Bultmann, Rudolf. *Kerygma and Myth*. Ed. Hans Werner Bartsch. New York: Harper and Row, 1961.

Burns, R. M. *The Great Debate on Miracles; from Joseph Glanvill to David Hume.* Lewisburg: Bucknell University Press, 1981.

Burrell, David B. *Aquinas, God, and Action.* Notre Dame: University of Notre Dame Press, 1979.

Burrell, David B. *Knowing the Unknowable God: Ibn-Sina, Maimonides, Aquinas.* Notre Dame: University of Notre Dame Press, 1986.

Burtt, E. A. *The Metaphysical Foundations of Modern Physical Science.* London: Routledge and Kegan Paul, 1924.

Catholic Bishops, Natonal Conference of. *The Book of Divine Worship.* Pocono, PA: Newman House Press, 2003.

Collingwood, Robin George. *An Autobiography.* Oxford: Oxford University Press, 1939.

Collingwood, Robin George. *An Essay on Metaphysics.* Oxford: Oxford University Press, 1940.

Collingwood, Robin George. *The Idea of History.* Oxford: Oxford University Press, 1946; 2nd ed., 1993.

Collins, Billy. "Introduction to Poetry." https://www.poemhunter.com/poem/introduction-to-poetry/.

Cooperman, Alan, Gregory Smith, and Katherine Ritschey. "America's Changing Religious Landscape: Christians decline as share of population; unaffiliated and other faiths continue to grow." Pew Research: www.pewresearch.org, 2015-05-12. http:// assets.pewresearch.org/wp-content/uploads/sites/11/2015/05/RLS-08-26-full-report.pdf.

Courtois, Stéphane, Nicolas Werth, Jean-Louis Panné, Andrzej Paczkowski, Karel Bartosek, Jean-Louis Margolin. *The Black Book of Communism: Crimes, Terror, Repression.* Trans. Mark Kramer and Jonathan Murphy, Harvard University Press, 1999.

Cross, F. L., ed., *Texte und Untersuchungen zur altchristlichen Literatur.* Band 88 (Berlin, Akademie-Verlag, 1964).

Cross, F. L. and E. A. Livingstone, eds. *The Oxford Dictionary of the Christian Church.* London: Oxford University Press, 1974.

Crossan, John Dominic. *The Cross that Spoke; the Origins of the Passion Narrative*. San Francisco: Harper and Row, 1988.

Damasio, Antonio. *Descartes' Error: Emotion, Reason and the Human Brain*. New York: Avon, 1995.

Deneen, Patrick J. "Unsustainable Liberalism," *First Things* 225 (2012/08–09) 25. Available online at https://www.firstthings.com/article/2012/08/unsustainable-liberalism.

Depew, David J. and Bruce H. Weber. *Darwinism Evolving; Systems Dynamics and the Genealogy of Natural Selection*. Cambridge: MIT Press, 1996.

Dix, Gregory, OSB. *The Shape of the Liturgy* London: Dacre Press, 1944. There are later editions.

Dodds, Michael J. *Unlocking Divine Action: Contemporary Science and Thomas Aquinas*. Washington, DC: Catholic University of America Press, 2012

Dreibelbis, Gary. "Moving Mountains and Money: A First Union Bank Commercial." Western Regional meeting of the American Academy of Religion, March 2001.

Dreyfus, Hubert L. *Being-in-the-World: A Commentary on Heidegger's "Being and Time," Division I*. Cambridge, MA: MIT Press, 1991.

Dreyfus, Hubert L. *What Computers Still Can't Do; A Critique of Artificial Reason*. Third edition. Cambridge, MA: MIT Press, 1992.

Dungan, David Laird. *A History of the Synoptic Problem; The Canon, the Text, the Composition, and the Interpretation of the Gospels*. New York: Doubleday, 1999.

Dupré, Louis. *Passage to Modernity; an Essay in the Hermeneutics of Nature and Culture*. New Haven: Yale University Press, 1993.

Eberstadt, Mary Tedeschi. *Adam and Eve After the Pill: Paradoxes of the Sexual Revolution*. San Francisco: Ignatius Press, 2013.

Eberstadt, Mary Tedeschi. "The Family: Discovering the Obvious." *First Things* 140 (2004/02) 10.

Eberstadt, Mary Tedeschi. "The Vindication of Humanae Vitae." *First Things* 185 (2008/08–09).

Eberstadt, Mary Tedeschi, "The Will to Disbelieve." *First Things* 190 (2009/02) 29.

Eliade, Mircea. *Cosmos and History; or The Myth of the Eternal Return. Le Mythe de l'Éternel retour: archétypes et répétition.* Paris: Gallimard, 1949. Trans. Willard Trask. New York: Harper, 1959.

Ellis, John M. *Language, Thought, and Logic.* Evanston: Northwestern University Press, 1993.

Embree, Lester, ed. *Encyclopedia of Philosophy.* Dordrecht: Kluwer Academic, 1997.

Episcopal Church, The. *The Draft Proposed Book of Common Prayer and Other Rites and Ceremonies of the Church*, "The Blue Book." New York: The Church Hymnal Corporation, 1976.

Fingarette, Herbert. *Self Deception.* London: RKP, 1969. 2nd edition, Berkeley and Los Angeles: University of California Press, 2000.

Foster, Michael Beresford, "The Christian Doctrine of Creation and the Rise of Modern Natural Science." *Mind*, 43 (1934) 446.

Foster, Michael Beresford, "Christian Theology and the Modern Science of Nature (I.)." *Mind*, 44 (1935) 439.

Foster, Michael Beresford, "Christian Theology and the Modern Science of Nature (II.)." *Mind*, 45 (1936) 1.

Friedman, Richard Elliott, *Who Wrote the Bible?* New York: Harper and Row, 1989.

Fuller, Reginald, *The Formation of the Resurrection Narratives.* New York: Macmillan, 1970.

Gadamer, Hans-Georg. *Truth and Method.* Second edition, Trans. Joel Weinsheimer and Donald G. Marshall. New York: Crossroad, 1989. The German original, *Wahrheit und Methode*, was published in 1960.

Gibson, William. *Shakespeare's Game* New York: Athenaeum, 1978.

Gould, Stephen Jay. *Rocks of Ages; Science and Religion in the Fullness of Life*. New York: Ballantine, 1999.

Greenfield, Gloria Z. "The Fight of Our Lives: Defeating the Ideological War Against the West." (A movie; 2018).

Griffith, Andy. "What it was, was Football." The Wiki dates it in 1953; it is on the Net. https://en.wikipedia.org/wiki/What_It_Was,_Was_Football, accessed 2019-07-09.

Hanson, Paul D. *The Dawn of Apocalyptic: The Historical and Sociological Roots of Jewish Apocalyptic Eschatology*. Rev. ed. Philadelphia: Fortress Press, 1979.

Haskell, David M. "Liberal Churches are Dying but Conservative Churches are Thriving." *Washington Post* online, 2017-01-04.

David Haskell, Kevin Flatt, and Stephanie Burgoyne. "Theology Matters: Comparing the traits of Growing and Declining Mainline Protestant Church Attendees and Clergy." *Review of Religious Research* 58 (2016) 515–541.

Hegel, G. W. F. *Phenomenology of Spirit*. Trans. A. V. Miller. Oxford University Press, 1977.

Heidegger, Martin. *Introduction to Metaphysics*. Trans. Ralph Mannheim. New Haven: Yale University Press, 1959.

Heidegger, Martin. *Sein und Zeit*, 1927. *Being and Time*. Trans. John Macquarrie and Edward Robinson. New York: Harper and Row, 1960. There is also a translation by Joan Stambaugh (Albany: State University of New York Press, 1996). Unless otherwise noted, references are to the Macquarrie and Robinson translation.

Heidegger, Martin. *The Fundamental Concepts of Metaphysics: World, Finitude, Solitude*. Trans. William McNeill and Nicholas Walker. Bloomington: Indiana University Press, 1995. The German was published in 1983.

Heidegger, Martin. "The Origin of the Work of Art." In *Poetry, Language, Thought*, ed. Albert Hofstadter. New York: Harper and Row, 1975.

Hennecke, Edgar, *New Testament Apocrypha* ed. Wilhelm Schneemelcher. Translation A. J. B. Higgins, George Ogg, Richard E. Taylor, R. McL. Wilson, 1963, Lutterworth Press, 1963. Original Mohr/Siebeck, 1959. Philadelphia: Westminster Press, 1963. Vol. One, *Gospels and Related Writings*. Vol. Two, *Writings Related to the Apostles; Apocalypses and Related Subjects*.

Heym, Stefan. *The King David Report*. London : Abacus, 1984, c1972; reprinted by Northwestern University Press, 1998.

Hick, John, *The Existence of God*. New York: Macmillan, 1964.

Hobbs, Edward C. "An Alternate Model from a Theological Perspective." In Herbert A. Otto, *The Family in Search of a Future*. New York: Appleton-Century-Crofts, 1970.

Hobbs, Edward C. "Gospel Miracle Story and Modern Miracle Stories." In *Gospel Studies in Honor of Sherman Elbridge Johnson*, ed. Massey H. Shepherd Jr. and Edward C. Hobbs, *Anglican Theological Review*. Supplemental Series, Number Three, March 1974, pages 117–126. On the Net at http:// www.pcts.org/ journal/miracle.html, .pdf, .dvi; also a softlink as http:// www.pcts.org/ journal/hobbs2002a.html.

Hobbs, Edward C. Instructional materials: "The theology of the evangelists, shared dimensions." No date, but my copy is from the late 1970s.

Hobbs, Edward C. Lectures in Houston, no. 4: "Can an apocalyptic prophet make sense in century 21?" Foundation for Contemporary Theology, March 23, 2002.

Hobbs, Edward Craig, "Recognition of Conceptuality as a Hermeneutical Tool." In F. L. Cross, ed., *Texte und Untersuchungen zur altchristlichen Literatur*. Band 88 (Berlin, Akademie-Verlag, 1964). Available online at http://www.pcts.org/journal/ hobbs2010a/ index.html.

Hobbs, Edward C. "The Gospel of Mark and the Exodus." University of Chicago PhD dissertation, 1952.

Hooker, Thomas. *The Soules Implantation into the Natural Olive.* London: R. Young, 1640.

Iggers, Georg G. *The German Conception of History: The National Tradition of Historical Thought from Herder to the Present.* Middletown, CT: Wesleyan University Press, 1968, 1983.

Iggers, Georg G. *Historiography In The Twentieth Century; From Scientific Objectivity to the Postmodern Challenge.* Middletown, CT: Wesleyan University Press, 1997.

International Commission on English in the Liturgy. *The Liturgy of the Hours*, usually known as "the Breviary." New York: Catholic Book Publishing Co., 1975.

Johnson, Roger A. *The Origins of Demythologizing. Philosophy and Historiography in the Theology of Rudolf Bultmann.* Leiden: E. J. Brill, 1974.

Kaufman, Gordon D. *Essay in Theological Method.* Oxford University Press, 1975; 3rd edition, 1995.

Kant, Immanuel. *Religion Within the Limits of Reason Alone.* (1793) Trans. Theodore Greene, Hoyt H. Hudson. New York: Harper and Row, 1960.

Kee, Howard Clark. *Medicine, Miracle, and Magic in New Testament Times.* Cambridge University Press, 1986.

Keener, Craig S. *Miracles: The Credibility of the New Testament Accounts.* Grand Rapids: Baker Academic, 2011.

Kelly, J. N. D. *Early Christian Doctrine.* 2nd ed. New York: Harper and Row, 1960.

Kenny, Anthony. "Aquinas and Wittgenstein." *Downside Review* 77 (1959) 217.

Kerr, Fergus. *Twentieth-Century Catholic Theologians.* Oxford, UK: Blackwell, 2007.

Kierkegaard, Søren. *Fear and Trembling and The Sickness Unto Death* Trans. Walter Lowrie. Princeton University Press, 1941, 1954.

Kierkegaard, Søren. *The Concept of Anxiety.* Trans. Reidar Thomte. Princeton University Press, 1980.

Kierkegaard, Søren. *The Sickness Unto Death. A Christian Psychological Exposition for Understanding and Awakening.* Trans. Howard V. Hong and Edna H. Hong. Princeton: Princeton University Press, 1980.

Kittel, Gerhard, ed. *Theological Dictionary of the New Testament.* Grand Rapids: Wm. B. Eerdmans, 1964 ff.

Kline, Meredith G. "The Old Testament Origins of the Gospel Genre." *Westminster Theol. J.* 38 (1975) 1–27.

Koyré, Alexandre. *From the Closed World to the Infinite Universe.* New York: Harper and Row, 1957.

Krentz, Edgar. *The Historical-Critical Method.* Philadelphia: Fortress Press, 1975. Reprint, Eugene OR: Wipf and Stock, 2002.

Kuhn, Thomas S. *The Structure of Scientific Revolutions.* Second edition. Chicago: University of Chicago Press, 1970. The first edition was published in 1960.

Kümmel, Werner Georg. *The New Testament: The History of the Investigation of its Problems* (1970). Trans. S. MacLean Gilmour and Howard Clark Kee. Nashville: Abingdon Press, 1972.

Laird, R. F. *The Boomer Bible: A Testament for Our Times.* New York: Workman Pub., 1991.

Lakoff, George. *Women, Fire, and Dangerous Things.* Chicago: University of Chicago Press, 1987.

Laycock, Joseph P., and Daniel Wise. "Review Essay: 'Our Secret in Plain Sight': Recent Scholarly Approaches to Paranormal Belief." *Religious Studies Review* 40 no. 2 (2014/06) 69.

Lewis, C. S. *Surprised by Joy: The Shape of My Early Life.* New York: Harcourt, Brace, and World, 1955.

Lewis, C. S. *The Abolition of Man; or Reflections on Education with Special Reference to the Teaching of English in the Upper Forms of Schools.* New York: Macmillan, 1947.

Lewis, C. S. *The Silver Chair* London: Geoffrey Bles, 1953.

Littleton, C. Scott, *The New Comparative Mythology: An Anthropological Assessment of the Theories of Georges Dumézil*. 1966; 2nd ed., 1973. University of California Press, 3rd ed., 1982.

MacIntyre, Alasdair. *After Virtue*. Notre Dame: University of Notre Dame Press, ca. 1981. Second edition, 1984. Third Edition, 2007.

MacIntyre, Alasdair C. "Epistemological Crises, Dramatic Narrative, and the Philosophy of Science." *Monist* 60 no. 4 (1977/10) 453–472.

MacIntyre, Alasdair. "Relativism, Power, and Philosophy." *Proceedings and Addresses of the American Philosophical Association* 59 no. 1 (1985/September) 5; reprinted in K. Baynes, J. Bohman and T. McCarthy, eds., *After Philosophy*, MIT Press, 1987, pp. 385-411.

MacIntyre, Alasdair. *Whose Justice? Which Rationality?* Notre Dame: University of Notre Dame Press, 1988.

Magurshak, Dan. "The Concept of Anxiety: The Keystone of the Kierkegaard-Heidegger Relationship." In Robert L. Perkins, ed., *International Kierkegaard Commentary*, Volume 8: *The Concept of Anxiety*. Mercer University Press, 1985.

Martin, Luther H. *Hellenistic Religions: An Introduction*. Oxford University Press, 1987.

McEvoy, James. *The Philosophy of Robert Grosseteste* Oxford: Clarendon Press, 1982.

Megill Allan. "Why was there a crisis of historicism?" *History and Theory* 36 no. 3 (1997) 416–430.

Mulhall, Stephen. *Philosophical Myths of the Fall*. Princeton: Princeton University Press, 2005.

Murray, John Courtney, S.J. *The Problem of God*. New Haven: Yale University Press, 1964.

Myers, Doris T. *C. S. Lewis in Context*. Kent, OH: Kent State University Press, 1994.

Neusner, Jacob, *Death and Birth of Judaism; the Impact of Christianity, Secularism, and the Holocaust on Jewish Faith*. New York: Basic Books, 1987. Atlanta: Scholars Press, 1992.

Nickelsburg, George W. E. *Resurrection, Immortality and Eternal Life in Intertestamental Judaism*. Harvard University Press (1972), revised 2006.

Niebuhr, H. Richard. *Radical Monotheism and Western Culture, with Supplementary Essays*. New York: Harper and Row, 1970.

Niebuhr, H. Richard. *The Kingdom of God in America*. New York: Harper and Row, 1937.

Niebuhr, H. Richard. *The Meaning of Revelation* (Originally published by Macmillan, 1941). Third edition. Louisville: Westminster John Knox Press, 2006. Citations unless otherwise noted are to the third edition.

Niebuhr, H. Richard. *The Responsible Self*. New York: Harper and Row, 1963.

Niebuhr, H. Richard. *Faith on Earth; An Inquiry into the Structure of Human Faith*. New Haven: Yale University Press, 1989.

Niebuhr, Reinhold. *The Nature and Destiny of Man*. Two volumes. New York: Scribners, 1941.

Noonan, John T. *Contraception*. Belknap Press, 1965, 1986.

Numbers, Ronald L. *The Creationists*. New York: A. A. Knopf, 1992.

O'Connor, Daniel, and Francis Oakley. *Creation: The Impact of an Idea*. New York: Scribners, 1969.

O'Neil, Tyler, "The Church of England's Vatican Envoy Doesn't Believe in the Resurrection of Jesus." *PJMedia* 2019-01-14; https://pjmedia.com/faith/the-church-of-englands-vatican-envoy-doesnt-believe-in-the-resurrection-of-jesus/. Accessed 2019-02-02.

Owen, H. P. *Revelation and Existence. A Study in the Theology of Rudolf Bultmann* Cardiff: University of Wales Press, 1957.

Pacholczyk, A. G. *The Catastrophic Universe*. Tucson: Pachart Publishing, 1984.

Perkins, Pheme, *Resurrection: New Testament Witness and Contemporary Reflection*. Garden City: Doubleday, 1984.

Perkins, Pheme, "The Resurrection of Jesus of Nazareth." Ch. 64 in Craig A. Evans ed., *The Historical Jesus: Critical Concepts in Religious Studies*, Vol. III, "Jesus' Mission, Death, and Resurrection." London: Routledge, 2004.

Phillips, D. Z. *The Problem of Evil and the Problem of God*. Minneapolis: Fortress Press, 2004.

Pilsner, Joseph. *The Specification of Human Actions in St Thomas Aquinas*. Oxford University Press, 2006.

Placher, William C. *The Domestication of Transcendence: how modern thinking about God went wrong*. Louisville, KY: Westminster John Knox Press, c1996.

Plantinga, Alvin. "Two Dozen or so theistic arguments." Lecture notes, undated. On the Net at http:// www.calvin.edu/ academic/ philosophy/virtual_library/articles/plantinga_alvin/two_dozen_or_so_ theistic_arguments.pdf.

Porter, Andrew P. *Basic Concepts of Biblical Religion: A Prolegomenon*. Xulon Press, 2016.

Porter, Andrew P. *By the Waters of Naturalism: Theology Perplexed Among the Sciences*. Eugene, OR: Wipf and Stock, 2001.

Porter, Andrew P. *Elementary Monotheism*, two volumes. Lanham, MD: University Press of America, 2001. Online at http://www.jedp.com/eln.pdf, alhr.pdf.

Porter, Andrew P. "History, Relativity, and Pluralism." *Budhi* (Manila) vol. 6, nos. 2&3 (2002) 223–234. Available online at http://www.jedp.com/hrp.pdf.

Porter, Andrew P. *In the Beginning, Exodus: The Bible Then and Now*. Eugene, OR: Wipf and Stock, 2008.

Porter, Andrew P. *Living in Spin: Narrative as a Distributed Ontology of Human Action*. Bloomington: Authorhouse, 2011.

Porter, Andrew P., "The Barbour-Smith-Gilkey Paradox: Historical Relativity in Natural Science and Historical Religion." *Theology and Science* 4 no. 1 (2006/April) 87–99.

Porter, Andrew P. *Unwelcome Good News: Providence in Human Life*. Eugene, OR: Wipf and Stock, 2004.

Porter, Andrew. *Where, Now, O Biologists, Is Your Theory? Intelligent Design as Naturalism By Other Means*. Eugene, OR: Wipf and Stock, 2007.

Porter, Andrew P., and Edward C. Hobbs. "The Trinity and the Indo-European Tripartite Worldview," *Budhi* (Manila) Vol. 3, nos. 2&3 (1999) 1–28. Available on the internet at http://www.jedp.com/trinity.html.

Rad, Gerhard von. *Old Testament Theology*, 2 vols. New York: Harper and Row. Trans. D. M. G. Stalker. The German originals were published in 1957 and 1960; translations in 1962 and 1965.

Rad, Gerhard von. "The Form Critical Problem of the Hexateuch" (1938). Reprinted and translated in *The Problem of the Hexateuch and Other Essays*. London: SCM, 1966.

Radner, Ephraim. "Same-sex marriage is still wrong; and it's getting wronger every day." The Anglican Communion Institute, 2013 July 17. http:// www.anglicancommunioninstitute.com/2013/07/ same-sex-marriage-is-still-wrong-and-its-getting-wronger-every-day/.

Ratzinger, Joseph. *Introduction to Christianity* (1968) Revised edition, San Francisco: Ignatius Press, 2004.

Reagan, Charles E. "Ricoeur's Diagnostic Relation." *International Philosophical Quarterly*, 8 (1968) 586–592.

Reisman, Sam. "Federal Judge Rules That Worshipping a Flying Spaghetti Monster Is Not a Real Religion." *The Mediaite*, April 13th, 2016, at http://www.mediaite.com/online/federal-judge-rules-that-worshipping-a-flying-spaghetti-monster-is-not-a-real-religion/.

Ricoeur, Paul. *Essays on Biblical Interpretation*. Philadelphia: Fortress Press, 1980. Available online at http://www.religion-online.org.

Ricoeur, Paul. *Freedom and Nature: the Voluntary and the Involuntary*. Evanston: Northwestern University Press, 1966.

Ricoeur, Paul. "The Model of Text: Meaningful Action Considered as Text." *Social Research*, 38 no. 3 (Autumn 1971) 529–555. Reprinted in Paul Ricoeur, *From Text to Action; Essays in Hermeneutics, II*. Trans. Kathleen Blamey and John B. Thompson. Evanston: Northwestern University Press, 1991.

Ricoeur, Paul. *The Symbolism of Evil*. Boston: Beacon Press, 1969.

Ricoeur, Paul. *Time and Narrative*. Three volumes. Chicago: University of Chicago Press, 1984–1985.

Rocca, Gregory. "Aquinas on God-Talk: Hovering Over the Abyss." *Theological Studies* 54 (1993) 641.

Rocca, Gregory. *Speaking the Unknowable God; Thomas Aquinas on the Interplay of Positive and Negative Theology*. Washington: Catholic University of America Press, 2004.

Rubenstein, Richard E. *Aristotle's Children: How Christians, Muslims, and Jews Rediscovered Ancient Wisdom and Illuminated the Middle Ages*. New York: Mariner Books; Reprint edition 2004.

Scott, Bernard Brandon, *The Trouble with Resurrection: From Paul to the Fourth Gospel*. Salem, Oregon: Polebridge Press, 2010.

Scott, Bernard Brandon, ed., *The Resurrection of Jesus: A Sourcebook*. Salem, Oregon: Polebridge Press, 2008.

Sheehan, Thomas. "Easter, Apocalypse, and the Fundamentalists." Part One, Part Two. *The Fourth R* 28-3 (2015/May–June) 3 and 28-4 (2015/July–August) 9.

Sheehan, Thommas. "The Resurrection, an Obstacle to Faith?" *The Fourth R* 8,2 (1995 March/April), pp. 3–9, reprinted in Bernard Brandon Scott, *The Resurrection of Jesus: A Sourcebook*.

Sheehan, Thomas. "How did Easter Originally Happen?" from *The Fourth R* 14:4 (2001/July–August) 3–8. Reprinted in Bernard Brandon Scott, ed., *The Resurrection of Jesus: a Sourcebook* Santa Rosa: Polebridge Press 2008.

Smith, Christian and Melina Lundquist Denton. *Soul Searching: The Religious and Spiritual Lives of American Teenagers.* Oxford University Press, 2005.

Smith, Christian, with Patricia Snell. *Souls in Transition: The Religious and Spiritual Lives of Emerging Adults.* Oxford University Press, 2009.

Smith, Janet E. *Humanae Vitae: A generation later.* Catholic University of America Press, 1991.

Smith, Janet E. *Why Humanae Vitae Was Right: A Reader.* San Francisco: Ignatius Press, 1993.

Sokolowski, Robert. *The God of Faith and Reason.* Washington: Catholic University of America Press, 1982, 1995.

Spencer, Bonnell, OHC. "The Vows." *Holy Cross Magazine*, vol. 9 no. 3 (1970/Autumn) 7–8.

Spielberg, Nathan and Bryon D. Anderson. *Seven Ideas that Shook the Universe.* Third Edition, New York: Wiley, 2006.

Stadler, Nurit, course syllabus. http:// pluto.huji.ac.il/ ~msstad/ AnthropologyOfMiracles.htm.

Steenberghen, Fernand van. *Aristotle in the West: The Origins of Latin Aristotelianism.* Louvain: Nauwelaerts, 1955.

Steiner, George. *Real Presences.* University of Chicago Press, 1989.

Stendahl, Krister. *Paul Among Jews and Gentiles, and other essays.* Philadelphia: Fortress press, 1976.

Strack, Herman L. *Introduction to the Talmud and Midrash.* New York: Athenaeum, 1978.

Strack, Herman L., and G. Stemberger, *Introduction to the Talmud and Midrash*. Trans. Markus Bockmuehl; Augsburg Fortress, 1992. There were earlier editions.

Strack, Hermann and Paul Billerbeck. *Commentary on the New Testament from Talmud and Midrash*. German original, 1922.

Talmud, Babylonian, the. The, general editor was rabbi Dr. Isidore Epstein. London: Soncino Press, 1978.

Thomas Aquinas. *In quator libros sententiarum*. There are many editions, some online. For the Latin of 1.8.1.1 ad 4, I probably consulted E. M. Macierowski, ed., *Thomas Aquinas's Earliest Treatment of the Divine Essence: Scriptum super libros Sententiarum, Book I Distinction 8* Binghamton University: Center for Medieval and Renaissance Studies, 1997.

Thomas Aquinas. *Summa Theologica*. Trans. by the Dominican Fathers of the English Province. New York, Benziger Bros., n. d.

Tilley, Terrence. *The Evils of Theodicy*. Washington DC: Georgetown University Press, 1991.

Tillich, Paul. *Systematic Theology*. 3 vols. Chicago: University of Chicago Press, 1951 ff.

Urban, Wilbur Marshall. *Language and Reality: The Philosophy of Language and the Principles of Symbolism*. London: George Allen and Unwin, 1939.

Ward, Benedicta, *Miracles and the Medieval Mind: Theory, Record and Event, 1000–1215*. Philadelphia: University of Pennsylvania Press, 1962, rev. ed., 1987.

Weeden, Theodore J. Sr. *Mark: Traditions in Conflict*. Philadelphia: Fortress Press, 1971.

Weeden, Theodore J. Sr. "The Heresy That Necessitated Mark's Gospel." *Zeitschrift für die Neutestamentliche Wissenschaft* 59 (1968) 145.

Weigel, George. *The Irony of Modern Catholic History: How the Church rediscovered itself and challenged the modern world to reform*. New York: Basic Books, 2019

Weinberg, Steven, *The First Three Minutes*. New York: Basic Books, 1977.

Welch, Claude. *Protestant Thought in the Nineteenth Century*. 2 vols. New Haven: Yale University Press, 1972–1985.

Westphal, Merold. *God, Guilt, and Death; An Existential Phenomenology of Religion*. Bloomington: Indiana University Press, 1984.

White, Thomas Joseph. "Catholicism in an Age of Discontent; The need for reason and mystery in Catholic apologetics." *First Things* (2016/November), online. https:// www.firstthings.com/ article/2016/11/ catholicism-in-an-age-of-discontent

Wiesel, Elie. *Night*. French original, 1958; English translation, New York: Avon Books, 1960.

Wilshire, Bruce. "Fifty Years of Academic Philosophy in the United States: Why the Failure of Nerve?" *Soundings* 67 (84/Winter) 411–419.

Wittgenstein, Ludwig. *Philosophical Investigations; The English Text of the Third Edition*. Trans. G. E. M. Anscombe. New York: Macmillan, 1958.

Wright, N. T. *The Resurrection of the Son of God*. Minneapolis: Fortress Press, 2003.

Index

abortion, 129
Achnai, oven of, 81, 231
Akiba, rabbi, 56, 61
ambiguity, 2, 8, 25, 27, 32, 43, 45, 47, 52, 69, 72, 76, 77, 80, 88, 115, 121, 123, 125, 133, 134, 138, 144, 156, 157, 161, 181, 184, 188, 189, 216, 225, 228, 229, 235, 243
    shows itself, 46
Amir, Alexander, 126
analogy
    in Aquinas, 84
Anderson, Bryon D., 175
Anselm, 75–77, 129, 134
anthropomorphic deity, 91, 92
anti-Jewish theology, 46–48, 51, 62, 217, 221
anti-Semitism, 47, 62, 240
Aphrahat, 21, 51, 214–218
apocalyptic, 150–151, 221
Aristotle, 66–74, 78, 86, 96, 174, 189, 227, 229, 242
    biology, 13, 71, 89, 90, 175
    causes, 89, 90
    forms, 178, 193
    logic, 122
    miracles, 70
    naturalism, 67
    nature, 5, 70, 78, 89, 125

arithmetic, biblical, 30
Arnold, Stephen, 108
artificial intelligence, 197
artificial personhood, 124, 197
Asimov, Isaac, 190
astronomy
    new, 88
    Ptolemaic, 89, 126
astrophysics, 70, 71, 95, 227
atheism, 196
    and Chalcedonian method, 97, 175
    and evolution, 96
    and nature, 176
    and proofs, 130, 131
    and unanswerable questions, 11
    Christianity as, 57–58
    New, 209, 247, 248
    scientific, 11, 91, 92
    secular, 115
atrocities, 34–36, 49, 62, 81, 196, 231, 250
Augustine, 52, 53, 78, 229, 242
Axelrod, Timothy, 144
Ayer, A. J., 131

Bacon, Francis, 89, 90
Bambach, Charles R., 109
Bar-Cochba, Simeon, 57
Barbour-Smith-Gilkey paradox,

137, 223
Barron, Robert, 105
Barth, Karl, 117, 119, 120
    Romans, 116, 117, 120
basic life orientation, 3, 5, 7, 26, 28, 43, 69, 80, 118–120, 128, 135, 149, 152, 160, 179, 184, 198, 209–210, 220, 225, 228, 231, 248
    definition, 7, 118, 119
Bauer, Ferdinand Christian, 104
Beck, Norman, 46–48, 51, 217
being-itself, God as, 130
being-with, 59, 60
    in Heidegger, 114
Bencivenga, Ermanno, 75
Benedict XVI, 247
Berger, Peter, 5, 55, 100, 136, 164, 228
    Adventures, 136
    bad faith, 168
    In Praise of Doubt, 136
    objectivation, 55
    Sacred Canopies, 128, 135
    Sacred Canopy, 6, 18–19, 102, 128, 164, 168, 239
    Social Construction, 6, 18–19, 135, 136
Bernard of Clairvaux, 184
Billerbeck, Paul, 59
biology, 94, 96
    autoimmune disease, 224
    creationism, 223
    evolution, 96, 97, 100, 111, 197, 200, 227
    social darwinism, 110
Blair, Alexander, 195
Bohr, Niels, 112
Boole, George, 87
Booth, Wayne, 144
Bowler, Peter J., 94
Boyarin, Daniel, 219
Brague, Rémi, 62
Brahe, Tycho, 88
Buddhists, 134
Bultmann, Rudolf, 118, 119, 121, 127, 128, 166, 168
    demythologizing, 118, 166, 168
    myth, 166
Burns, R. M., 92
Burrell, David B., 84, 117, 118

Cajetan, 84–86, 117
Calvin, John, 86, 88
Calvinism, 227
Cantor, Georg, 77
Cauchy, Augustin-Louis, 213
Chalcedon
    council of, 10, 70, 78
Chalcedonian method, 10–13, 69, 70, 72, 80, 83, 95, 97, 102, 106, 118, 140, 150, 175, 176, 203, 213, 220, 229, 237, 244, 250
    outside Christology, 5
Chambers, Mark, 108
Chomsky, Noam, 122
Collingwood, R. G., 72, 107
    and Troeltsch, 108
    Idea of History, 107, 108, 110
    idealism, 107
Collins, Billy, 4
Common Documents, definition, 9
communism, 196
conceptuality, 80, 104, 118, 119, 141, 156, 160

Constantine, 98
  Donation of, 103
contraceptives, 129, 202–207
Cooperman, Alan, 164
Copernicus, 88
cosmogony, 91
cosmology
  and theology, 71
  astrophysical, 71
  Babylonian, 104
  secular, 217
Courtois, Stéphane, 196
creationism, 99, 126, 169, 176, 197, 198, 223
critical history, historical and cultural relativity, and religious pluralism, 5, 129, 185, 187, 212, 237, 239, 250
Crossan, John Dominic, 162
culture-protestantism, 101

Darwin, Charles, 94–97, 99, 227
Dawkins, Richard, 200
Deism, 13, 105, 160
Deneen, Patrick J., 194, 196
Denton, Melina Lundquist, 198
Depew, David J., 94
Descartes, 86, 242
  cartesian anthropology, 197
  cartesians, 111, 112
  naturalism, 202
  philosophy, 125
Dilthey, Wilhelm, 109
distributed system, 125
Dix, Gregory, 56, 182
Dodds, Michael, 71, 72
Dostoevsky, Fyodor, 101
Douay-Rheims, 47

Dreibelbis, Gary, 145
Dreyfus, Hubert, 125
DSMAAGL, 96
DSMNR, 96
Dumézil, Georges, 185
Dungan, David Laird, 104
Dupré, Louis, 93, 225, 232
Durkheim, Émile, 135

Eberstadt, Mary, 205
Egypt, 9, 10, 20, 29, 31, 40, 42, 221, 222, 229
Einstein, Albert, 112
Eliade, Mircea, 217
Ellis, John, 192
Embree, Lester, 125
environmentalism, 122, 197, 198, 249
Eucharist, 56, 87, 182, 221
evolution, 227, 245, 249
Exposure, Limitation, and Need, 15, 44–46, 63, 64, 138, 152, 153, 155, 184–187, 211, 212, 222, 250

Fingarette, Herbert, 128, 197, 225
Flying Spaghetti Monster, 210
football, 3, 4
form criticism, 142, 143, 155, 246, 247
formal cause, 71, 72, 89, 90, 192, 193, 211
forms, ideal, 178
Fortinbras, 240, 247, 248
Foster, Michael Beresford, 90–92, 175, 232
Frege, Gottlob, 87
Fregean logic, 122, 225
Friedman, Richard Elliott, 26

Index 271

Fuller, Reginald, 142, 161
Fundamentalism, 98, 99, 242
 Five Fundamentals, 127
 Princeton, 99

Gadamer, Hans-Georg, 14, 119, 122–124, 136, 143, 144, 153
 hermeneutical circle, 143
Galileo, 126, 223
Gibbon, Edward, 108
Gibson, William, 32, 33, 238
Gilkey, Langdon, 176
global warming, 197, 249
Gnosticism, 26, 150
Gould, Stephen Jay, 222
Greenfield, Gloria Z., 226
Griffith, Andy, 4

halakah, 50, 59, 60, 219, 220, 231
Hamlet, 16, 17, 32, 160, 240, 241, 244, 248, 250
Hanson, Paul D., 151
Harnack, Adolf, 23, 63
Harris, Sidney, 159
Harvey, Van, 105
Haskell, David M., 164
healing touch, 173
Hegel, G. W. F., 99, 100, 110, 113, 196
Heidegger, Martin, 5, 24, 109, 112–115, 122, 133, 135
 anxiety, 113, 133
 artificial intelligence, 124
 being-in-the-world, 114, 124, 193
 being-with, 177
 hermeneutical circle, 123, 143
 meanings of being, 86, 200
 mistake in definition of Dasein, 177
 other people, 59, 218
 vorhanden, 115
 worldhood, 114, 135
 zuhanden, 115, 124
Heisenberg, Werner, 112
Herodotus, 107
Heym, Stefan, 36
Hick, John, 130, 131
Hippolytus, canon of, 56
historicism, 105, 108, 109, 115, 128, 141, 142
Hittite suzerainty treaties, 236
Hobbes, Thomas, 195
Hobbs, Edward, 8, 15, 41, 43, 44, 63, 64, 118–120, 144, 145, 147, 149, 154, 185, 239, 257
 on conceptuality, 16, 18, 80, 104, 119, 156, 166
Homer, 229
Hooker, Thomas, 86
Hoyle, Fred, 70, 71
Humanae Vitae, 203, 205
Humboldt, Wilhelm von, 108
Hume, David, 79, 92, 108, 200
Huxley, Thomas Henry, 94
Hyrcanus, Eliezer ben, 60, 61

Iggers, Georg, 108
Incarnation
 at Chalcedon, 11
 social construction, 220
individualism, 193–196
informalism in religion, 199, 209
interpersonation, 102, 128, 177–179, 182, 234

irony, 11, 122, 128, 144–146, 148, 150, 153, 156, 157, 159, 161, 191, 221
    in comics, 191
    in the Gospels, 40
    irony-challenged, 156, 179, 180
Islam, 196
    conquests, 81

John of Damascus, 92, 118
Johnson, Roger, 118, 166
joke, 148, 153
Josephus, 57
Judah ha-Nasi, 58
Judaism, 196
Justin Martyr, 57

Kübler-Ross, Elizabeth, 186
Kümmel, Werner Georg, 104
Kant, Immanuel, 99, 101, 111–113
kashrut, 46, 50, 51, 59, 150, 155, 220
    not works righteousness, 59
Kaufman, Gordon, 22
Kee, Howard Clark, 79
Keener, Craig, 170, 174
Kelly, J. N. D., 62
Kenny, Anthony, 68
Kepler, Johannes, 88
Kerr, Fergus, 117, 131
Kierkegaard, Søren, 24, 113, 115, 131, 133, 136, 177, 207, 218
Kline, Meredith, 41, 55
Krentz, Edgar, 103–106

Laird, R. F., 246
Lamarckian evolution, 97, 227

Landau and Lifshitz, 157
language
    home in the universe, 8, 19, 72, 96, 228
language-capable life, 243, 245
Larson, Gary, 166
Lawrence of Arabia, 33
Laycock, Joseph P., 174
Lewis, C. S., 6, 132
    Screwtape Letters, 238
Life of Brian, 41
Littleton, C. Scott, 185
Locke, John, 195
Luckmann, Thomas, 6, 55, 100
Luther, Martin, 47, 86

MacIntyre, Alasdair, 146, 229, 240
    After Virtue, 204
    Epistemological Crises, 123
    relativism, 137
    Whose Justice? Which Rationality?, 229, 241
Macquarrie and Robinson, 114
Magurshak, Dan, 113, 133
Maimonides, 117
Marcionite
    crisis, 62–63
    theology, 16, 23, 24, 82, 100, 106, 168, 171, 176, 180, 188, 198, 202, 209, 216, 217, 234, 236, 243, 250
Markan whiplash, 148, 171
Marlowe, Faust, 2
marriage, gay, 204, 206
Martin, Luther H., 8
martyrdom, 221
Marxism, 192, 196, 198
McEvoy, James, 91
mechanics

of history, 110
orbital, 110
quantum, 112, 189, 190, 213
statistical, 33, 190
Megill, Allan, 109
memetics, 197–199
Mendel, Gregor, 94
Mendelssohn, Moses, 98, 99
Mesopotamia, 9
metanoia, 43, 44, 146–148, 153–156, 160, 161, 163, 165, 169, 187, 236
Michelangelo, 30
mimesis, 199
Mishnah, 41, 46, 58–61, 218, 236
modalism, 64
monophysite theology
    and anxiety, 23
    Christology, 12
    divine action, 12, 13, 24, 82, 83, 97, 102, 105, 106, 116, 117, 139, 140, 159, 160, 165–168, 170, 172, 174–176, 180, 188, 198, 200, 209, 211–213, 221, 224, 234, 236, 237, 239, 243, 248, 250
    generalized, 237
    intramundane, 117, 200
    outside Christology, 5
Monty Python, 41
Moses, 42, 160
    covenant, 214, 215, 218
    in Deuteronomy, 20
    the conquest, 201
    the Law, 30
    the Name, 23, 28, 29, 178, 229
Mudge, Lewis, 170

Mulhall, Stephen, 179
Murray, John Courtney
    four questions, 57, 73, 74, 76, 238, 244
    on the Name, 23, 28, 29, 178, 230
Myers, Doris, 190, 191
mystery, 37, 83, 84, 95, 116, 143, 158, 167, 176, 181, 239, 243
    of nature, 223
    the mystery of faith, 149
myth, 152, 172, 230
    Genesis, 27
    in philosophy, 179
    science as, 152

naiveté
    Lewis Mudge, 170
    naive, 126, 127, 168
    Paul Ricoeur, 242
    pre-scientific, 232
    primary, 95, 126, 167, 170
    secondary, 170
    tenacious, 126, 127, 168, 170, 232
naturalism, 82, 139, 188–190, 200, 209
    definition, 125
    miracles, 92
    not phenomenology, 125
Neo-orthodox theology, 98, 99, 101, 111, 112, 115–121, 123, 131, 201, 239, 247
neolithic, 8
Neoplatonism, 186
Neusner, Jacob, 59, 98, 100
Newman, Barnett, 31
Newman, John Henry, 214, 238

Newton
  calculus, 213
  method, 144
  physics, 71, 111, 189
Nickelsburg, George, 151
Niebuhr, H. Richard, 38, 45, 57, 101, 119, 121, 178, 186, 211, 212, 216, 225
  revelation, 105, 244
Niebuhr, Reinhold, 216
nihilism, 5, 50, 93, 123, 132, 136, 186, 200, 201, 211, 236
nominalism, 66, 92, 93, 122, 123, 190–192, 200, 209
Noonan, John T., 206
Numbers, Ronald, 100

O'Connor, Daniel, 194
O'Neil, Tyler, 127, 128
Oakley, Francis, 194
objectivation
  and Limitation, 169
  and myth, 165–167
  and subjectivity, 174
  apologetics, 158, 165, 171
  as evasion, 18, 128, 172, 188, 222, 236, 242, 244
  comforts of, 183
  Gospel of Peter, 162, 164
  historicism, 152, 158, 160, 169
  in literalism, 127, 128
  in proofs, 128
  irony, 180
  monophysite thinking, 139, 203
  of choice, 171
  of clearings, 181
  of faith, 22, 138, 152, 158, 161, 168, 172, 175, 181, 232, 241
  of the supernatural, 170
  Peter Berger, 55
  platonist, 136
  Resurrection, 153, 156–158, 180–183
  signs and wonders, 156, 250
  unlike hermeneutic circle, 184
ontology
  distributed, 69, 95, 125, 133, 149, 168, 211, 220
  nanomind, 24, 188–196, 209, 211, 220
    definition, 196
  part and whole, 148, 149
  systems, 125, 149, 189, 190, 193
other-personhood, 219
Otto, Herbert A., 44, 63, 120
Owen, H. P., 166

Pacholczyk, A. G., 70, 199
paganism, 240
pagans, 64, 68, 135
parables of Jesus, 144, 149
Parlapiano, Gary, 2
Pelagius, 227
Persian period, 21, 34, 35, 54
Pew Research, 164, 165
phenomenology, 24, 66, 73, 74, 76, 80, 111, 112, 124, 125, 201, 230, 231, 242, 249
Phillips, D. Z., 37, 74, 97, 178
phlogiston, 136, 164
Pius IX, 100
Placher, William, 73, 83–88, 92, 94, 95, 97, 117
plagues (Exodus), 154, 155, 170, 171, 174

Planck, Max, 112
Plantinga, Alvin, 132
Plato, 132, 242
Platonism, 66, 112, 123, 125, 136, 137, 191, 201, 214
pluralism, 186, 214
Polycarp, 57
polytheism, 57
Porter, Andrew P., 44, 63, 64, 120, 185, 186, 212, 223
pre-scientific worldview, 78, 127, 170, 174, 230
predestination, 97, 227
Psalms
    Exodus in, 63
    of lament, 218
    seeking God, 75, 76
pseudo-Dionysius, 73, 118

Rad, Gerhard von, 29, 32
Radner, Ephraim, 206
Ranke, Leopold von, 141
Rankean history, 128, 142, 154, 155
realism
    moderate, 66, 190, 191
redaction criticism, 247
Reisman, Sam, 210
religion
    exilic, 7, 8, 151, 172, 209
    historical-covenantal, 8, 10, 20, 36, 48, 172, 229, 231
    mimetic, 8, 82, 199
    world-affirming, 3, 7, 9, 26, 33–36, 43, 65, 135, 141, 151, 152, 176, 180, 209, 219, 221, 223, 224, 230, 233, 239, 240, 248–250
    of nature, 7–9, 25, 209, 229

responsible liberty of interpretation, 22, 37, 48–53, 58, 60, 61, 81, 123, 150, 217, 221, 222, 231, 235, 237, 239, 242, 247
Ricoeur, Paul, 55, 56
    model of text, 55
    naiveté, 170, 242
    narrative, 189
Ritschey, Katherine, 164
Rocca, Gregory, 57, 73, 74, 118
Rubenstein, Richard E., 67
Russell, Bertrand, 124

sacred canopies, 6, 24, 48, 49, 80, 134, 135, 180, 198, 222, 231, 236, 237, 239, 241, 242, 250
Sagan, Carl, 176, 200
Schleiermacher, Friedrich, 99, 101, 111, 112, 122, 143, 241
    Speeches, 100
Schrödinger, Erwin, 112
Schweitzer, Albert, 104, 115
scientism, 73, 82, 93
Scott, Bernard Brandon, 146, 156, 161, 180
Scotus, John Duns, 85
Searle, John, 122
Septuagint, 28, 56, 62
Shakespeare, 16, 32, 33, 238
Sheehan, Thomas, 5, 151, 156, 157, 165, 180, 181
signs and wonders, 148, 154–157, 160, 161, 166, 168–171, 174, 223, 236, 248, 250
Smith, Christian, 198
Smith, Gregory, 164
Smith, Janet, 205, 206

Snell, Patricia, 198
socialism, 196
Sokolowski, Robert, 116, 202
Sophocles, 229
source criticism, 103, 247
Spencer, Bonnell, OHC, 169, 170
Spielberg, Nathan, 175
Spinoza, Benedict, 102
Stadler, Nurit, 174
Stalin, Josef, 36
Stambaugh, Joan, 114
Steiner, George, 220
Stemberger, G., 58, 59
Stendahl, Krister, 47, 51
Strack, H. L., 58, 59
Stuhlmacher, Peter, 106
Suarez, Francisco, 85, 86
Superman, 171
supernatural
    modern, 11, 135, 170, 174, 180, 201, 209, 244
    Scholastic, 12, 13, 67, 69
Swinburne, Richard, 132

Talmud, 58–61, 98, 107
    Achnai, oven of, 49, 60–61, 221
    Berakoth 60b, 45
Taylor, Charles, 24
Terrien, Samuel, 36, 38
The Far Side, 166, 167
Theodosian Code, 219
Thomas Aquinas, 74, 92
    analogy, 84, 85
    and ambiguity, 72
    and Aristotle, 66, 67, 71, 74
    and confessionality, 67–69
    and Scotus, 85
    and Suarez, 85
    divine action, 67
    Eucharistic hymns, 87
    gratia non tollat naturam, 12, 13, 67, 70, 141, 175
    human unknowing, 68, 73, 84, 87, 242
    knowing and naming God, 238
    moderate realism, 242
    non-existence of God, 57
    on faith, 80, 86, 87
    on language, 74
    thick darkness, 57, 74
Thomism, Leonine, 134
Thucydides, 107
Tilley, Terrence, 37
Tillich, Paul, 119, 130, 131
Tomaso de Vio, 84
totalitarians, 198
transhumanism, 197
transphysical, the, 159, 180
tribalism, 230
Trinity, 15, 44, 63–65, 120
tripartite ideology, 65
    definition, 64
    Indo-European roots, 15, 64, 185
    Trinity, 44, 63–65, 120
tritheism, 65
triumphalism, 40, 134, 139, 198, 214
Troeltsch, Ernst, 108, 109, 115
    Historismus, 108, 109
    miracles, 141, 174, 175
typological interpretation, 41, 62
    Exodus typology, 40–42, 52, 149, 154, 155, 164, 171, 215

ultimate reality

Index

definition, 202
shows itself, 3, 10–14, 79, 118, 172, 179, 181, 203, 211, 233, 234, 244
Ultramontanism, 98–100
unanswerable questions, 11, 15, 39, 71, 74, 84, 118, 122, 165, 176, 186, 236, 243, 244, 250
uncanniness, 72
universalism, 230, 231
univocation, 24, 84, 85, 117
Urban, Wilbur Marshall, 190, 191

Valla, Lorenzo, 103
van Steenberghen, Fernand, 67
Vatican I, 134
via negativa, 73, 92
volokinesis, 92
Vulgate, 28, 47

Ward, Benedicta, 78
Weber, Bruce H., 94
Weber, Max, 135
Weeden, Theodore J., Sr., 54, 139, 149
Weierstrass, Karl, 213
Weigel, George, 99, 204
Weinberg, Steven, 97
Welch, Claude, 100–102
Wellhausen, Julius, 104
Westphal, Merold, 7, 8, 10, 20–22, 28, 29, 52, 59, 137, 151, 171, 172, 183, 199, 217, 218, 226, 230, 233
Whitaker, William, 87
White, Thomas Joseph, 134, 214
Whitehead, Alfred North, 112, 124
Wiesel, Elie, 183

Wilberforce, Samuel, 94
Wilshire, Bruce, 112, 201
Wise, Daniel, 174
Wittgenstein, Ludwig, 122, 191
fideism, 136
moderate realism, 68
Wright, N. T., 158–160

Yahwist, 26, 27, 230
idols, 38

Zijderveld, Anton, 136